GEORGE HAMMELL COOK

Geo. H. Cook
Nov. 9. 1887

GEORGE HAMMELL COOK
A Life in Agriculture and Geology

Jean Wilson Sidar

RUTGERS UNIVERSITY PRESS
New Brunswick   *New Jersey*

Library of Congress Cataloging in Publication Data

Sidar, Jean Wilson.
   George Hammell Cook : a life in agriculture and geology.
   Includes bibliographical references and index.
   1. Cook,   George   Hammell,   1818-1889.   2. Agriculture—New   Jersey—
History. 3. Geology—History. 4. Geology—New Jersey. 5. Rutgers University,
New Brunswick, N. J.—History.
S417.C636S5   630'.92'4 [B]   76-15950
ISBN 0-8135-0827-4

For
Ruth Dewey Wilson
and
James Kirkwood Wilson

CONTENTS

PREFACE

In this biography of a simple but quite remarkable man my primary goal (as I suppose to be the case with most biographers) has been to present as honest and complete an account as I could of George Hammell Cook, his beliefs and ambitions, his work, his family, his friends, his failures and his successes. Cook has long been highly respected among New Jersey agriculturists and geologists and I hope that now that the story of his life is between the covers of a book, his fame may spread somewhat beyond the boundaries of the state, for in his time Cook was recognized both nationally and internationally as a leading educator, agriculturist, and geologist.

I have tried to place Cook's work in the context of nineteenth-century developments in higher education, agricultural experimentation, and geology. He was deeply involved in the collection of geological data during a period when the future of the science depended not so much upon the formulation of hypotheses as upon the development of a tradition and procedures for massive and patient accumulation of factual details. It was in the establishment of the high standards of the New Jersey Geological Survey in such activities as the first tracing of the course of the terminal moraine of the Wisconsin glacier across the state, the production of the first set of state topographical maps in the nation, and the meticulous mapping of the greensand marl beds that his work was especially valuable. In another dimension of the responsibility of the Survey was his insistence that the work of the state agency be used to improve the quality of life of the people of the state. This was not common in his day.

He was similarly ahead of his time in his ambitions for the land-grant college, envisioning it not as a trade school for farmers and engineers but a place where the nation's future leaders in agriculture, engineering, and the sciences would be trained in the fundamentals of science and all the apparatus of the educated life.

Cook's accomplishments in agricultural science were limited not by a lack of imagination or leadership, but by a lack of funding. He saw clearly the kind of experimentation which scientific agriculture had to undertake and took as many steps in that direction as his resources allowed.

All of Cook's efforts on behalf of higher education, agriculture and science show him to have been deeply involved in the nineteenth-century combination of escalating industrialization and scientific advance which was to make the United States of the twentieth century the most technologically advanced nation in the world.

For those who have kept Cook's memory green he has assumed the proportions of a secular saint because of his selfless devotion to the welfare of the people of New Jersey and to the advancement of science. My investigation of his letters and papers has not disturbed that image although I hope I have managed to write of him as a fallible human being.

My chief source of information has been the cook papers in the Alexander Library of Rutgers University. Cook was a saving man and his wife, Mary, and later his daughters, Emma and Anne, saved almost all his books, journals, papers, letters, and notebooks. When Anne died in 1937 the collection was bequeathed to the University. In addition, Cook's reports for the Rutgers Scientific School and the New Jersey Geological Survey provided detailed information. I am indebted to Mr. Halsey Thomas, a great-nephew of Mrs. Cook's, and to Cook's granddaughter, Mrs. Margaret Cook Thomson, for permission to use their family papers.

I am especially grateful to the late Charles Collins; to Philip Alampi, New Jersey Secretary of Agriculture and Secretary-Treasurer of the New Jersey Agricultural Society, for the grant which made the writing of this biography possible; to the Dean of Douglass College and the Chairman of the History Department for granting me a year's leave of absence; and to Edward J. Bloustein and Karl Metzger who several years later allowed me to take a six-month's leave of absence.

In my research I was helped by many people over the years and my thanks go to all those unnamed herein. Donald Sinclair, Curator of Special Collections of Alexander Library, Rutgers University, William Miller Archivist of the University, and members of their staff, Clark Beck, Anthony Niccolosi, Irene K. Lionikis, and Harmony Coppola, were extraordinarily helpful. I have appreciated the comments on various chapters made by Richard P. McCormick, John C. Greene, Wayne Rasmussen, William Jordan, Kemble Widmer, and the late Carl

Woodward. I wish to thank my husband, Alexander G. Sidar, Jr., for his constant encouragement and his financial contributions to the project. For their patient and expert help with the typing of numerous drafts I am indebted to Thelma Van Cise, Lynn Van Cise, Donna Szilagyi, Kathleen Dewan, and, especially, Marie Kantra.

Jean Wilson Sidar

New Brunswick, New Jersey
April 1976

FOREWORD

According to Thomas Carlyle, a well-written life is almost as rare as a well spent one. Under that criterion, I can recommend *George Hammell Cook, 1818-1889: A Life in Agriculture and Geology* as a rare book indeed and one that deserves a wide audience.

Scholars with an interest in the development of geology and agricultural science or in the growth of higher education in nineteenth-century America will find here an account of a pioneer in these fields. For the general reader, this biography is an absorbing narrative of an engaging, colorful, and energetic man who could take as his motto "make things go."

For those of us who have been a part of the Rutgers community as students, faculty, staff, or alumni, the life of George H. Cook holds a special significance. In 1971, the University's newest undergraduate college, formed from the College of Agriculture and Environmental Science, was named in his honor. But despite this formal recognition, I believe we had tended to lose sight of the remarkable human being behind the distinguished name, a man whose energy and vision served Rutgers well at a critical stage in its 210-year history. Jean Wilson Sidar's book is thus a very real contribution to our understanding of the Rutgers heritage.

In addition to her academic training in history, Mrs. Sidar has brought to this work a practical experience with the ways in which individuals shape the decision-making process within institutions. Many of the battles fought by George H. Cook for public higher education are remarkably similar to those Mrs. Sidar has witnessed as Secretary of the University. With the advantage of this unique background, she has produced a biography well attuned to the realities of the political process.

Mrs. Sidar also describes the state of geology and agricultural science during Cook's life, and his important contributions to these fields. Cook had the good fortune to embark on a scientific career at a time when the amateur and the dilettante were giving way to the trained professional, and when significant advances were being made in the standards of basic research and the techniques for the dissemination of scientific knowledge.

Again, this sympathetic yet well-balanced biography deserves a wide audience; but I know that it will hold a unique appeal to all who have followed George H. Cook at the institution he loved and served so well.

Edward J. Bloustein
President
Rutgers University

WITH GRATITUDE TO
CHARLES AARON COLLINS

The foresight and generosity of a Burlinton County farmer helped make this book possible. Charles Aaron Collins of Moorestown entrusted a fund to the New Jersey Agricultural Society for a book on an agricultural subject to be selected by the Society's Board of Trustees.

After reviewing various proposals, the Trustees decided that the story of the life and work of George Hammell Cook, for whom Cook College is named, would be appropriate. Dr. Cook's investigations in several disciplines of the natural sciences beneficially touched the lives and welfare of city dwellers as well as farm families.

A principal regret is that Charles Collins did not live to read this book, which is the product of ten years of research and writing. However, we are fortunate that publication in 1976 coincides with celebration of the bicentennial of the birth of the State of New Jersey and the United States of America.

The life of Charles Collins was devoted to the arts and sciences of farming in which he was eminently successful. Along with that pioneer American scientific farmer, George Washington, he believed that agriculture is the "noblest and most necessary occupation."

Charles Collins descended from English Quaker farmers who settled in southern New Jersey soon after 1700. Although their religious convictions forbade their bearing arms, they helped to fight two invaders of America—France and Britain—with their farms' production of food for the patriot armies. Succeeding generations produced leaders in education and government, as well as agriculture.

Charles Collins contributed with distinction to many uplifting programs in his community, county and state, perhaps most notably as a member of the Board of Managers of the New Jersey Agricultural Experiment Station and the State Board of Agriculture. Significantly, Dr. Cook was a founder of both agencies.

No personal credit for his part in making this book was requested by Charles Collins. Characteristically, he would have rejected any suggestion of credit. The Agricultural Society and Rutgers University would have it otherwise, hence this page of grateful acknowledgement.

Phillip Alampi
Secretary-Treasurer
New Jersey Agricultural
  Society

GEORGE HAMMELL COOK

1818-1839
The Early Years

For a young man coming of age in the 1830s, the United States was an exciting place to live. Born on a small farm in Morris County, New Jersey, George Hammell Cook had grown up like thousands of other farm boys in the early days of the nation. Theirs was the life that produced the legend, beloved of nineteenth-century America, of the honest, good-natured, hard-working young man from the country whose sturdy farm background and steadfast Christian faith provided him the perseverance to achieve fame and fortune in the great world beyond the farm. The legend was not entirely untrue.

The most adventurous or land-hungry young men were often lured by the forests, rivers, and plains of the western frontier; but an ambitious youth who wanted to stay nearer home could also find excitement and a hope of eventual wealth and importance in the new field of railroading, in the risk of business and banking, or in struggling with the problems of machines and men in the proliferating factories. George Cook found himself led in yet a different direction—toward the newly developing scientific professions where he discovered that a scholarly young man with a scientific bent could also find a place in the dynamic bustle of the young nation. Science, long known best as a hobby for ministers and doctors, was beginning to find its place both in college curricula and in industry. Industrialists were coming to realize that men with scientific training could adapt their knowledge of basic principles to new techniques and processes for mines and factories. Two centuries after Francis Bacon's death, his concept of science as a source of marvelous discoveries which could be put to the use of mankind was stronger than ever. In New Jersey Cook was to become the leading example of the Baconian tradition. Ultimately his influence spread beyond the confines of the state. Not only did he probably contribute more than any other in his century to the prosperity of the state and the welfare of its citizens, he achieved a place of leadership in national and international circles of geologists and agriculturists.

There was nothing in Cook's early life to suggest that he was to play such a prominent role. The small farm where he was born on January 5, 1818, lay a few miles north of Hanover in the section called Hanover Neck. Early in the eighteenth century a handful of families of English stock had bought land along the west bank of the Passaic River from the early Dutch purchasers, who had themselves but recently procured it from the Lenni Lenape Indians and the East Jersey proprietors.[1] Refugees from the rocky soil of New England, the new settlers were happy to find in the foothills of Morris County an easier climate and a somewhat more productive soil than New England could offer. This outpost of the Puritan frontier at Hanover was built in the pattern of many early New England towns, with houses grouped in a small cluster and the farm fields spread around them. This was the old pattern of the English medieval village, and it served well as a protection against the possible hostility of the Indians.

New Jersey's Lenni Lenape, however, never disturbed the villagers, and farmhouses built later at Hanover Neck were more widely scattered.[2] The first settlements in Morris County were the hamlets of Hanover and Whippany but in a few years villages and farms appeared at Morristown, Chatham, and Madison. Mills of all kinds were built wherever there was a watercourse. The inhabitants mined their own iron ore and took it to their own furnaces for smelting. Small factories were started, like the shoe factory Josiah Quinby built in 1800 at Hanover. Although the region took care of its own material needs, before the Morris Canal was opened in 1824 the lack of cheap transportation meant that few products could be sold in outside markets.

Population increased slowly in Hanover Township. By 1820, when it included much more territory than it now does, only 3,505 souls were counted.[3] The village of Hanover hardly seemed to grow at all. As late as 1852 George Cook's young brother Henry could write that although other towns seemed to have new buildings and improvements, no new home had been built in Hanover since he could remember. "The rapid march of progress," wrote Henry, "has left it in the lurch."[4] In the 1830s Hanover consisted of a few houses around the blacksmith shop, the shoe factory, the general store run by Mr. Ely, and the Presbyterian Church.[5]

For many years after the first settlement, Hanover villagers who wanted to attend church services had to go to Whippany by horseback, farm wagon, or sleigh. This was a source of much annoyance and some discomfort, especially to the ladies riding in open wagons who were forced to turn their cloaks inside out or throw their shawls over their heads to protect their best bonnets from the rain. As protection against the cold of winter, travelers carried small footstoves filled with live coals which were replenished from homes along the way and passed back and forth during the Sunday services.[6] It was fifty years before the Hanoverians could afford to build a church of their own. They purchased the land for forty pounds from George Cook's great-great-grandfather—"ten acres lying on the right hand of the road as we goe to Ephraim Prides."[7] The church provided most of the intellectual stimulation as well as spiritual guidance for the Kitchells, Balls, Elys, Hoppings, Cooks, and other local families, who were fortunate in having a succession of able pastors.[8] The skepticism of the more sophisticated circles of the eighteenth century never penetrated to the countryside and there was no debate about the validity of the Bible or the authority of the preacher. Personal salvation was the burning question. Not only was this the most important religious question; it meant more to the village and farm folk than did health or success in business or social life.[9] While "respectable" families the country over abided unquestioningly by the standards set forth by the churchgoers for their social and business behavior, Hanover was particularly noted for its church-centeredness. Almost a century later, the reputation of the inhabitants was so impressive that the author of a study of the Passaic Valley took pains to mention their conscientious churchgoing and their great honesty in business matters.[10]

Cooks had lived in this quiet, careful community since 1747 when Ellis Cook came from Southampton at the eastern end of Long Island and "bought of Cornelius Drake of Hanover a farm of 110 acres lying on the south side of the road to the old 'iron works' and extending from Passaic 62 chains westerly."[11] Ellis Cook was a product of four generations of Long Islanders, descendants of an earlier Ellis Cook who had come from England and joining the company of Edward Howell from Lynn, Massachusetts, had settled in Southampton in 1640. The Cook property in Hanover was augmented during the years by inheritance and purchase. Cooks remained modestly prosperous small farmers for the most part but George's great-grandfather (another Ellis) kept an inn at Hanover for a time.[12] This latter Ellis was the most renowned member of the family. Before the Revolution he had served as a member of the Morris County Committee of Correspondence and in 1775 he was sent as a delegate to the Provincial Congress of New Jersey.[13] As a lieutenant colonel in the eastern battalion of the Morris County militia he was given the task of protecting the records of the East Jersey Proprietors when Perth Amboy was threatened by the British.[14] Known as "Captain Cook" he is reported to have been a "man of lofty character." He served three years in the Council and fourteen years in the House of Assembly of the state of New Jersey.[15]

Ellis's grandson, John Cook (George's father), was a sturdy farmer, of whom his son later wrote, "he knew not what it was to give up for any kind of hardship."[16] Greatly respected by his sons, who deferred to his wishes as to their vocational pursuits even when they were grown, he remains a shadowy figure. There is no letter from him among the many saved by his son. Nor is there a letter from George's mother, Sarah Munn Cook, though both are consistently mentioned in terms of love and respect in the correspondence of their children.

Sarah's brother, Dr. Jephtha Munn of Chatham, was a favorite uncle of George's and had a greater early influence on him than anyone else. Dr. Munn, a leading physician in the state, had been one of the organizers of the county medical society in 1816 and was made a Fellow of the State Medical Society in 1828. Munn's letters to George show him to be a man of wide interests and much ability. A farmer as well as a doctor, he was fond of experimenting with different kinds of manures and various methods of fertilizing, all of which he wrote about at length to his nephew. He was also active in politics and was elected to the state senate in 1835 where he served as vice-president. As an active Mason and one time Grand Master of the Masons in New Jersey, one of the high points of his life came when he was chosen to give the welcoming address for a brother Mason, the Marquis de Lafayette, during the hero's visit to Newark in 1824.[17]

Family tradition has it that Lafayette's visit also provided the most momentous event in young George's life. As the great carriage rolled over the dusty road from Morristown to Newark, seven-year-old George was among the awe-struck children who were permitted to leave their schoolroom and line the fence to watch the old gentleman pass. Such an exciting event came seldom in the small boy's life. Most of his early memories concerned simple activities on the farm and in the family circle. He later remembered as a dramatic incident a day when the fire in the kitchen fireplace went out and he was sent running to a neighbor to get live coals to start it up again.[18]

John and Sarah Cook were fortunate in having a large number of children. A daughter, Margaret, died when she was four, but five sons, Isaac, David, George, Henry and Matthias, and two daughters, Mary and Eliza Joanna, lived to grow up. In letters written when they were young

men living and working away from home, Isaac and George revealed
their reserved but affectionate family feelings. Isaac wrote that though
they used to have childish quarrels, he thought they had "as much
affection for each other as is common among mankind."[19] George
recalled the happy days when the children gathered around the table;
David rode around on a broomhandle horse and the rest of the children
bothered their parents with their noise and romping.

As soon as the boys were old enough they began to help on the farm,
where John Cook, like his neighbors, had to struggle to raise enough to
feed his family and livestock. In a typical year, he cultivated twenty-one
and a half acres: three acres of wheat, four of rye, five of oats, eight of corn
and one and one half of potatoes plus the hay fields.[20] Some year he also
grew flax which then had to be pulled, rotted, dressed, spun, woven into
cloth and hand-sewn into shirts and gowns.[21] The family kept chickens,
pigs, cows, horses, sheep, and oxen which had to be butchered, milked,
shorn, shod, or otherwise taken care of. Wool from the sheep was carded,
spun, woven into cloth, and fashioned into garments. Most of the
responsibility for cloth and garment-making fell to the women. Cook
later remembered that it took weeks and months of their time and
consumed their strength and energy. The memory left him with a lasting
respect for any process which could lessen these wearisome chores and a
proper scorn for those who wished to return to the simpler pursuits of an
earlier day. George's mother and sisters also grew vegetables in a garden
near the house, planted flower beds, and persuaded the men to put in
fruit trees and berry patches.[22]

As farm machinery was nonexistent, the tasks of plowing,
harrowing, and rolling were done by the Cook sons walking behind the
oxen or horses pulling the simplest of ploughs or other farm tools. In
these early years on the farm George developed the capacity for hard
work that remained one of his outstanding characteristics. He never
abandoned the hours of the farmer and habitually rose at five or six
o'clock to begin his day's work. In spite of his sharp memories of the
hardships of farm life he remembered the joys too, and years later when
he was teaching in Albany his love for the farm remained so strong that
he urged Matthias and Henry to fill their letters with all the minor
details of the farm activities. Henry obligingly recounted the succession
of farm duties, reminding his brother that in the spring they had first
sowed the oats, then the corn, and finally the potatoes. By the second
week in June all this was done and then they were busy hoeing the corn
and potatoes to keep down the weeds until finally the haying and
harvesting began in late July. Henry concluded with some acerbity, "I

can remember the time when these things were not matters of story to you."[23] John Cook sold livestock and vegetables when he could, but broom corn was the principal cash crop on the farm.[24] Money was always scarce and it was difficult to find enough to pay the mortgage. For a while, in an effort to augment his income, John Cook tried his hand at running a distillery.[25] The family managed to get along with very little cash. After George had left home, his sister Mary wrote to ask him to lend her some money to pay off a debt at Mr. Emmell's shop in Morristown, promising that their father would pay it back as soon as possible.[26] Despite their financial problems, the Cooks always managed to have newspapers and books in the house. Even after they left school, Mary, Henry, and Matthias tried to improve themselves by reading books and practicing their penmanship at home.[27]

As young men the Cook sons thought that farming was the only conceivable life in spite of its difficulties and limitations, but they faced the obstacle common to many farm sons. Farmers needed sons to work the land, but as the boys grew up the farm became too small to support more than one or two and few farmers could afford to purchase land for their sons. When young men reached eighteen or twenty they began to look around for jobs clerking in a store, learning carpentry, blacksmithing, surveying, or working in a manufacturing shop. They hoped to raise money to buy a farm or to learn a trade that would enable them to earn money while they farmed. George's older brothers Isaac and David learned blacksmithing. In 1836, when he was twenty-three, Isaac left home for Tuscumbia, Alabama, where Matthias Munn, his mother's brother, lived. Isaac's health was not good, and the family hoped that he would grow healthier in a warmer climate. He soon found a job in the railroad shops and had a little extra money to spend. David stayed on the farm doing blacksmithing when he could and eventually accumulated enough money to buy himself a farm and blacksmith shop. Henry, Matthias, Mary, and Joanna Eliza remained on the farm and never married.

In spite of their attachment to the land, farm boys often were permanently drawn away by their desire for adventure, prestige, and money, or by the needs of the new factories for mechanics and the new railroads for surveyors and engineers. When George Cook turned twenty in 1838, the country was suffering from the effects of the Panic of 1837. Unsound speculation in western land and the collapse of railroad and canal-building schemes had led to bank failures. Men were thrown out of work, farmers lost their markets, and many small shops and factories went bankrupt. Although the effects of the depression lingered on for

more than ten years the chance of success loomed larger in the
imagination of the young men than did the possibility of failure.
George's chance came when he was offered a job on the Morris & Essex
Railroad (where his uncle Jephtha was a director).[28] He welcomed the
opportunity to earn some money and learn the "engineering business."

George's educational background, though sketchy, was better than
that of the majority of young men at the time. While he was growing up
the entire cost of schooling in New Jersey fell upon parents.[29] They paid
between $1.50 and $2.00 tuition per quarter year at the district school to
cover the salary of the schoolmaster. Powder for making ink, slates, slate
pencils, and the large penny sheets of paper that the children wrote on
all had to be privately purchased. Pens were fashioned from quills found
in barnyards or along the banks of the streams. In 1829 the legislature of
New Jersey had appropriated $20,000 to be distributed to the districts
according to the number of students taught.[30] This did not cover the
entire cost of tuition and in any event was repealed the next year. Many
children did not attend school at all, either because the financial burden
was too great, or because their parents did not see any use in education.
Some, and John Cook was one, were willing to have their sons continue
their education if they showed enough desire to do so, but thought that
their daughters ought not to go beyond the district school. A report of
1828 estimated that twenty-five to fifty children in each district had no
schooling. Morris County was reported to have exceptional educational
advantages because there was a district school in every neighborhood.

Even at its best, the education provided by the district schools was
rudimentary and uneven. Teachers, usually men except during the
summer when young women were hired to teach small children, came
and went with appalling rapidity, frequently hastened onward by the
district board because of chronic drunkenness.[31] If they were not
dismissed because of incompetence, they found a better job after a year or
so. The length of the school year was frequently shortened because there
was no teacher. Eliza Joanna Cook once wrote to her brother that she had
had a "play spell" for two months because Mr. Woods, the teacher, was
ill and had to stop working.[32]

Emphasis in the schoolroom was on reading, spelling, writing, and
arithmetic with a smattering of "historical catechism," geography, and
grammar.[33] Occasionally a particularly able teacher would for an extra
fee give lessons in botany or astronomy to interested pupils before or
after school. Sometimes when a teacher had a special talent or hobby he
might add a subject like elocution or astronomy to the curriculum.[34]
Students progressed at their own rate, depending on the books available

and their own desire to study. When she was about nine, Eliza wrote to George that she was studying Olney's *Geography* and had been through it twice. Students apparently did not mind repeating the same book many times and the practice did insure a relatively complete command of the material covered. In the same letter Eliza reported that they had a new reading book, the *Mount Vernon Reader,* and no longer did their reading practice in Hale's *History of the United States.* She thought she might study Smith's *Grammar* that quarter, but had not yet started. Her enthusiasm for the new teacher, Mr. White, was considerable because she had been going to school for a week and had not been whipped once![35]

The casual and uncertain nature of the schooling stimulated the educational appetites of some students. When Eliza was ten, a dispute over a teacher of the district school led one group of parents to set up another school in an abandoned store in Hanover which they called the "select school." Drawers formerly used by the shopkeeper were turned upside down for writing desks and the fathers put together rough benches. The unorthodox arrangements led to some approved modern techniques—Eliza was particularly pleased because the chairs were not fastened to the floor which made it "very handy to move them as they wanted."[36] Her attachment to the school was intensified because she feared that her father thought she had had enough schooling. She quoted an unidentified author, "I love it, I love it, and who shall presume to chide me for loving our old school room."[37]

George was more fortunate than his sister. When he was eighteen his father allowed him to live with his uncle Jephtha in Chatham for one quarter of the year so that he could study with Thomas B. Dooley at the "Old Academy."[38] One of the thousands of such academies formed as private corporations during the nineteenth century, this forerunner of the high school included practical as well as classical subjects in its curriculum.[39] It was here that George laid the foundation for his future work on the railroad by studying surveying and geometry.

Social life in Hanover moved at the same leisurely pace as did education. Small parties and calls upon friends and relatives accounted for most of it. Young ladies especially spent weeks or months at a time visiting distant relatives. Between the long visits the young people journeyed by horseback, buggy, or sleigh to see relatives in Chatham, Bloomfield, or Newark. Sleigh rides by moonlight were particularly favored. As they reached their late teens and twenties, the Cooks began to participate in camp meetings, debating societies, lyceums, and singing schools in Hanover and surrounding communities.[40] David joined a singing school with fifty members that was financed by the male singers who each paid one dollar a night to cover the stipend paid to the leader. Female members were admitted free while spectators had to pay twelve and a half cents.[41]

One night Mary and David Cook and their cousins Joanna and John Munn visited their Uncle Joseph Munn in Bloomfield to witness a ball. The country cousins were entranced by the dancing at this marvelous event. David wrote, "The way they made the dust fly was a caution."[42] When the twenty couples sat down at eleven o'clock to an "elegant supper" the Munns and the Cooks had a glass of wine and returned home thoroughly enchanted with their experience.

A more familiar social affair was the Fourth of July Sabbath school outing. In 1840 Sunday Schools from Madison, Genungtown, Parsippany, and Hanover gathered in Whippany where the ladies of Hanover distinguished themselves by the splendor of their banner. While children from other churches carried banners of plain muslin, Matthias Cook and the boys from Hanover proudly bore a blue-trimmed white satin masterpiece with the message, "His banner over me was love."[43]

After the spring of 1836 George left these simple pleasures behind. With $2.09 in his pocket he went to board in Orange and work as a surveyor in the building of the Morris & Essex Railroad for Major Ephraim Beach, veteran of the War of 1812 and chief engineer of the Morris Canal.[44] George liked boarding the train in Orange and riding out to the end of the line where he worked to complete the survey of the company's right-of-way. He easily made friends with other young men working on the railroad, especially J. B. Bassinger, L. N. Vibbard, and Elihu W. Cotes.[45] He did not, however, greatly improve his financial condition. Like many nineteenth-century railroads the Morris & Essex had economic problems. The line was planned to run from Morristown to Newark but the exact route was changed several times to please or attract investors.[46] As costs mounted the directors had to borrow money privately. Then they began to have trouble with the strap rail track where cars ran on a thin metal rail mounted on timber. This "strap" occasionally came loose and curled under the wheels, piercing the bottom of the car. Although the problem was eventually solved and the road completed to Morristown, the railroad's economic problems meant that employees had trouble collecting money due them. George had apparently been so eager to start work that he neglected to find out who was to pay his wages. Lacking cash, the railroad eventually paid off its employees with some of the notes due it but George found that not only did the notes not cover the money owed him, but it was impossible to collect them. He tried for several years before he finally gave up. Major Beach was not particularly successful in his business ventures, but the opinion among Cook's friends was that Beach himself was not in want. Isaac wrote that it would not hurt Beach to pay George himself, but "these poor rich folks are the poorest kind of poor."[47] However, as there were no other jobs available, George continued to work for Beach and with Cotes surveyed land for a proposed extension of the line to Easton. This work was soon completed and by October 1837 George had returned to Hanover and was casting about for other work. He surveyed a wood lot for a local farmer, performed odd jobs for his neighbors, and thought of joining Isaac in Alabama.

Before anything materialized he heard from Major Beach again. This time it was from New York State where Beach was chief engineer on the Canajoharie & Catskill Railroad. The company, organized by Judge Thomas B. Cooke of Catskill and eight other men, planned to build a railroad from Canajoharie on the Erie Canal to Catskill on the Hudson River, thus connecting the canal and the existing Utica & Schenectady Railroad to the Hudson River.[48] In response to a terse note, "If you wish to be employed upon the C & C come now and I will furnish you work," George left home on June 9, 1838, taking the train to New York City and the steamboat *Swallow* for the trip up the Hudson to Catskill.[49] To mark the step he began keeping a diary in which he documented his adventures.

The country around Catskill was unknown to him but two of his old friends, J. B. Bassinger and Elihu W. Cotes, were already working on the Canajoharie & Catskill and George settled in with them at Mr. Roggen's boardinghouse at Oak Hill. He was made assistant in charge of the second division under Major Beach and the assistant engineer, Lewis J. Germain, and was responsible for directing a rodman, a chainman, and an axman. After the surveying was finished, sections of the line were let out to various contractors who cleared land, built embankments, and graded the course for the tracks. They hired their own men and worked under the direction of Beach and his assistants. Printed orders issued to the engineering corps set forth in quasi-military style the discipline under which they operated.[50] Ranks were so clearly distinguished that the chief engineer was not to be addressed unless the head was uncovered. Discipline extended even to dining and sleeping arrangements in the boardinghouse, where workers could take their seats only after their superiors had been seated and the choice of a bed was made in order of rank. Questions could be asked of superiors only if orders were not understood. No suggestions were permitted and inferiors could interrupt only with permission.

George's job was to oversee the contractors in his section; survey the route of the railroad bed; designate land to be cleared and the way it was to be done; and, with his helpers, stake out the next stretch to be cut. He showed the contractors how far to carry their embankments and urged them on when the work seemed to go too slowly. He enjoyed working outdoors but the days were long and hard and to his great distress he usually fell asleep about nine o'clock. This made it difficult to follow the study plan he had mapped out for himself although he still rose at 5:30 or 6:00 A.M. to review Euclid, Comstock's *Chemistry*, Gumere's *Surveying*, or some of his other books in the hope that he might find a way to go on with his schooling the following winter. To improve his writing style he wrote regularly in his diary.[51]

George and his friends talked of their chances of getting another job in surveying when the Canajoharie & Catskill was finished and of other possibilities that might be open. Cook thought he might like to study with his uncle Jephtha and become a doctor or go to the Fairfield Medical School in New York State. Lewis Germain spoke enthusiastically of the Rensselaer Institute in Troy, New York, saying that it was not like the colleges which made students concentrate on Latin and Greek but focused on the sciences and offered a degree in civil engineering. He was sure Cook would do well there and would like the life and the studies.[52]

George's self-doubt and his determination to improve himself were especially evident in his religious life. He read the Bible regularly and worried about the state of his soul. Because he shared with most churchgoers of his class and generation an unquestioning faith in the reliability and relevance of the biblical accounts of the life and significance of Jesus of Nazareth, he was greatly concerned about his chance of salvation. He worried about the question his friend and former schoolmaster, Lucius Barrow, posed, "Do you hope you have an interest in Christ?"[53] Cook wrote of his doubts of his worthiness saying that he *did* dare to hope he had an interest in Christ, but that he had not united with the church in case he was wrong. In his diary he cautioned himself not to fail to stand for the right as he would be held accountable on the last day and he "feared that his feelings were not as they ought to be on the important subject of religion and eternity."[54] Church membership was not taken for granted in the Cook family or in most families at that time—a personal religious experience rather than traditional support of the church by the family was the criterion for membership. A letter from

Isaac noted with approval a revival of religion in Hanover and hoped that it would "reach to our house among those who I esteem most on earth that all may become the followers of the Lord Jesus."[55] George's mother was a communicant of the Hanover Presbyterian Church and he had been baptized there but his father was not a member. Nowhere did George ever write specifically of having had an overwhelming personal revelation but a letter written later by a lifelong friend, William Gurley, makes it clear that at some time he had had such an experience.[56]

With this kind of preoccupation it is not surprising that one of the most constant of George's activities was churchgoing. He usually went to two church services on Sundays—his youthful daring prompted him to take advantage of his absence from home to sample Episcopal and Methodist services. For a time he was particularly attracted to the Episcopal form of worship, studied the Prayer Book and noted in his diary that he intended to practice until he could find his place in the service more readily. A few months later, however, he confessed that it was a relief to enter a well-filled Presbyterian church. It seemed like home, and he thought, was "almost the only church that seems like a house of worship to me."[57]

It was doubtless George's self-conscious preoccupation with religion and with his own character that led him into a positive response to the increasingly popular temperance movement. The nineteenth-century reign of the "respectable" with its condemnation of the pleasures of the flesh had not yet settled immovably upon the middle class, but reaction to the widespread heavy drinking of the early nineteenth century had led to a flourishing movement to restrain or abolish it. Getting people to sign temperance pledges was a favorite method of discouraging drunkenness. George and his two friends, Cotes and Vibbard, signed a pledge in which they agreed that because the use of "ardent spirits" was immoral and besides that unnecessary, they would abstain from partaking or serving of such.[58]

The other tempter, tobacco, was considered less iniquitous and therefore was harder to resist. George recorded that on October 9, 1838, he smoked his first pipe of tobacco and found that it did not make him ill. He felt that he did not want to be a habitual smoker but thought that it would be useful to know how to smoke without getting sick.[59]

As for girls, George had a normal interest in them and, indeed, was the recipient of a mildly bawdy document written by one of his fellow workers testifying to his probable prowess in amatory matters.[60] He was rather particular, however, and seldom found any young ladies who pleased him. At the conclusion of a ride to visit four young women who lived near Oak Hill he remarked sourly in his diary, "I for my part was not very well pleased."[61] He was on very friendly terms with his cousin, Joanna Munn, who admired him greatly and with whom he corresponded while at Catskill. George's awareness of his own shortcomings made him very sensitive of the effect his actions might have on others. Once he wrote regretfully in his diary of having inadvertently insulted a man at tea. He scolded himself for not "paying that attention to strangers which I ought."[62] On another occasion he deeply regretted his part in a practical joke in which he and his companions tied a fellow worker's bed sheets into knots.

Living away from the farm and earning their own money led both George and Isaac into purchases that they feared the family at home would not understand. Isaac justified a certain extravagance in buying clothes with the thought that if they did not dress as well as their companions they would be considered miserly. George had been talked into buying a gold watch from Major Beach for the enormous sum of $85. He thought this was probably inexcusable.[63]

George's self-doubts did not keep him from enjoying his free time. He swam with his friends at a nearby pond after work on hot days, took walks, visited the homes of new friends in the neighborhood, and went looking for strawberries. A more venturesome outing on the Fourth of July saw George, Cotes, Germain, Bassinger, and some other friends travel by stagecoach to Cairo and thence by train to Catskill. Here they spent the night and the next morning left Catskill on the steamboat for Poughkeepsie. George walked up to the main part of the town, which he pronounced to be "altogether very pleasant" with "paved streets and the buildings in good repair."[64] After an hour the adventurers got back on the steamer, where they had dinner while sailing back up the Hudson in a violent wind and rainstorm.

After his pleasant summer in the Catskills George was sorry to learn that no new work on the Canajoharie & Catskill would be started before the next spring.[65] He stayed on the job through November while the company made explorations for a possible new railroad line in an area near Middleburgh and he figured estimates of the work that had been done the two months previous. By December 10, however, he was out of work and undecided as to where he would spend the winter. The country was still in the throes of a depression and very little work was available. He was determined not to go home to be a burden on his family. He thought of joining Isaac in Alabama but Isaac wrote that times were harder there than they had been the year before. The purchase of the gold watch seemed especially foolish to him now, for such a large amount of money might have supported him for the whole winter and enabled him to continue his education at an academy.

Cook at twenty was somewhat old to think of beginning further study in a period when many young men went to college at the age of fifteen, especially since he had had a minimum of formal education. It is doubtful that his years at the district school and his quarter year at the Old Academy in Chatham had prepared him sufficiently for most colleges even in that age of minimum requirements. On the other hand, he had had first-hand experience as a surveyor and had developed exemplary habits of work and study. Remembering how enthusiastic Lewis Germain had been about the Rensselaer Institute and having nowhere else to go, he set out for Troy with a vague plan to visit the school and a hope that he might find work.

1838-1846
The Rensselaer Institute

George Cook arrived in Troy on December 18, 1838, to find that there were no jobs available for aspiring young engineers. In the long run this disappointment proved to be a stroke of fortune for he decided on an alternative that was to be much more common a hundred years later; when he couldn't find work, he went to school. Thus almost by accident he began an association with Amos Eaton who, more than anyone else, set the pattern for his future career.

When Cook went to see Eaton at the Rensselaer Institute he had barely enough money to enroll in the Institute for the winter term. He confessed to Isaac his unhappiness at the prospect of not earning any money that year. His conscience still bothered him about the extravagant purchase of the gold watch. Isaac reassured him: "From my knowledge of your studius [sic] habits [I am sure] you will never regret the time and money you will spend at that institution."[1] Although there is no evidence to support the notion, it would have been quite in character for Eaton to let Cook enroll with nothing but a hope that he would eventually pay his debt. Eaton's habit of extending credit to students was largely responsible for the chronic financial troubles of the Institute. Except for the first five years of its existence during which it had been subsidized by Stephen Van Rensselaer, the school was always short of money.

Nevertheless, small, insecure, and poverty-stricken as it was, with Amos Eaton as its head it provided the best training available in applied science. Although Eaton was aging and in failing health when Cook arrived, he was still a powerful and flamboyant figure—a man whose energy, enthusiasm, and occasional flashes of brilliant insight were so much above the ordinary that common men thought him a genius. He had not begun the teaching of science as a profession until he was over forty years old and had seen a career as lawyer and land agent come to a disastrous end. An accusation of forgery and fraud in land deals (which Eaton explained to Cook was the work of his enemies) led to a conviction and sentence of life imprisonment. During his years in prison in Manhattan, a sympathetic jailer allowed him to study botany. Even in this unconventional setting Eaton's teaching talents found an outlet. He began to teach botany to the keeper's young son, John Torrey, an unusually gifted boy who later became one of America's outstanding botanists.

Eaton remained in prison for four years before New York Governor Daniel D. Tompkins pardoned him on condition that he leave the state. Determined to make a new career for himself in the field of science, he went to Yale where he studied geology and mineralogy under Benjamin Silliman. Until 1817 (when Governor DeWitt Clinton granted him a complete pardon that allowed him to return to New York State) he spent his time in New England giving public lectures. He became a popular lecturer on the wonders of science and the marvelous benefits which it could bring to mankind. Williams College, his alma mater, gave him an M.A. degree in 1817 and in 1818, at the request of Governor Clinton, he delivered some lectures on geology before the New York State legislature. Thus thoroughly returned to respectability and energetically embarked upon his Baconian mission to persuade men of the rewards of scientific development, he came to the attention of Stephen Van Rensselaer, the wealthy and powerful owner of the great Van Rensselaer estate which covered more than a thousand square miles along the Hudson River. Surely one of the happiest products of the aristocratic tradition, Stephen Van Rensselaer was kindly, concerned for the people who lived on his lands, active in civil life, and fully aware of the responsibilities of great wealth. He was drawn to Eaton because he wanted to help the tenants on his vast lands to adopt more scientific and efficient methods of farming. Under his patronage and the direction of the short-lived Central Board of Agriculture of the State of New York, Eaton carried out a geological and agricultural survey of Rensselaer and Albany counties. Rensselaer was so impressed with Eaton's survey that he hired him to make a survey of the fifty-mile strip of land along the line of the Erie Canal and sponsored him in a series of lectures on chemistry, natural philosophy, and natural history for the working people of the area. Both men were so caught up in the marvels of science that they confidently expected that when common folk witnessed demonstrations of chemical experiments they would be inspired to apply the methods and principles of science to "the common purposes of life.''[2]

Response to the talks was encouraging, but Eaton and Van Rensselaer agreed that a more sustained effort was necessary in order to accomplish the kind of metamorphosis they had in mind. Van Rensselaer decided in 1824 to finance the establishment of the Rensselaer School "to qualify teachers for instructing the sons and daughters of farmers and mechinics . . . in the application of experimental chemistry, philosophy, and natural history to agriculture, domestic economy, the arts and manufactures.''[3] He hoped that the City of Troy would eventually help support it. Unfortunately, the school was not a great success. The citizens were willing enough to be titillated and awed by startling scientific demonstrations and lectures but they were not interested in giving money to support scientific education. Eaton and Van Rensselaer had to come to the school's assistance more often than had been expected. The tuition fees Eaton collected never amounted to more than $800 a year as he was so little able to resist extending credit to students that sums as high as $700 were sometimes outstanding.[4] He himself subsidized the school by the sale of the textbooks which he wrote on many scientific subjects.

Eaton bore not only the financial burden of the school but after the first four years, when he had the capable assistance of Lewis Caleb Beck, he had had to carry the whole academic burden with only part-time, sporadic, and inadequate assistance. The continuation of the school thus meant great personal effort and sacrifice for him; a sacrifice which was the greater because of a series of family tragedies and because of his chronic asthma and other respiratory problems. Although the financial and emotional responsibilities for his large family weighed heavily on Eaton, he refused to abandon the Institute for more lucrative pursuits. In addition, he gave as many public lectures on science as he could manage, frequently without costs to the audience. Earlier he had written, "I do not know a person in the world but myself who would become a successful scientific pedlar. I have learned to act in such a polymorphous character that I am to men of science a curiosity, to ladies a clever school master, to old women a wizzard, to blackguards and boys a shewman and to sage legislators a *very knowing man.*''[5]

Eaton was undeniably a master teacher and he made the Rensselaer Institute unique. Long-established colleges like Harvard and Yale and smaller institutions such as Union, Williams, and Rutgers provided for instruction in science to the extent that they were able, while medical schools taught those sciences necessary for the practice of medicine. But Rensselaer was the only institution that from its beginning had focused on teaching science as a foundation for careers in engineering, chemistry, scientific agriculture, mining, and the newly developing industries of railroading and manufacturing. Not only was the goal of education different at Rensselaer, the method of teaching, too, was different. When students at Princeton and Yale studied science under John Maclean or Benjamin Silliman they concentrated on memorizing texts and occasionally watched the professor conduct an experiment. Most of the time they listened to lectures. As late as the 1870s, it was rare to find students at Harvard participating in laboratory work or even observing experiments.[6] At Rensselaer Eaton was convinced that the best way to teach was to do away with as much dull memory work as possible. His students performed their own experiments in chemistry and physics and he sent them into the field to search for botanical and geological specimens. Strongly believing that the best way to learn is to teach he demanded that they regularly prepare lectures for presentation to their fellow students.

In his insistence on practical laboratory work for students and in the "practice-teaching" techniques he was far ahead of his time, but it was more than teaching methods that made him a great teacher. He had an infectious enthusiasm and self-confidence that implanted in his students a lasting interest in science. Even though they might enter nonscientific fields after they left the Institute, they kept up an exchange of botanical and geological specimens and wrote to each other of their collections and their new finds.[7] Reorge Perkins Merrill, in *The First One Hundred Years of American Geology*, called the decade 1820 to 1829 the "Eatonian Era" because Eaton was "the most prominent worker as well as the most profuse writer of the decade."[8] Though Merrill acknowledged that Eaton had shortcomings as a theoretician, he concluded, "Yet the Rensselaer School, where Eaton was teaching, was and continued to be for many years, the chief training school for American geologists. Fortunately, his students were taught to *think* and not to blindly follow."[9]

Eaton's greatest strength was in geology and many of the outstanding geologists of the nineteenth century were products of the Rensselaer Institute. Cook studied at the Institute at two different times, first from December 1838 to March 1839 and later from March 1840 to September 1840. During the winter of 1839 he was enrolled in the course in civil engineering. This program required that students know trigonometry, conic sections, mensuration, hydrostatics and hydrodynamics. They also learned the use of the level and compass in laying out roads, railroads, and canals; how to run curves and stake them out; how to calculate for excavations and embankments and how to direct the construction of bridges and waterworks. They had to become proficient in calculating the height and pressure of the atmosphere as well as the heights of hills and mountains and were instructed in how to make topographical surveys and how to describe geological formations.[10] George already had learned much of this while working on the railroads and was able to finish the course in one term. By March 1839 he had a C.E. degree and a letter from Eaton testifying to the fact that he had been "a diligent student and is well qualified to teach engineering or work in the profession [because he had been] well fitted when he entered and considerably versed in field practice." and because "his diligence and progress in his exercises . . . were uncommonly great."[11]

George thoroughly enjoyed his studies, met a number of congenial young men (among them William Gurley of Troy) and acquired professional status. But this status did not help him to find another railroad job in New York and he returned to New Jersey. Unfortunately, the effects of the Panic of 1837 lingered on. Not until the 1850s did railroad construction gain impetus again. George kept hoping that Major Beach would have work for him on the Canajoharie & Catskill. However, when no word had come by July, he decided to teach school— a stopgap often employed at the time by desperate young men who had some education but no money or prospects.

Probably because of the influence of his Uncle Jephtha Munn, he was offered a job at the "Old Academy" in Chatham. He wrote to tell Beach that he was going to take the job but added that he could arrange to leave with a few days notice if work on the railroad materialized.[12] While teaching in Chatham he lived with the Munns and, the railroad business being what it was, he registered his apprenticeship in the study of medicine with the New Jersey Medical Society and began to study with his uncle. He liked living with the Munns and wrote in his diary that he had "found a home and friends such as I can never reasonably expect to meet with again."[13] But he did not enjoy teaching school as he was poorly paid and the students were hard to discipline. When the maneuvering of one Squire Burnet caused him to be "turned away" after three quarters of the year (because the Squire had another candidate for the job) George was glad enough to give up being a schoolmaster.[14] His experience with teaching was so distasteful that he turned down a job as schoolmaster at Madison which would have paid him more money.

Again Cook traveled up the Hudson looking for work on the Canajoharie & Catskill. But there were still no jobs. When he stopped at

Rensselaer he found that Eaton needed an assistant for the summer term. This was a more palatable kind of teaching than grammar school and in addition he would be able to study for the Bachelor of Natural Science degree. Eaton gave him a contract that made him an "assistant professor," provided room and lodging, paid four dollars a week for twenty-four weeks and allowed him to continue his studies.[15] George was to teach surveying and engineering, help out when he could in geology, botany, chemistry, mineralogy and zoology, and was responsible for the conduct of the students.[16] Even with this opportunity, George did not look upon teaching as an especially desirable profession and had by no means given up hope of finding work on a railroad or studying medicine. He weighed the possibility of going to the Fairfield Medical College in New York State the following fall. With good reason he could later write, "I have always been the creature of circumstances, going just as the time seemed to dictate."[17] Nevertheless, he *acted* as though his dearest wish was to become a scientist, recording in his diary (with his customary passion for self-improvement) a determination to make the most of this opportunity by rising to study every morning at five o'clock. The drive to extract the last ounce of benefit from every situation was to push him further than any high-flown ambitions he might have nursed.

Though teaching and studying at the Institute was a fortunate chance for George, Amos Eaton also had cause to thank fortune for sending a young man of Cook's ability and temperament to help him in his declining years. Eaton was badly in need of help. His school, upon which he had lavished his efforts, energies, and what substance he could, was discouragingly often in need of donations to keep it going. His health, never hardy, by the winter of 1840 (when he was sixty-four years old) had been increasingly undermined by frequent attacks of asthma and what Cook called "tisic" (the country name for phthisis or pulmonary tuberculosis).

When Cook began his duties as an assistant professor at Rensselaer in 1840 there were five students enrolled, two of them Eaton's sons, Cuvier and Humboldt.[18] More young men drifted in as the term went on and the ranks were increased by a number of ladies who enjoyed collecting botanical specimens and were anxious to learn. Even so, the largest number enrolled at any time during that year seems to have been about twenty. This did not displease George for the fewer the students, the more time he could spend upon his own studies.[19]

From the very first day (when he had to conduct the opening exercises of the school because Eaton was busy elsewhere) Cook exerted considerable influence upon the institution.[20] He was instrumental in reviving an old regulation requiring practice in composition, first infecting the students with his enthusiasm and then procuring Eaton's approval. Every week each student wrote a "composition" and read it before the rest of the school. Eaton criticized them all immediately and publicly.[21] George admitted to Isaac that he did not enjoy being criticized before the whole school, but he felt the operation worthwhile because he was very anxious to improve his writing.[22]

The organization of the curriculum was haphazard—not for Amos Eaton the carefully structured catalogue of courses with descriptions, credit hours, prerequisites, and hours of meeting that has since become standard. He taught according to his mood and the students' interest and took advantage of the chance or planned visits of scientists and the talents of members of his household to augment his curriculum. The usual procedure was to have lectures in the morning and field work in the afternoons. The lectures were delivered by Eaton, Cook, the students themselves, or a visiting dignitary. Dr. John Wright lectured on the circulation of the blood; Douglass Houghton, state geologist of Michigan (a graduate who had assisted Eaton in 1828), came for a visit and lectured on geology.[23] Every Saturday morning students were examined orally on the week's work. Usually Eaton or "the Professor" as his students called him pursued one subject for several weeks though this concentration might be interspersed with lectures on other topics. Cook records that during one week in April 1840, the students calculated water pressures under different conditions on Monday morning and that afternoon went out surveying with compass and lead. On Tuesday the students lectured. Wednesday they stayed in and worked examples. Thursday Cook again taught surveying, and took the students out to work with level and sextant. No afternoon exercises were carried on that day because they returned too late. Friday was again devoted to surveying, the students spending their time after the morning exercise calculating surveys.

During the following weeks, Eaton lectured on botany, zoology, and geology. A month after the term began he attended to such administrative details as recording the names, birthdates, and home addresses of the students. Eaton's system required each student to assume a great deal of personal responsibility for what he accomplished. Cook's diary shows that he finished Bakewell's *Geology* April 30 and planned to begin it again the next day along with Gray's *Botany*.[24] This repetition when added to the oral examinations and student lectures insured a solid knowledge of the material offered. George rejoiced in the rigorous program—he once wrote to Isaac with great pleasure and satisfaction that he arose at 4:30 A.M. and worked until 10:30 P.M. But, he reassured Isaac, "no student of this institution ever hurt himself with study, there is too much out of door exercise collecting plants, minerals, bugs, birds, etc."[25] The geological tour taken at the end of each summer was the most elaborate excursion afield. In 1840 it was Cook's responsibility and for ten days he led the students across river, valley, and mountain in New York and New England studying geological formations at first hand.

During the summer term that year the burden of teaching and the conduct of the school fell increasingly upon the young assistant. In April, shortly after Cook arrived, Eaton had become extremely angry while scolding someone and had a fit of coughing which raised blood and altogether made him so unwell that Cook had to conduct the examination of students that morning. The next night Eaton had an alarming attack of bleeding. His family feared for his life, and he was cautioned by his physician to keep very still if he wished to recover. "The professor is much better today," wrote Cook in his diary, "he is, however, interdicted by the physician from all conversation. He, however, manages to talk most of the time. And he got out once today to call the dog and set him on a cow in the field so imprudent is he. . . ."[26] In his sober way, George recorded his determination to profit by this example and learn to control his passions.

Eaton's indisposition gave George so much experience that he wrote to Isaac, "I should not be afraid to lecture before common folks on chemistry now, I have had an excellent chance this summer. The professor on account of ill health has been obliged to leave the laboratory frequently. At such times I have to give the lecture and experiments to the class and about a dozen ladies who attend the morning lectures. I generally get along without any trouble though I cannot make much of a speech."[27]

At the end of the summer of 1840 George received the degree of Bachelor of Natural Science and reached another crossroad. He was still juggling the possibility of careers in medicine, engineering, farming, and teaching. He thought of going to Alabama to join Isaac, or of taking a job teaching natural science at Maryville College in Tennessee (urged on him by a minister friend from Hanover). He was also considering the chances of getting a job on the Erie Canal where his friend E. W. Cotes was working. It was as difficult as ever for him to make up his mind. He wondered if Eaton might want him to remain another year. Eaton's usual practice had been to keep his assistant (a student who had finished the first year's course) only one year but because of his health he finally decided to ask Cook to stay on for a second year.[28] At first George thought he would be able to find a good job elsewhere and he had almost decided not to stay unless he could get more money.[29] But by October nothing better had turned up. Eaton's attacks grew more frequent; it was clear that he badly needed an experienced assistant and Cook was glad of a chance to show his gratitude to the old man.[30] In the previous year Cook had found that he could really manage quite well with $4.00 per week plus room and board. Even after he paid his expenses for the geological trip he had as much money left as when he had arrived. He hoped to make some extra money helping Eaton with his public lectures on geology and decided that the additional training would make it worthwhile even if he lost money.

Through the course of the winter Cook found that he was, indeed, learning a great deal. His duties were lighter because no field work in surveying or botany was carried on in the winter and teaching mathematics and helping Eaton set up apparatus for chemical experiments left ample time for study. His help in Eaton's public lectures was noted in the *Troy Daily Mail*: "The Senior Professor will have an assistant of experience to fill his place when needed. He will also prepare for all experiments and prevent every auditor from being annoyed with disgusting gases."[31] During one of the experiments a gas bag exploded. No one was injured and in later years Cook liked to tell his children the exciting story.[32]

Under Eaton's sponsorship Cook was elected a member of the Troy Lyceum of Natural History, became a member of the committees on botany, geology, and mineralogy and was made chairman of the committee on paleontology. He and William Gurley also studied conchology with a local doctor.

During the winter of 1840-41 at Eaton's suggestion Cook took an extra job assisting the science teacher at the Troy Female Seminary.[33] Later that year the science teacher left and Cook was delighted to be hired in his stead. This famous school, founded by Emma Willard, was at the time run by her son, John Hart Willard, although Mrs. Willard still exerted considerable influence. In many ways Cook's position at the Troy Seminary was a better one than that at Rensselaer. The seminary was very highly thought of and successful—much more successful financially than Rensselaer. Cook was paid $400 for his seminary job but was perhaps even more pleased at being allowed to spend five hundred dollars on new equipment for the laboratory (on which the seminary had already spent $1500).[34] Cook's records show that among the things he bought with the $500 was a compound microscope, a camera obscura, a horseshoe magnet, quicksilver, glass tubes and flasks, lead pipe; nitric, oxalic, and sulphuric acids, a galvanic battery and specimens from a slaughterhouse he used to illustrate physiology lectures.[35] He also taught geology, physics, and chemistry and in the spring took his students into the fields on botanical rambles. Fortunately, much of his teaching at the seminary was scheduled during vacation periods at Rensselaer.

In 1841 major difficulties developed for the Institute. Seven years earlier the school had been moved from its original location on the Old Bank Place, which belonged to Eaton, to the Van Der Heyden Mansion—a property which he had leased. Now the owner planned to sell the land for the building of small houses.[36] In May, therefore, the school moved back to the Old Bank Place which had been rented for the seven years. "A more filthy set of tenants never lived," wrote Eaton. To make the place habitable for the school everyone had to "labor like slaves"—scrubbing, papering, plastering and carting away rubbish.[37]

Dirt and disorder were not the greatest problems. As usual, the major difficulty was lack of money. The house at Old Bank Place was mortgaged and Eaton could not keep up the payments. Stephen Van Rensselaer, who had held the mortgage, might have been indulgent (as he always was with Eaton), but he had died in 1839 and the mortgage had passed to his son William. William and his brother Alexander were sympathetic to Eaton but they demanded that the citizens of Troy assume financial responsibility for the school.[38] The citizens of Troy remained unconcerned but fortunately for Eaton the mortgage was assumed by his son, Daniel Cady Eaton (then thirty-seven years of age and a successful businessman in New York City) and Daniel Cady, Eaton's brother-in-law of Johnstown, New York, who had become a justice of the State Supreme Court.

The school struggled on. At Cook's suggestion the students arranged to have Eaton's portrait painted.[39] The painting was acclaimed by some as the finest portrait in Troy and had "the superior merit of being an accurate likeness of the venerable old man."[40]

George's increasing satisfaction with his jobs and his life in Troy was disturbed in June 1841 when a heartbroken letter came from his sister, Mary, telling him that Isaac had died.[41] George hurried home and wanted to go to Alabama at once, but his family persuaded him that there was no reason to make the long trip; Isaac had been buried even before the letter announcing his death arrived in Hanover. The following April the family got word that Isaac's personal property had been sold to cover the funeral costs. George immediately sent fifty dollars to buy back his watch and papers and eventually received Isaac's letters.[42]

He kept them for the rest of his life. Although they had been apart for several years, their letters show the strong brotherly love they both felt. Just before Isaac's death, George had written to say how much he appreciated Isaac's counsel because he felt he had made no really close friends since he had left home.[43] Even in the family he thought only Isaac could understand the needs of a young man away from home because only Isaac was in the same situation. The two brothers shared a feeling of responsibility for their younger brothers and sisters and together had planned to send Eliza Joanna to Emma Willard's school the next winter.

In the fall George's multitudinous responsibilities at Rensselaer were somewhat lightened by the arrival of his brother Henry. Though their father could ill afford to spare Henry from the farm (Matthias was already away working for his cousin Mary Munn Belknap's husband as an apprentice in his store and candle-making shop), the opportunity seemed too good to miss. Eaton, in his peculiarly involved and wordy way had arranged the matter. In a memorandum he began by describing George as "aspiring, energetic, and efficient," and suggested that Henry could live in George's room and George could pay two dollars per week for his board. For this Eaton thought George could get from Henry "services for which nobody knows what you may get if he does not stay. Pay nothing for tuition, fees, etc. . . . You will (and always did) have much fall on you. He will, of course, aid you much."[44]

In November 1841 Eaton recognized Cook's increased importance in the school by making him junior professor. Between them they worked out a new financial arrangement. Eaton's memorandum on this was even more complicated than usual. He suggested that Cook get his room, board, laundry, and one fourth of the income of the school (which Eaton estimated at $800). That would give Cook $200 for the forty-two-week school year. To this would be added whatever he received from the Troy Female Seminary. Another memorandum written by Cook (who had lost the original) reports that Eaton said that he would take $533 and Cook would get $267.[45] Cook wrote, "He further stated that he thought I had better stay with him one year longer if I could only come out even at the end of the year and that I would never regret it. He also said that he only wished to live and if I preferred a stated sum as salary he had no objection."[46]

As junior professor, Cook taught chemistry and mathematics and directed engineering and botany field work and the geological tours.[47] He also gave the public lecture series by himself that winter. As the *Troy Whig* explained, "An evening course of experimental lectures in chemistry to commence soon. Mr. Eaton's health will not admit of his giving the course. It will be conducted by Prof. Cook."[48]

The old "wizzard and shewman" advised Cook on the best way to begin the lectures: Avoid the usual introductory lecture, he said, because "the uninstructed derive no benefit from it, on account of the facts referred to being unknown to them . . . and those who have given any attention to it are already prepared for entering upon the course."[49] Accordingly, Cook began with a demonstration of six experiments, presumably the most sensational and interest-grabbing he could manage. He showed the effect of heat on iodine, the burning of phosphorus in oxygen, the burning of sodium on water, and three demonstrations that showed the application of chemistry in testing various ores of iron. But he was not pleased. It seemed to him that such demonstrations were unsatisfactory because they "did not have sufficient point."

Eaton's health became progressively worse during the winter. His asthmatic seizures forced him with increasing frequency to abandon the classroom to Cook in the middle of a lecture. In the spring he was stricken with his final illness and in May he died. For Cook Eaton's death was a personal as well as a professional loss. As his friend Cotes wrote, ". . . he was an invaluable friend to you, perhaps a better one than almost any other you can mention. He seemed to identify your interest with his own."[50]

The wonder is that the Rensselaer Institute did not die with Eaton's death; during the eighteen years of its existence only his inspiration and determination had kept it going. Certainly many thought it would now be closed. The trustees were forced to put a notice in the *Troy Whig* to the contrary:

Rensselaer Institute. This institution will *not* be suspended in consequence of the death of Professor Eaton. The Rev. Dr. Beman, trustee, will exercise a supervisory care over its interests. Dr. Wright, one of our most distinguished naturalists, will assist in the Department of Natural History, and Professor Cook, the able and popular associate of Professor Eaton, will act as Principal. With such an array of talent, the Institute will prosper, we doubt not, as in times past, and continue to send forth to the world young men distinguished for their proficiency in the sciences.[51]

This was a fine, brave statement, but the school's troubles with finances and location were by no means settled. Very few students applied for admission. There was some talk of moving the school to Schenectady. The Van Rensselaers still felt that the citizens of Troy should assume responsibility for the school. The state legislature of New

York, petitioned by Eaton in 1841 to establish a professorship, was disinclined to help.[52] For a time the trustees hoped that James Hall might take over the position of Senior Professor. Hall was a graduate of Rensselaer, a former assistant of Eaton's and at the time was working with the New York Geological Survey. A brilliant and hard-working geologist, Hall eventually came to be revered as the foremost American paleontologist and stratigrapher of the time, but he was often arrogant and abrasive.[53] In September, Hall wrote a long letter to Cook, outlining ambitious plans for the distribution of teaching duties between them. Hall would lecture on geology, chemistry, and "any other subject convenient," while Cook would be in charge of mathematics and the literary department.[54] It is possible that Hall gave some lectures (though there is no clear evidence) but he seems never to have had more than a sporadic connection with the school.[55] Cook ended up teaching geology and chemistry as well as everything else.[56]

Though Hall was older and better known than Cook, it is very likely that during that crucial period Cook's conscientious and methodical efficiency was more necessary for the continued existence of the Institute than Hall's brilliance. Nevertheless, it was by default that the trustees decided to name the twenty-four-year-old George Hammell Cook senior professor of Rensselaer Institute. He himself was well aware that his term at the Institute studying civil engineering, the term studying natural science and the three terms assisting Eaton had ill prepared him to take over the responsibility of the entire school and teach the wide variety of subjects Eaton had taught. One of his former students, Calvin Park, wrote to encourage him, "If you would decline the situation which offers decided advantages . . . because you thought yourself incompetent . . . why I say that you do not 'know yourself.' "[57]

Whatever his disadvantages of youth and insufficient preparation, Cook had the temperament to cope with the problems of the school and he was (as Eaton had not been) moving in the direction that American science was then taking—toward specialization and professionalism.[58] Though circumstances at Rensselaer forced him to teach many sciences, as soon as possible he focused on chemistry and geology and, if his finances had permitted, would have specialized even more narrowly. Perhaps Cook's greatest contribution to the Institute was to simply keep it going. But he also had some clear ideas of what he wanted the school to become. Without changing its orientation toward applied science, he was very anxious to build up the "literary department" in order to make a well-rounded curriculum.[59]

To broaden his knowledge of science and technology Cook

undertook a series of trips to scientific and industrial centers in New Haven, West Point, Newark, Philadelphia, and Boston. At Yale he met Benjamin Silliman and Denison Olmsted. He found Silliman to be as excellent a lecturer as he was reputed to be and arranged to exchange geological specimens with Olmsted. The best documented of Cook's trips was the one he made to Boston in December 1843. He filled an entire notebook with a detailed account of his ten-day stay, getting up at five o'clock some mornings to write down the events of the previous day before he joined his landlord and the other guests for morning prayers.

Armed with letters of introduction from trustees of Rensselaer Institute, Cook was able to meet a wide range of Boston's notables, from the famous surgeon Dr. John Collins Warren (who later became the first person to use ether in a public operation) to a suspicious glassblower at the New England Glass Company who suspected that Cook was from a rival firm trying to "steal his art." Cook finally convinced the glassblower of his connection with Rensselaer and bought from him a number of glass items for the laboratory.

One of his most interesting mornings was spent with Dr. Charles T. Jackson, whose laboratory was a mecca for students of analytical chemistry.[60] (The abstemious Cook wrote in his diary that it was there he drank the first coffee he had taken in two years.) Jackson, though brilliant, was a man of erratic personality, inclined to make harsh judgments about fellow scientists, and quite willing to share Boston's scientific gossip with his new acquaintance. He obligingly showed Cook around his laboratory, explaining his equipment and the techniques he used. Cook was particularly impressed with a spirit lamp which heated glass for making bulbs and bending tubes and with Jackson's method for washing filters. In this process he "used a common dropping tube with an India rubber bag attached to the upper end and then forced the liquids in or out by compressing or enlarging the bag."[61] Among other helpful tips, Jackson told Cook that he imported his pure potash and soda from Europe and kept distilled water in a green glass retort because this was the only way it would remain pure.

In this period when the distinction between amateurs and professionals in the scientific world was not yet clearly drawn, Jackson impressed Cook with his conviction that scientists "should use scientific terms and not condescend to the ignorant."[62]

With Jackson, Cook visited the American Academy of Arts and Sciences and the Boston Society of Natural History. At the Society of Natural History Cook found out that conchology was "all the rage" and was impressed by the informal way in which the members talked with each other about matters of scientific interest. The two were among the three hundred who gathered at the Masonic Temple to hear Henry Darwin Rogers lecture on geology. This should have been the high point of the trip, but George commented with disappointment that the lecture "was not clearly arranged and . . . too much encumbered with new names, new theories, and facts of a popular character . . . scarcely necessary in a lecture before an audience of the learning of this."[63] Rogers's platform technique was also disturbing to Cook, who found that he was "by no means as dignified as he might be—constantly running about on the platform—in many cases with scarce any object apparent."[64]

During his ten days in Boston Cook also found time to visit a foundry, a soap factory, a lamp factory, a gas works, the Bunker Hill Monument, the Boston prison, and the Boston hospital where he watched three operations—all performed without benefit of anesthesia.

When Cook returned to Troy he found that Amos Eaton's personal property and the apparatus and library of the Institute had been sold at auction for $382.26.[65] Fortunately the property was bought by Thomas Brinsmade, a trustee of the school and left with Cook so that he continued to use it for the instruction of the students.

In spite of all the uncertainties and in the midst of the lingering economic depression the trustees of the Institute, led by the Reverend Dr. Nathan S. Beman and Brinsmade, were determined to keep the school going. To the sale of Eaton's personal effects had to be added the loss of the building which housed the school itself. The Old Bank Place now belonged to Daniel Cady Eaton. He offered to rent it for $100 a year or sell it outright for $3,000 but William van Rensselaer and his brothers were still determined that the city of Troy should take some responsibility for the school. In a letter to Cook, van Rensselaer said that the "doings of the Common Council . . . are not satisfactory and besides nothing [has] been done in the way of contributions from the citizens and no measures having been taken to unite the school and the Troy Academy . . . we are compelled to give up the whole business and if the school cannot sustain itself without us, let it be abandoned."[66]

Either this determined stand or the persuasive powers of Cook and the trustees convinced the Common Council and the citizens of Troy that if they did not support the school it could not continue. Faced with this prospect both responded; the Council deeded to the Institute a building which had formerly been used to house an "infant school," the Trojans subscribed $1,260 to build a laboratory and the Troy Lyceum decided to hold its meetings and store its scientific collections at the

Institute.[67] William van Rensselaer was sufficiently encouraged by this support to contribute $6,500. Invested at 7 percent this was the Institute's first endowment and produced an income of $455 every year. The trustees repurchased Eaton's apparatus and equipment and during the winter of 1844 Cook raised some money from a series of public lectures on chemistry.[68] In addition the New York State Board of Regents contributed a small sum from the State Literature Fund.

All these developments would have been fruitless if the number of students had continued to dwindle. After Eaton's death the enrollment dropped sharply—from seventeen graduates in 1841 to nine in 1842. The nadir was reached in 1843 and 1844 when only three men graduated each year.[69] Samuel Resneck in his history of Rensselaer Polytechnic Institute has pointed out that this decline was due in part to the decline in public works that accompanied the economic depression of the 1840s. In 1845, however, there were five graduates and the number had increased to eleven by 1846.[70] There were always more students than is indicated by the number of graduates as many came for a short term or took only one or two courses. In 1846, for example, there were seventeen students in the geometry class alone and Cook confidently expected more during the summer term.[71] Friends in Syracuse, Boston, and Philadelphia were trying to interest acquaintances. Cook journeyed to Newark to try to recruit students there. These combined efforts brought twenty-eight students for the summer term, including William Hall, brother of James Hall, and a brave fellow from Surinam by the name of Nicholas Gerard van Meerteen who spoke no English.

It was remarkable that as young and inexperienced a man as Cook was able to keep the school going through the combined catastrophes of the death of Eaton, the loss of the building, and the reorganization of the school. By 1846 George was optimistic about the school's prospects.[72] He had the personal satisfaction of knowing that his work with students was appreciated. The distinguished Unitarian clergyman, Samuel Joseph May of Syracuse, whose son was a student at the Institute, wrote: "I am so much pleased with the progress he seems to have made under your instruction that I am very much inclined to send him back to pass the next term also with you."[73] Gratitude was also expressed by a former student, David Collin, Jr., who wrote, "I shall always feel indebted to you for your kindness and faithfulness toward me while I was with you in imparting those principles which I did not then appreciate as since I left and had it been in my power I should have returned and spent another year with you. . . ."[74]

The esteem in which the City of Troy held George Cook may be judged by a letter from J. Barber at the Troy *Whig*, introducing a stranger who wished to meet the scientific men of the city. Barber sent him to Cook, saying that he knew "but one really deserving of the name of a man of science in this our city."[75] With William Gurley Cook sparked a revival of the Troy Lyceum of Natural History and was made corresponding secretary.[76] He continued to give public lectures, spoke before various lyceums and the Agricultural Society of Rensselaer County on "The Benefits of Science to Agriculture" and he talked to the Young Men's Christian Association of Troy on "The Supposed Conflict between Religion and Reason." He continued to correspond with his uncle Jephtha Munn on scientific agriculture and their letters were full of questions and comments about the value of combining salt with lime, the fertilizing qualities of greensand marl, the Scottish agriculturists in Edinburgh who had hired a chemist to analyze soils and fertilizers, and similar topics.[77]

With all his professional and scholary activities George managed to continue teaching at the seminary. There he met Mary Halsey Thomas, a graduate who had returned as a teacher. The daughter of William Thomas, innkeeper, postmaster, and farmer of Chatham-Four-Corners in Columbia County, New York, Mary was a young woman of exceptional ability and determination. Her father assumed that a few years at the district school was sufficient education for a girl but as soon as she finished those years Mary taught in the school until she had saved enough money to enroll in the seminary.[78] When she ran out of money she borrowed enough to see herself through. After her graduation she taught at the seminary for a year and then spent a year teaching in Stroudsburg, Pennsylvania, where, she wrote home, she had "twenty-five scholars—all dunces."[79] Fortunately, the next year she was able to return to the seminary where she taught Latin, astronomy, arithmetic, and chemistry.[80]

When George's friends heard he was teaching at the seminary, one wrote, "I hear you are having a happy time among the Ladies of the Seminary. Look out for them or you are a 'gone Coon.'"[81] His friendship with Mary, however, blossomed very slowly and for a time George was discouraged enough to think of renouncing female company altogether—which was such an unlikely event that another friend wrote that he could not believe that George would not "cultivate the softer, tenderer feelings of your nature. Alas, that I should live to hear you foreswear the company of the ladies. Why I should as soon think of myself becoming a lady admirer as you ceasing to be one!"[82] If Cook did indeed "foreswear the company of the ladies" it was only for a short time for later that year Joanna Munn wrote coyly: "How we should love to have you here tonight, perhaps you are otherwise engaged just at this present time, out on a *moonlight walk* but not if it rains there as it does here. I apprehend rather wet for my cousin M. (it is to be). How are you progressing? You have always got along so smoothly with all your undertakings that I hope and doubt not this will be like the rest."[83] Even so, not for another year and a half did word begin to filter through to their families at Hanover and Chatham that George and Mary were planning to be married. Joanna wrote reminding Cook of his promise to let her know the day and the date but said she had seen Mary Cook, who had said nothing, "so I am inclined to think the matter will be kept very still."[84] The wedding took place late in March 1846 but a month later Dr. Munn was still uninformed for he wrote: "A friend at my elbow intimates that a rumor has been on the wing some time past that you are actually married and yet no evidence of the alleged fact has reached us by any acknowledgement of the same either from you or yours, or the public prints in these diggings. Has Madame Rumor been fibbing?"[85]

After their marriage Mary and George set up housekeeping in Troy in a rented house at 44 State Street, which Mary described in a letter to her brother Nathan: "[It has] a back piazza, a grape vine is trained upon it and beyond the little space before the wood house is divided into beds and a few flowers are opened to the 'Sun of Spring.' There is a currant bush on one side and a gooseberry on the other trained against the fence. Both now give promise of fruit but the poor peach tree, the pride and ornament of the garden, droops sadly."[86]

George's account book shows that he and Mary bought all manner of household equipment, including a set of white glazed china with soup plates, fluted coffees, a soup tureen, pitcher, and pickle dish; three bedsteads; a feather bed; six bolsters; three mattresses and twenty-five chairs—six "cottage" chairs, six maple chairs, six painted chairs, six mahogany chairs plus a Boston rocker and a sofa! The total bill came to $215.38 and as Cook did not have that much on hand, he had to borrow the money from his friend William Gurley.[87]

After her active and intellectually stimulating life as a teacher, Mary was not particularly pleased with her role as a housewife. She confided to her sister Patty, "I confess I almost hate housekeeping—there are so many petty vexations, so many little things, I do hate them—it's out now."[88] Fortunately she was able to continue at the seminary, where she taught for a time after her marriage, and she also helped George with his teaching preparations. She wrote Patty, "This week my employment has been more agreeable. Monday and Tuesday preparing specimens for the solar microscope. Wednesday and Thursday writing a table of chemical tests, which is very interesting and pleasant. There is enough to occupy me a week longer if I revise what is already done."[89]

Mary and George were well suited to each other. In addition to their common interests in teaching and science, they were both deeply religious and shared an enthusiasm for increasing their general knowledge. Both had a decidedly practical turn of mind and a strong sense of duty. In writing to her younger brother James, Mary advised, "Knowledge in these days is more than power, it is wealth and respectability, be sure you get a large share of it."[90] This somewhat materialistic advice was modified by her strong Calvinistic conviction of the dignity of work. She told James that an intelligent farmer was inferior to no man. "Your own character and attainments will give dignity to whatever your work might be," she wrote. She also advised him to remember his patriotic duty and prepare himself in case his country called him to be a governor, ambassador—or even President.

George and Mary Cook attended church regularly and held daily family prayers as did most respectable middle-class Protestant families. Their religious interests were broader than the average, however—one day George brought Mary Pascal's *Pensées* in the original French to translate.[91]

During the winter of 1845-46, two Albany men, Benjamin Nott (brother of Eliphalet Nott, president of Union College and of the Board of Trustees of the Rensselaer Institute until 1845) and John Paige Pepper, an inventor, enlisted Cook's aid to help them perfect two products Pepper had invented. These were described as "a valuable substance possessing the properties of Porcelain," and a kind of black glass.[92] Nott and Pepper hoped that Cook could help them find a way to glaze iron.[93] If he succeeded he was promised $500 but if he did not, he was to get nothing.[94] There is no evidence to show precisely what experiments Cook performed but he was successful. They called the glazed iron "argillo" and shortly after his marriage Cook, Pepper, Nott, and four other men (including Amos Dean, an Albany attorney who put up the money) formed a corporation to "carry out improvements and establish in this city or elsewhere . . . a manufactory . . . of Glass, Enamel, and Porcelain."[95] The company had a modest beginning—only ten shares of stock at $1,000 were issued. Pepper and Nott held five shares and each of the other five held one. There is no evidence as to where Cook got the money for his share. Perhaps he used some of the five hundred dollars. In any event a receipt shows that sometime in 1846 he paid $875 which was the balance of his payment.[96] The company was named the Albany Glass Enamel and Porcelain Company. J. K. Paige was made the president and Benjamin Nott secretary. Located in the southern part of the city on the corner of Broadway and Ferry Street, the company produced doorknobs, handles, vases, and decorative vessels of various kinds.[97] Cook wrote of the knife handles of argillo that they were, "hard, strong, and suspectible of a very high polish, equalling the agate or carnelian in beauty."[98]

Cook expected that his connection with the glass company would be a sideline to his work at Rensselaer and the seminary and in August he led nine young men on the Institute's annual geological tour, first climbing Mt. Marcy and then exploring the area around Glens Falls and Crown Point. He resumed his duties at Rensselaer on his return but the glass business began to demand more and more of his time.[99] He had to travel to Albany for board meetings and took the responsibility for purchasing firestones and a twenty-horsepower engine.[100] Finally the board asked him to be the full-time manager of the works and he decided to try his hand in industry.

Before he left Rensselaer in October he found his successor. His first choice was his old friend from the Canajoharie & Catskill Railroad, Lewis Germain, then teaching at St. Mary's Hall in Burlington, New Jersey.[101] Unfortunately Germain was not at the school when Cook's letter arrived and the bishop (who apparently ran the school) opened the letter thinking it had something to do with school business. Before Germain ever saw the letter, the bishop had a letter written to Cook saying that he was about to make Germain head of the mathematics department and could certainly not allow him to leave the school.[102] Germain later told Cook that it had been a "source of constant regret" that he could not take the position.[103] (No one seems to have been disturbed by the bishop's high-handed behavior.)

The next man Cook thought of was Benjamin Franklin Greene, who had come to the Institute as a student in November 1841 and had studied there during the difficult months just before and after Eaton's death. His training therefore was primarily under Cook's tutelage. The two had kept up a correspondence through the following years about their jobs and their collections of botanical and geological specimens. Greene was professor of mathematics and natural philosophy and vice-principal of Washington College in Chestertown, Maryland.[104] The trustees took Cook's advice and offered Greene the position of senior professor, which he gladly accepted. (He soon changed his title to "Director.") During his years at Rensselaer he developed engineering curricula which served as a model for engineering education throughout the country.[105]

Even after Cook left Rensselaer, his interest in the school continued. As long as he lived nearby he regularly accepted Greene's invitations to act as an examiner during the students' examinations. William Gurley later became a trustee of the Institute and kept him informed of important developments. In 1859 Greene, who had performed brilliantly as a professor and planner, ran afoul of the trustees because of his personality and his questionable management of school funds. After his resignation the trustees asked Cook to return as director but by that time he had been teaching at Rutgers College for five years and he declined their offer.[106]

In 1846, however, Cook had decided to give up teaching and make his fortune as a glass manufacturer. As a mark of recognition and gratitude the Rensselaer trustees conferred a master's degree upon him. He and Mary moved across the river to Albany with high hopes.

3

1846-1853
Albany: The Glass Works and the Albany Academy

Until the latter years of the nineteenth century glassmaking was not a noticeably prosperous undertaking in America. The industry was expanding in the 1840s but because it was still primarily a handcraft industry demanding a high degree of skill, expansion meant the formation of many small companies rather than the growth of large factories. Many of these small companies were so poorly managed that they soon failed.[1] Unfortunately, this was to be the case with the Albany Glass, Enamel and Porcelain Company that George Cook had joined with such optimism.

Cook's first action after leaving Rensselaer was to go to Boston to inspect the New England Glass Works—one of the few large flourishing glass houses in the country. Mr. Howe, manager of the Glass Works, proved to be very cordial; allowed Cook to inspect everything except their lead works; and provided information about the kind of clay they used, the construction of their furnaces and presses, and the cost of equipment.[2] But he was discouraging about the Albany company's chances for success. He told Cook that glass houses everywhere were failing; four flint houses had gone under in South Boston, and in Philadelphia a Mr. Leybert had lost $30,000 in a glass house. Furthermore, he warned Cook that the New England Glass Works had made knobs like the argillo one Cook brought along to show him but they had not sold and he still had some in stock. He especially advised against trying to manufacture plate glass because the process was very expensive. Glass companies in Europe that made plate glass kept their process secret and, as it cost about half-million dollars to set up a plate glass works and required a great deal of labor (and labor cost twice as much in the United States as in Europe), no one had yet tried to make plate glass in America. There was not much consolation in Howe's assurance that after Cook and his associates had spent thirty or forty thousand dollars they would know these things by experience. The interview was discouraging but on Howe's advice Cook ordered molds and presses from H. N. Hooper & Co. on Commercial Street so his visit to Boston was not entirely unsuccessful.

Soon after Cook returned to Albany, he and Mary moved into a house at 45 Ferry Street, and he settled down to manage the glass house.[3] The Cooks' family and friends greeted the new products with enthusiasm and were optimistic about the prospects of the glass works. But problems developed. William Arthur of Lansingburgh complained that many of the bottles he had ordered broke and their contents spilled.[4] He thought the glass was too thin. On the other hand, Lewis Germain wrote from Burlington that he had seen some samples of argillo which were much admired and which he pronounced to be beautiful specimens of art.[5] Cook wrote to a friend in Boston who had ordered doorknobs that the black knobs with roses "were taking the market wherever they were offered."[6] Mary's brothers, Nathan and James, and George's brother Henry came to live with them and work at the glass factory.[7]

In September 1848 a son, Paul, was born to George and Mary and the following spring the family, including Henry, James, and Nathan, moved to a larger house at 304 South Pearl Street.[8] Mary enjoyed her new home: "It is so pleasant that however much I am disturbed downstairs I can hardly go up as far as my room without recovering my equanimity. The air is delightful and it is almost as quiet as on the hill in Chatham. Besides, the pleasure of a kitchen on the ground and going outdoors to hang something on real bushes to dry—everything smells so sweet and fresh I run out with everything I can lay my hands on."[9]

But matters in the glass factory deteriorated. It had been undercapitalized from the beginning and the directors were soon forced to borrow money. Cook signed a promissory note for $408 and, along with the other stockholders, one for $3,585.[10] In an effort to boost sales, he reluctantly gave up his position as manager of the works and devoted himself to sales promotion. This proved to be an unwise move, for more problems developed at the works and deliveries lagged.[11] Then came a complicated series of financial maneuvers in which Cook sold his stock to Amos Dean and John Paige Pepper for one dollar and the next week bought a fifth of two shares of stock transferred to Dean and Pepper from two other stockholders.[12] The company continued for some time under the new organization but financial problems continued and payment was refused on the two notes.[13]

Even while he was involved in glass-making, Cook had kept up with academic and scientific matters. He continued to collect specimens, made some analyses of ores, and acted as an examiner at the final examinations of students at both Rensselaer Institute and Union College.[14] He did not, however, accept the offer of publishers W. S. Stedman of New York and Elias Gates of Albany, who wanted to put out a new edition of Eaton's botany textbook while his name was still recognized and respected. Dr. Leonard at Rensselaer had begun the revision, but had decided that too much work would be involved. Gates wrote to Cook asking him to "leave off glass-making and help Dr. Leonard. You have the patience and perseverance to carry on that part which requires hard labor and constant application and more than this I could wish you to be associated with him on account of being able to advise with him as to arrangement."[15] Gates promised to pay him well but Cook had just received an offer to teach at the Albany Academy. After but two years in the enticing but risky world of industry, he decided that he belonged in the academic and scientific community. His earlier hopes of making a fortune had changed to disillusioned fears of bankruptcy. He was willing to settle for a secure living and the hope that he could begin to pay off his debts.

To land on his feet at the Albany Academy was extraordinarily good fortune for Cook. As its most eminent alumnus and ex-professor, Joseph Henry, head of the Smithsonian Institution, commented at the 1851 meetings of the Association for the Advancement of Science: "The Albany Academy was and still is one of the first, if not the very first, institution of its kind in the United States. Its system of education is more extensive and more thorough than that of many colleges in our country."[16]

Like the Rensselaer Institute, the academy had benefited from the support of the Van Rensselaer family. Philip S. Van Rensselaer, brother of the "Old Patroon," was mayor of Albany when the academy was established by the Common Council in 1813.[17] Stephen himself was one of the first trustees and the first classes had been held in a building rented from Killian K. Van Rensselaer.[18] In contrast to Rensselaer Institute, however, the real strength of the school was the support of the citizens and government of the City of Albany. An original public subscription of over $5,000 had been increased by a city contribution of over $5,000, and the city ultimately underwrote the construction of a school building costing $90,000.[19] The school, whose graduates were frequently accepted as juniors or seniors when they went on to college, was particularly distinguished in the scientific field. For thirty years the principal had been Dr. T. Romeyn Beck, who also taught at the Fairfield Medical College and had participated in the New York Geological Survey. He started the teaching of chemistry in the academy and initiated a system of meteorological observations.[20] Joseph Henry, while science professor from 1826 to 1832, performed experiments with electromagnetism which laid the basis for the invention of the telegraph.[21]

The academy had been started in the rash of academy-founding that began in the latter half of the eighteenth century. Before this time children had customarily gone either to Latin grammar schools to be trained as gentlemen and prepared for college or to district schools where they learned the rudiments of reading, writing, and arithmetic and then began an apprenticeship in a business or trade. As businessmen became increasingly affluent and influential, it became apparent that neither system answered the needs of their children, who were destined to take their places in an entrepreneurial or managerial aristocracy. The answer to their needs was filled by the academy.

At Albany Academy, similar though superior to most academies, alternative courses of study were offered. The most ambitious program took eight years and included Latin, Greek, mathematics, physics, chemistry, logic, moral and mental philosophy, rhetoric, history, and evidences of Christianity. By 1848 French and German had been added as electives. An "English" or a "Mathematical" course in five years provided the same studies as the full course, except that Latin and Greek were omitted, while the "Mercantile" course took four years, omitted courses in higher mathematics as well as Latin and Greek, and added a few commercial subjects.

By 1848 the school had been through several lean and prosperous cycles, following the course of the general economic fluctuations of the country. In 1848 it was beginning to feel the winds of adversity from another source. A new trend was discernible in the world of education. The public schools, which always had been less expensive and now were improving their quality, began to offer competition to the academies. Albany had no high school but the district schools were providing better education than they had earlier and a state normal school had been established there. Falling enrollments and decreased tuition income at the academy reflected these changes. At about the time Cook began to look about for a new job, the trustees of the Albany Academy embarked upon a massive reorganization in hopes of strengthening the school enough to counteract the downward slide. The Reverend Dr. William H. Campbell was appointed principal; most of the teachers resigned; Romeyn Beck was to lecture on physiology and physical geography; the

Reverend John Sessions was hired to teach English; and George Cook was made professor of mathematics and natural philosophy. Later David Murray was added to the mathematics faculty and the Reverend William Miller to the English and religion faculty.

The convergence of Cook, Campbell, and Murray at the academy brought together a particularly congenial and effective combination— one which was to be repeated several years later at Rutgers College. Campbell was a dynamic, red-haired Scot, a Presbyterian minister who had taught with great success at Erasmus Hall in Brooklyn and who had served as pastor in churches in Chittenango, East New York, and Albany before coming to the Academy as principal.

At the academy Cook found the teaching more demanding than at Rensselaer. There were many more students (230 in 1848) and they were much younger. He was unaccustomed to dealing with boys of nine—the age of the youngest pupils. Nevertheless he was successful enough so that when Campbell left in 1851 to accept a position at the Dutch Reformed Theological Seminary in New Brunswick, New Jersey, Cook was made principal.

During Cook's first few years at the academy, he and Mary continued to live at the house on South Pearl Street. Here in October 1849 a daughter, Sarah, was born. Two years later they had a baby who lived only a few hours and in 1852 a son, John Willard, was born.[22] In his account book George recorded details of life at South Pearl Street. One important detail was his garden. Lettuce, pumpkins, squash, tomatoes, cabbages, and two hundred asparagus plants went into the garden, and George was careful to note the precise date when the garden was planted and the day they ate the first lettuce. His flannel underwear was a matter of particular concern and was credited with the therapeutic and medicinal powers reserved at a later day to such substances as wheat germ and Vitamin C. In 1849 he had delayed putting it on until November 3 and paid the price by catching a fever. He resolved that thereafter he would put it on before the equinox.[23]

George and Mary became members of the Second Presbyterian Church, where he was soon made superintendent of the Sabbath School and served as superintendent of the Mission Sunday School.[24] During his years in Albany, Cook undertook teaching and research activities outside his regular responsibilities at the academy. He began to teach again at the Troy Female Seminary and beginning in 1850 gave a series of eighteen chemistry lectures there each winter, traveling across the river every Monday and Thursday afternoon after classes at the academy ended.[25] He also undertook various small jobs analyzing mineral ores, peat, and other substances and, his energies apparently not thus exhausted, in 1852 began lecturing at the Albany Medical College. Dr. Lewis Caleb Beck, a brother of T. Romeyn Beck had been teaching a course there in inorganic chemistry and when his health began to fail, he persuaded Cook to take over part of his teaching responsibilities.[26] The organization of the course was rather disjointed because Beck was also teaching science part time at Rutgers College in New Brunswick, New Jersey. Beck began at the medical school in the middle of February and lectured twice a day for a week. Then he left for New Brunswick and Cook took over and lectured for six weeks after which Beck returned and lectured twice every other day and once on alternate days for four weeks. In this manner the full number of sixty lectures was delivered to the students. Cook taught the general principles of chemistry and inorganic chemistry while Beck taught organic chemistry, poisons, and applications of chemistry to medicine. In the spring of 1853 Beck died and Cook completed the course. Forty-seven medical students presented a testimonial to him in which they thanked him for "the able and instructive manner in which this important subject has been presented to us."[27]

While Cook was in Albany a group of scientists and citizens began a movement to start a new university in the city. Led by James Hall, and Harvard professor Benjamin Peirce, they sought the support of science professors from various colleges for the establishment of a great scientific university affiliated with the Albany Medical School.[28] Each professor would remain at his original post but arrange his schedule so that he could spend three months of each year teaching at Albany. Thus the very best scientific men in the northeast (who felt insufficiently valued at their own colleges) would cooperate to provide an outstanding scientific education. Among those interested in the plan were Louis Agassiz, Harvard's famous professor of geology, and Luther Tucker, publisher of the *Country Gentleman*. An act of incorporation was passed April 17, 1851, and a circular published in 1852 (listing Cook as professor of elementary chemistry).[29] Mrs. Blandina Dudley contributed money for the Dudley Observatory. The plan, however, was opposed at Harvard and in New York City, where investigations were beginning for the establishment of a new polytechnic school. When the state failed to provide any money for scholarships the great university foundered although the Observatory, the Albany Medical School, and the Albany Law School survived.

Cook was more successful in a project he undertook for the salt industry of the state. In 1850 the New York State legislature appropriated $3,000 for experiments and analyses of the Salt Springs at Onondaga, New York, and Cook was appointed at a salary of $600 to conduct them.[30] His first task was to find a way of removing impurities from salt produced at the Onondaga springs. Analyzing and comparing the Onondaga salt with salt produced elsewhere, he discovered an unacceptably high lime content. Lime was used to precipitate oxide of iron from the salt and was permitted by law but when manufacturers used too much their salt became chalky white, soft, spongy, and slightly alkaline.[31] This was obviously unsatisfactory and state inspectors were authorized to destroy salt with too high a lime content. Cook recommended the use of alum instead of lime. This had been used for some time in England but American manufacturers were reluctant to change and three years after his first report he was still urging the use of alum.[32]

After two years of experimentation and study Cook began tests comparing boiling with solar evaporation as a means of preparing salt from brine. He also investigated the use of salt for preserving meat and determined the economic benefits of using coal rather than wood as the fuel. In 1852 the legislature sent him to England, Belguim, France, and Holland to study European salt-producing methods. His annual report for that year gave details of various European procedures, the geology of the Cheshire rock salt mines and English labor practices, the hiring of boys and women, wages relative to those in other industries, and current prices.[33] He wrote also about French salt springs and the making of salt from sea water by solar evaporation and reported on Belgian and Dutch refineries where British rock salt and crude sea salt were prepared for market. In the course of his travels he distributed copies of his own reports on the Onandaga Salt Springs. A letter from one M. De Grimaldi at one of the French installations pronounced it to be "very remarkable" and from the Cheshire mines James B. Lobb wrote to thank him for hints on salt manufacture.[34]

In 1853 the legislature failed to appropriate money for the continuation of the salt studies and this activity and supplemental income for Cook came to an end. A letter from his brother Henry suggested that there might be benefits from the newly acquired leisure,

I think you do manage to keep yourself pretty well supplied with something to do. I suppose your lectures at the Medical College were on Chemistry, of course. The lectures with the preparations required must have taken all the time that you could spare from the Academy. Now they are over I should think you would feel much more like a person who could take time to look around him or maybe to write a long letter to your friends at home . . . if in the quarreling of the legislature you should be forgotten, a little more leisure than you have had for the past 2 or 3 years would be the consequence, which I do not think you need regret.[35]

However, the failure of the "great university" to materialize in Albany and the cessation of his work on salt made George more receptive to an offer which came from Rutgers College.

4

1853-1862
Rutgers College

During the late spring and summer of 1853, President Theodore Frelinghuysen and the Board of Trustees of Rutgers College in New Brunswick, New Jersey, had been trying to find a professor of chemistry and natural science to succeed Lewis Beck. They had decided that interest in science at the college had increased to such an extent that a full-time professor was now needed. William Campbell, who was a professor in the Dutch Reformed Seminary and taught rhetoric and belles lettres at the College, had known Cook when they worked together at the Albany Academy. This, plus the fact that Cook had been senior professor at the Rensselaer Institute, and principal of the academy and had taken over Beck's responsibilities at the Albany Medical School, made him an obvious possibility. In July Cook received a letter from Campbell asking him to pay an informal and secret visit to New Brunswick to look over the situation.[1] Perhaps only partly in jest, Campbell wrote that Frelinghuysen seemed determined to have Cook although he, Campbell, had opposed that appointment as much as possible because it would be such a loss to the academy. Campbell promised that his salary would be higher than what he was getting at the academy and his duties less arduous. Furthermore there was greater prestige in teaching in a college; he could expect to be able to do more advanced scientific work and the trustees had promised to purchase $2,000 worth of scientific equipment. In addition to all this, George, as a "Jerseyman" by birth, retained a loyalty to his native state, and would be happy also to live nearer his family. But there were arguments against going to Rutgers. The greatest of these was Mary. She did not want to leave Albany, where she was near enough to her home for frequent visits with her family and could count on help from her mother and sisters during her child-bearing years. She agreed with her brother Elijah, who thought that George would never be content to teach in an institution which had fewer than one hundred students.[2] She also felt a not-infrequent female resentment against disrupting the nest. However, as a dutiful nineteenth-century wife she knew her place, and she neither raged nor sulked when George decided on the move to Rutgers. But she could not help referring occasionally to a few signs that seemed to her to portend the working of a "charm" that would bring Cook back to New York State where she really felt he belonged. She cheerfully reported that after he had left the academy, the mother of one Homer Wheeler, a student, announced that her son felt that now Mr. Cook was gone he didn't like any of the teachers and would drop out.[3] But Cook had made up his mind and his resignation from the academy took effect at the Christmas holidays.

The nine teachers at the academy wrote Cook a letter of appreciation which, even allowing for the exaggeration on such occasions, provides an insight into the nature of his talents as an administrator:

... While we would congratulate the institution which has secured your services, we would without flattery assert our consciousness of the loss we have experienced. For the last five years you have discharged here the duties of Professor of Mathematics and Natural Philosophy, and for the last two years, those connected with the office of Principal; and while the proficiency of your scholars and the general prosperity of the Academy, attest your success as a teacher, and your tact as a presiding officer, we, your fellow laborers, are rejoiced to bear witness to your urbanity and courteous consideration of our respective interests. We have no reminiscences connected with the relations we have sustained to you, which are not sources of grateful and pleasing recollection— and we assure you that the history of your administration as principal of the Albany Academy, will be one that we shall all love to contemplate.

It is the sincere wish, as it is the prediction of each one of us, that your fidelity and energy may, in your new field of labor be amply remunerated—that in the superior scholarship of your students and your eminence in the departments of science to which you have devoted yourself, you may find the reward promised to those who are faithful in the discharge of duty.[4]

Similar letters came from a group of students at the academy who presented him with a plate and thanked him for his "uniform kindness to them and for his unwearied exertions to promote their improvement and welfare."[5] The trustees, the minister, and session of the Second Presbyterian Church and other groups expressed similar sentiments of congratulations and regret.

With such knowledge of his security and success at the academy and his wife's opposition to the move, it is not surprising that Cook himself had some reservations. He decided, however, that he would plan to stay at Rutgers for five years as a trial period. At the end of that time he planned to take stock and decide whether to stay or look for another place.[6] Rutgers College in 1853 had achieved somewhat more security than the Rensselaer Institute had when Cook was struggling to keep it going in the 1840s, but it was not as prosperous or stable as the academy. Proud of its heritage as one of the nine colonial colleges, it had failed to achieve the size or success of such other colonial colleges as Yale, which usually had about four hundred students or the nearby College of New Jersey in Princeton with an average of 250. Rutgers was always hoping to reach a secure enrollment of one hundred. Chartered originally in 1766 as Queens College, it was a product of dissension among ministers of the Dutch Reformed Church, some of whom wished to have a college of their own so that they might be able to educate ministers in America rather than having to send their young men to the Netherlands for their education.[7] This group was opposed by others who preferred the status quo or wished to have a professorship in New York's King's College. The factionalism that ensued impeded the development of the college for many years after the dispute originated.

It proved to be so difficult to raise money for the new college that it did not open until 1771 and the first student was not graduated until 1774. By that time the Revolution was brewing and only the devotion of the tutor, John Taylor, and a small band of students kept it alive at all. Periodically classes were abandoned so that students and tutor could take up arms at the approach of the British forces but they always managed to set up classes somewhere again. For some forty-five years after the Revolution the college continued to have problems staying in operation and twice shut down altogether for several years. In 1825, renamed Rutgers College in honor of a much respected philanthropist of the church and with the help of the General Synod of the Dutch Reformed Church and the Theological Seminary, it reopened its doors and never closed them again.

Primary emphasis in the curriculum was placed on the study of classical languages and various aspects of Christianity but since 1809 the trustees had considered essential the teaching of natural philosophy (physics and astronomy). The charter itself included in the scope of the college "the liberal and useful arts and sciences." In 1829 a report of a Trustee Committee on the Professorates, chaired by the Reverend John Ludlow had urged, "We cannot pass from the literary institution without expressing the *strong conviction* which is felt, that the church ought not to rest in her efforts until two more professors be added to the present number. It should be our ambition to make this a *First Rate Seat of Science.*"[8]

Cook's salary was set at $1,600 and he planned to take up his duties during the Christmas holidays. Campbell wrote, "I am very happy at the prospect of having you so soon with us. I don't think you will regret it but on the contrary will bless God for your enlarged sphere of usefulness . . . ."[9] Frelinghuysen had written that he thought the prospects of the college encouraging and that life in New Brunswick was pleasant as there was a "small but excellent" society away from fashions but also removed from the cold ceremonials of great cities."[10] Unfortunately, the events of the next year were so distressing and, in one case, so tragic for the Cooks that it might well have seemed that the decision to move to New Brunswick was taken under an evil star. Finding a house was the first problem. The house they had expected to rent turned out to be too small so they rented rooms with the Misses Dumont at their boardinghouse on Albany Street and the furniture was put into storage. However, this arrangement proved to be too difficult for Mary and she, Paul, Sarah and Johnny returned to New York State to stay with her parents in Chatham. Here a saddened household awaited them as Cornelia, Mary's sister, lay dying of consumption.[11] After Cornelia's death in January, the young Cooks and their mother stayed on in Chatham until March. Mary worried about the health of Johnny and Sarah. She wrote to George, "I felt quite anxious . . . when I have such thoughts I like to read your letter and know that the prayer of love rises for us to Him who is over all God of the sea."[12]

In another letter, she revealed her unhappiness at her inability to keep up with her husband's fearful efficiency. "The author of *Sunnyside* was a housekeeper after your own heart—she had a plan for everything—even written plans for the distribution of household labors and bills of fare for every meal for weeks in advance . . . . I wish your wife had such capabilities."[13]

By March, when Mary and the children returned to New Brunswick, George had made some unfortunate discoveries about the faculty at Rutgers. There were only five full-time professors including Cook. Professor Theodore Strong, who had started teaching mathematics in 1827, had been excellent but was aging rapidly as was John W. Proudfit, professor of Greek. William Irvin taught Latin and Charles von Romondt was professor of modern languages. These were aided by professors from the seminary who taught logic, rhetoric, belles lettres, and Evidences of Christianity. Unfortunately, with Cook's ability to "look at all things *as they are*," as his friend Austin F. Park had once written, he could not fail to observe the lethargy and indolence of the other professors.[14] He wrote about it to William Miller at the Albany Academy, who replied sympathetically that it seemed that "Fogyism was of the rankest kind."[15] Miller urged Cook to try to raise the standards, expressing confidence that he could do so in his own department, but fearing that many of the professors were too far gone to be improved. His counsel was that in the end students would thank the professor who made them work.

Mary was similarly distressed. She wrote, "I am sorry you have fallen among those who are too indolent to keep you in countenance" and also "sorry you have made such discoveries in the college—I hope you will not be led by bad examples about you to lose your integrity as a teacher and I can't say that I have any fears that you will."[16]

As upsetting as these things were, much sadder days were in store for the Cooks. In May the family moved into a rented house at 3 Elm Row but almost immediately Cook started to build a house on the corner of College Avenue and Bartlett Street, where he had purchased land from James and David Bishop.[17] Mary's brother James, a carpenter, brought his wife and came to stay in New Brunswick while he worked on the house which at that time was on the outskirts of the town.

Shortly after they had moved into their new home the saddest blow came to the young parents. Their small son Johnny died. He was then just two years old and had been a particularly lively and attractive baby in spite of a succession of illnesses. For Mary, the presence of her brother and sister-in-law was a comfort through the grief-stricken days that followed. For them both, their deep faith was a source of greater help.

These difficult times were made no easier by the fact that Mary did not like New Brunswick very much. New Brunswick was primarily an industrial town although in an earlier day the prosperity of the town had depended upon commerce. Farmers from Somerset and Hunterdon counties had brought their produce to the banks of the Raritan River, there to be loaded on river boats bound for the markets of New York City. But the building of the Delaware and Raritan Canal in the 1830s meant that products could be loaded farther inland and activity on the New Brunswick docks began to diminish. At the same time factories for making wallpaper, carriages, hosiery, and cotton cloth were built and foundries, machine shops, planing mills, sawmills and rubber factories flourished. Such industrial activity brought an influx of a variety of European ethnic groups to labor in the factories. In 1860 the census listed seventeen countries as diverse as Hungary, Bohemia, Ireland, and India as places of national origin for New Brunswick residents.[18]

New Brunswick's greatest problem in 1854, according to the local newspaper, the *Fredonian*, was the unpaved streets.[19] These became muddy with the slightest rain and in addition were filled with all kinds of debris—dirt, rubbish, glass, horse droppings and other filth. Many feared that the water which stood in the gutters would bring about illness and epidemics, especially during the warm weather. Even so, there was considerable opposition to the paving of George Street, the main thoroughfare. The *Fredonian* editorialized that the ladies would probably begin to appreciate the paved road when they discovered how much cleaner their skirts would stay.

Because the town was on the Raritan River, the residents were able to take advantage of the pleasures of river travel. Though the Camden & Amboy Railroad and the New Jersey Railroad offered somewhat more reliable transportation to New York City, they were expensive—a round trip ticket on the Camden & Amboy cost five dollars.[20] When the river was clear of ice it was a favorite means of transportation and pleasure— especially for a picnic jaunt to Staten Island.[21]

The benefits of gas lighting had been brought to the city the year before the Cooks arrived and they had it put in their new home, but the water supply was deplorable. They were far enough out of town to be assured of a pure well, but many of the wells that supplied the townspeople were contaminated by seepage from the waste material from the higher area. The result was recurrent epidemics of typhoid fever.[22] Cook was soon asked to test the wells of the town. He compared their water with that from the Lawrence Brook and the Raritan River and found that the town wells had far more solid material than the brook or the river.[23] It was not until 1867, however, that the city built waterworks at Weston's Mills and pure water was made available.

All things considered, the move to New Jersey was an unhappy one during the first year but matters improved in the years that followed. A daughter, Emma Willard Cook, was born in 1854 and another, Anne Bigelow Cook, in 1857. In 1859 a baby was born but only lived thirty-six hours and Robert Anderson Cook was born in 1861, the year before their oldest child, Paul, entered Rutgers as a freshman at the age of fifteen. After her first uneasiness at settling in a new community Mary began to enjoy New Brunswick and made friends among the faculty families and townspeople and took a particular interest in the town library. In 1859 George wrote to C. Y. Lansing in Albany that he would like him to see what four years had done for Mary's original antipathy to the city.[24]

George became involved in a number of community and church activities. He served as an elder in the Second Dutch Reformed Church, was a member of the New Brunswick School Board, joined the Natural History Society of New Jersey and the New Jersey Agricultural Society, and was made assistant geologist on the State Geological Survey. He continued to perform chemical analyses for the salt manufacturers in New York State, the New Jersey Zinc Company, and others and wrote an article on New Brunswick for the *New American Cyclopedia.*

While the Cooks grew to enjoy living in New Brunswick, problems at the college continued to distress them. An important feature of the town, the college at this time had but three buildings. Old Queens, the original building, was used in part as a residence. In the center were the classrooms (some of them shared with the seminary), while living quarters for professors were located in the wings. The President's House, with chimneys at each of its four corners, was the second building and the third, Van Nest Hall, built in 1848, housed a chemistry laboratory and a museum established by Beck as well as the two student literary societies. The buildings stood on the crest of a small hill near the river surrounded by a large grassy area with trees, around which had been built a cast-iron fence. Although the college was important to the city, New Brunswick could hardly have been a "quaint old college town," as the words of the old song go. Even in the mid-nineteenth century the town was more industrial than collegiate. College professors were sometimes important and influential citizens and useful when it became necessary to have an oration delivered—but there were only four or five of them and less than a hundred students and the city boasted some ten thousand inhabitants.

Enrollments at the college remained small, reaching a peak of 124 in 1861.[25] Under Theodore Frelinghuysen as president it languished, unhappily beset by financial and faculty problems. Some professors were incapable of maintaining discipline in the classroom and many of them were getting old.[26] The modern language teacher, Charles von Romondt, was such a poor teacher that one of the trustees jocularly urged Cook, who was making a trip to Pennsylvania, to see if he couldn't find a church that would take von Romondt and thus solve two problems.[27] Old Dr. Theodore Strong, the mathematics professor, was having great difficulty in carrying out his customary responsibilities. The trustees resolved to urge von Romondt to retire and Strong to have an assistant.[28] Both refused.

In the letter to C. Y. Lansing of Albany assessing his first five years at Rutgers, Cook noted that although the number of students had increased since the advent of President Frelinghuysen in 1850, he was now over seventy and too feeble to take a strong position of leadership in the raising of money.[29] The trustees had resolved again and again to raise funds for an endowment, but their endeavors, though helpful, were not sufficient. Consequently the professors were poorly paid. Cook said that his salary was insufficient. While he was assistant geologist he was able to save some money but when that job ended and his family grew larger, he was barely able to manage. The college's lack of money had made it impossible for the trustees to fulfill their promises that he would have a salary of $1,600 and $2,000 to purchase apparatus for his department. He was, therefore, hampered in his teaching of the sciences, which depended upon up-to-date equipment. In part this lack had been remedied by his own exertions and those of some trustees. Benjamin Taylor of Bergen was particularly interested and he often traveled around (sometimes accompanied by Cook) to visit Dutch Reformed churches and wealthy friends of the college.[30]

The salaries of many faculty members were below even the minimal $1,100. In 1859, the Latin professor, William Irvin, who, said Cook, was good and popular, usually received only $500 although some years they were able to pay him $1,000.[31] The Greek professor, John Proudfit (apparently neither as good nor as popular as Irvin) was getting $1,000— not enough to tempt a good man to come in his place. Cook himself rarely received his salary when it was due and once had to wait six months to be paid.

In 1859 the Board of Trustees decided to make an effort to improve academic matters at the college.[32] Dr. Strong asked Cook to make a list of all the "philosophical" (having to do with physics), chemical, and astronomical apparatus and indicate the new equipment most necessary to upgrade each department.[33] It became clear during this effort that no one had ever decided which subjects should be taught by Cook as professor of chemistry and natural science and which by Strong as professor of mathematics and natural philosophy. Strong also taught mechanics and astronomy and, said Cook, because there was no apparatus to illustrate optics and acoustics, it was immaterial who taught it. But in case they acquired the apparatus he thought it should be taught as physics rather than as mathematics.

The basis of Cook's advice was the Smithsonian Report for 1856, which included a "Syllabus of a Course of Lectures on Physics" by Joseph Henry.[34] Cook thought chemistry should be included as a "natural science," which also included natural history (geology, botany, zoology, physiology, and the cognate sciences). Numerous lists of possible divisions of the sciences among Cook's papers attest to the efforts he made to arrive at a satisfactory categorization. He finally came to the conclusion that the divisions in natural science were more conventional than real and that final decisions as to teaching were usually made according to the desires and capabilities of the teachers in the various colleges.[35]

In the spring of 1859 the trustees appointed a committee to examine the "present exigencies of the College, ascertain what measures are needed for its permanent establishment and report some definite action for the Board."[36] As a result of this action, Dr. von Romondt was persuaded to resign and Gustavus Fisher was engaged as professor of modern languages. He received no salary and was expected to secure his living from students' fees. Strong was semi-retired, teaching only seniors for the two years before his resignation in 1861. Irvin soon resigned also.[37] To replace these professors, the Reverend Marshall Henshaw, principal of the Dummer Academy in Massachusetts, was appointed to teach mathematics and natural philosophy and DeWitt Ten Broeck Reiley of the class of '57 became professor of Latin. For a few years a new professorship of English literature and language was filled by John Forsyth but after he left no one was hired to take his place until 1880. Dr. Proudfit also retired and Howard Crosby was appointed to teach Greek. Cook was the only professor teaching in 1859 who remained in 1862.

In 1856 Cook had received an honorary doctorate from New York University. The honorary doctorate as a measure of academic distinction was more important in this earlier period than it has since become as there were no earned doctorates in the country until after Yale awarded the first one in 1861. Cook's professorial title was soon changed to professor of chemistry and natural history and he was finally able to add a number of pieces of equipment to the science laboratories including a Ruhmkorff Induction Coil, a new cistern, pumps, and a sink and drain for the laboratory. Much of this was paid for by contributions from trustees and by the proceeds of a series of public lectures which Cook gave in New Brunswick.

Some light is thrown upon Cook's teaching responsibilities by an examination of the faculty minutes listing examinations.[38] In June he was scheduled to examine the sophomores in botany and the juniors in nonmetallic chemistry and physiology. In February he had examined the juniors in electricity, heat, and magnetism, the seniors in organic chemistry, and the sophomores in pneumatics and hydrostatics. All examinations were traditionally oral though Cook was soon to recommend that they be written. A lack of equipment had prevented Cook from adopting the Rensselaer plan which required each student to perform his own experiments. Instead, demonstrations were given when the apparatus was available. Cook could conduct geological field trips, however, and they proved to be popular with students.

All the students lived in town in private rooming houses because there were no dormitories. The college catalogue, making a virtue of necessity, advertised the advantage to young men of living in respectable homes of the community and thus avoiding the danger of corruption from four years of living with rowdy boys.[39] The civilizing effect of the respectable homes of New Brunswick was not so great, however, as to materially improve the behavior of the young men. Over the years they not only persisted in roistering in oyster bars and billiard saloons in town but some of them drank intoxicating liquors and occasionally had to be suspended or dismissed for drunkenness.[40] Considering the relatively small number of students (rarely more than thirty in a class even counting those who did not graduate), the faculty, whose salaries depended in large part upon the payment of tuitions, were somewhat cavalier in the number of suspensions, dismissals, and expulsions they handed down.[41] To be sure, many of these were later rescinded upon promises to do better in the future. Such lively pranks as throwing firecrackers into classrooms and tying Professor von Romondt's door on the outside so that he could not leave the room were only a few of the undergraduate inspirations.[42] Because Cook was apparently the only faculty member who did not propose to put up with this behavior, he was more often than not charged in faculty meetings with the responsibility of searching out culprits, finding proof of their misdeeds, and admonishing them.[43] Such lapses as traveling to nearby Bound Brook or Plainfield without permission, neglecting their studies, cutting classes, or sneaking out of the compulsory chapel exercises all required his attention.

The high point of student misbehavior as far as Cook was concerned occurred at 3 A.M. on the morning of June 18, 1862—the night before commencement. This was the time the students chose to favor Cook with what had come to be known as a "Calliathumpian Serenade."[44] The Cook family awakened to the sound of hideous noises produced by a mob who shouted, whooped, wailed, and finally tore down their fence and threw pieces of it and other missiles at the door and walls of the house. It is not clear whether this episode was inspired by student resentment of Cook's disciplinary functions or just mindless hell-raising. Whatever the cause, Cook was not one to quietly wait out the storm. Tearing out of his house in a rage he grabbed the nearest figure and hit him on the head with a "club."[45] The victim, Isaac S. Taylor, had been a student at Rutgers but was then studying law in Jersey City. Unfortunately, he was also the son of Benjamin Taylor who had so selflessly canvassed the parishes to raise money for the college. After a few days, Isaac wrote to Cook demanding an apology, on the grounds that he had merely been strolling by and had not engaged in the destruction of Cook's property.[46] Cook replied that 3 A.M. was a strange hour to be strolling about and it was even stranger that he should happen by the Cook house at the same time that the mob did.[47] With great forebearance, Cook regretted Isaac's part in the outrage and hoped that it was merely a temporary deviation. Three or four other men who were seniors were threatened with expulsion but at the last minute the trustees and some members of the faculty relented and they were allowed to graduate.

Some idea of the attitude of students and the course requirements is provided by an exchange of letters between Cook and a student named Trevainon Haight.[48] Haight had failed an examination and was to be re-examined in the fall, but wrote to complain that he would cheerfully take another examination with Cook if that were the only one, but, he said, "if you all insist on another examination my vacation will be nothing but a studing [sic] up from beginning to end & I now wish to ask you if you will not excuse me promising to pass perfectly satisfactorially [sic] to you in future."[49] Cook's reply was that although Haight's behavior had been acceptable he had been unprepared to recite several times and

there were two bad features in your examination, one was not understanding the subject well, and the other was an attempt at copying from the blackboard what should have been learned. . . . In regard to your examination next fall, I have told the President, that I am entirely willing to examine you upon one topic only (Iron, its ores and manufacture) which was assigned to you at examination. . . . The study of that topic will not fill up much of your vacation. You were wrong in your description of the different kinds of iron,—you did not give the composition of iron ores correctly, and in your account of the manufacture, you did not show a proper knowledge of the significance of chemical symbols, equivalents, etc.[50]

This seems a modest enough request by a professor but it was somewhat unusual for the professors to make any demands upon students and alumni sometimes complained that they had not been adequately prepared. A letter to Cook in 1863 from a graduate working in Cuba shows him to have been more demanding, "Every day, my dear doctor, the lessons you taught us prove more valuable, to me at least, and if it will in any degree compensate for the pains you took in teaching us rest assured of the fact."[51]

To stimulate interest in natural history Cook started a Natural History Society in 1857 and served as its first president. One of the principal objects of the society was to build a "cabinet" or museum. The nucleus was Lewis Beck's collection which had been purchased for the college after his death. At commencement time alumni and friends were urged to inspect the museum and attend the anniversary meeting of the society at which supporters and local scientists read papers. The society's doings figured prominently in the pages of the *Rutgers Quarterly* and testified to great student and alumni enthusiasm.[52] The collection, in which any kind of specimen was welcome—mineral samples, stuffed birds, fossils—grew more rapidly than expected. One enthusiastic member wrote from Scotland proposing to chip pieces of rock from historic sites, while another sent two large albatrosses taken off the Cape of Good Hope on his way to Amoy (China).[53] Rutgers also received collections of specimens from the Smithsonian Institution. The success of both the museum and the society depended upon Cook's initiative and drive. As an editorial in the *Rutgers Quarterly* proclaimed: "With such an untiring and zealous leader as Dr. Cook it cannot fail and to him is its success mostly due. As a Caesar in the kingdom of nature, our wishes towards him are expressed in the language of Horace: 'Serus in coelum redeas diaque. . . .'"[54]

Cook's abilities were still appreciated in Troy also and in 1859 when the trustees became displeased with the management of the Rensselaer Polytechnic Institute by Benjamin Franklin Greene they offered the job to Cook at a salary of $2,000—more, they said, than they would pay anyone else.[55] But Cook decided to stay in New Brunswick, writing to the president of the Rensselaer Board of Trustees, Thomas Brinsmade, that he felt the trustees of Rutgers had a claim upon him because they had recently made improvements in the laboratory that were based to some extent upon his presence at the college and in addition they had promised to raise his salary.[56] He expressed his gratitude to the trustees of Rensselaer whose confidence in him had lasted through an absence of thirteen years.

1854-1860
Early New Jersey Geological Surveys

One reason for Cook's decision to stay in New Jersey may have been his hope that the New Jersey Geological Survey might be resumed. When he first came to Rutgers he found that his new job did not take all his time nor did it supply enough money for his growing family. After his profitable experience with the salt industry in New York State he was on the lookout for a similar opportunity in New Jersey. His chance came when in 1854 the legislature approved a new state geological survey and named William Kitchell, an old friend of the Cook family, state geologist. Cook's Uncle Jephtha took pains to see that his nephew's qualifications for a position on the survey came to the attention of Governor Rodman Price and George was appointed assistant geologist.[1] Thus at the age of thirty-six, George Cook found a focus for his energies and ambitions. Throughout the remainder of his life his concentration on the geology of New Jersey and his work in the related field of agriculture made him the outstanding nineteenth-century figure in New Jersey in both fields and one of the most respected geologists and agricultural experts in the nation.

Cook was fortunate in finding his life's work in geology and agriculture. In spite of his limited formal education he was able to join the newly emerging professionals in both fields as an equal.[2] The day when any doctor or minister who enjoyed rock collecting was welcomed as a colleague into the circles of professors and scientists was fast disappearing but geology and agriculture had not yet achieved that exalted status wherein all save those who have the prescribed graduate training are excluded. In their practical application both geology and agriculture had long histories. Man had made use of rocks and minerals since prehistoric times and had been formulating theories about the origin of geological phenomena at least since Thales and Anaximenes but throughout the medieval and Renaissance centuries minerals were still being classified in such unsatisfactory ways as alphabetically or by color and the theories were more remarkable for their evidence of a vivid imagination at work than for their relation to demonstrable facts.[3]

By the beginning of the nineteenth century, because of the work of such men as Agricola and Gesner in the sixteenth century and Abraham Werner and James Hutton in the eighteenth century, geology was beginning to develop the orderly classification of data which is the necessary prerequisite to the emergence of a modern science. A geological survey that examines systematically the rocks, minerals, and topography of a given area is a necessary step in the accumulation of this basic data. Such surveys had been made in parts of Italy, France, Germany, and England during the eighteenth century while in 1749 in the British colonies in North America, Lewis Evans made a map of the Middle Atlantic region delineating geological divisions with remarkable accuracy.[4] Among later maps one by William Maclure (a Scot whom Benjamin Silliman later called the "father of American geology") was particularly notable for its hand-coloring of geological formations.[5] Evans's map had been accompanied by a booklet of geological notes and a number of other writers, notably the Swedish Peter Kalm, the Hessian physician Johann David Schoepf and Samuel Latham Mitchill, physician and professor at Columbia College, also had published geological information about America.[6] But the beginnings of the meticulous square-mile-by-square-mile description of a given area are more clearly seen in the efforts of Benjamin Silliman in New Haven, Connecticut, and Amos Eaton in New York State. Expeditions sent out by the federal government (of which the Lewis and Clark trek to the Pacific is the most famous) usually included geologists, botanists, and other scientists, but the activities of these men, especially in the earlier expeditions, was often incidental to military or strategic purposes.

Eager geologists were willing to spend their leisure time tramping over hills and plains and writing up their findings for Archibald Bruce's *American Mineralogical Journal* or Benjamin Silliman's *American Journal of Science and Arts* but it was not until public money became available that extensive topographical and mineralogical surveys could be carried through on a large scale. State legislatures for the most part were unwilling to fund long-term surveys until after the Civil War, although twenty-nine states initiated short-term geological surveys before then.[7] A partially successful effort at a state-supported survey was made by Denison Olmsted in North Carolina in the 1820s but

Massachusetts was the first state to carry through a full survey. Directed by Edward Hitchcock, professor of chemistry and natural history at Amherst, the Massachusetts survey was completed in 1841. The report was an impressive work in four volumes, with large numbers of plates and woodcuts.[8] Most outstanding among early state surveys was New York's with its two thousand pages, eighty-two plates and numerous maps.[9] Published in 1843 after seven years of work, it established American nomenclature for a series of Palaeozoic strata.

The lever by which the public and state legislatures were moved to support geological surveys was economic self-interest. Geologists themselves were at least as much interested in mapping formations, cataloging rocks, and theorizing about problems of origins as they were in discovering new and profitable mineral sources. But arguments used to get financial support for the work leaned heavily upon economic benefits to come. When directors of state surveys failed to produce economic benefits they ran the risk of losing the support of their legislatures.[10]

New Jersey provided for its first geological survey in 1835 after governors had for several years urged that one be established. In his message of 1832 Governor Peter D. Vroom suggested that, like the railroad and canal building then going on, a geological survey would add to the state's wealth.[11] By demonstrating the possibility of "new avenues to prosperity and comfort" in New Jersey it would attract new settlers and discourage old residents from leaving. In 1832 the legislature ignored Vroom's suggestions, but his successor, Samuel L. Southard, reiterated the plea and Vroom, re-elected in 1835, urged it even more strongly. Finally the legislature responded and appropriated $1,000 to hire a qualified man to conduct a geological and mineral survey. Two thousand dollars a year was appropriated for each of the following two years. The governor appointed Henry Darwin Rogers, who was one of a family of four brothers, all distinguished in science, and is primarily remembered for his theories on mountain building.[12] In 1835, the year he was hired by New Jersey, he was appointed professor of geology and mineralogy at the University of Pennsylvania and the next year became director of the survey of Pennsylvania. For several years he kept all three positions—a considerable responsibility even for the 1830s when the posts were less demanding than they later became.

The New Jersey survey was a slight work compared to the Pennsylvania one, which, after a good many financial vicissitudes was finally published in 1858 in two enormous volumes running to over fifteen hundred pages and including numerous color prints, scenic sketches, geological sections and a splendid table of contents, index, and glossary.[13] Compared to this impressive effort Rogers's 1840 geology of New Jersey seems hardly more than a pamphlet.[14] Nevertheless, it was important because it represented for the first time in one volume a geological treatment of the entire state in an organized manner.[15] The finished work had three hundred pages and a colored map, but it lacked prints, a table of contents, and an index.

Rogers began by drawing five straight lines (traverses) crossing the geological formations of the state. He then worked his way along the routes of the traverses, exploring the land for several miles on each side.[16] On the basis of these explorations he drew geological sections to illustrate the formations along the five lines. These accompanied his preliminary report, which included a chapter on the Highlands and on the counties of Middlesex, Monmouth, Burlington, Gloucester, Salem, Cumberland, and Cape May.

In the completed work Rogers divided the state into four geological regions:[17]

1. The coastal plain; that section of the state south of a line drawn between New Brunswick and Trenton. In modern terminology this is designated as partly of the Cenozoic Era and partly of the Cretaceous Period of the Mesozoic Era. Rogers labeled the entire plain "Alluvial."

2. The Piedmont region; the next northerly division including Union, Essex, Hudson, the northern part of Middlesex and Mercer, and most of Somerset and Bergen counties. This is now designated Triassic. Rogers called it Middle Secondary.

3. The Highlands; the northern part of Passaic, Morris, and Hunterdon counties and the southern part of Warren and Sussex. These are the oldest rocks in New Jersey and the term used currently is Precambrian. Rogers called it Primary, though most geologists of the period seem to have preferred "Primitive."

4. The Ridge and Valley province; the northwestern part of the state which includes the northern parts of Sussex and Warren counties. Now termed Palaeozoic, Rogers designated the section as "Older Secondary Rocks."

Although he used different terminology, Rogers made the divisions approximately where contemporary geologists place them, put them in the same relation in age to each other, and made the divisions more precisely than had any previous geologist.

Most of Rogers's report was devoted to economic geology. In the southern part of the state the most economically significant formation was that of the great beds of marl which stretch across the state from

Raritan Bay on the east, southwesterly to the Delaware River near Salem.
Rogers located the beds and analyzed the marl. Although it has long
since given way to artificially prepared chemicals, in the nineteenth
century marl was a valuable fertilizer. The first recorded use in New
Jersey was in 1768 near Marlboro on the farm of Peter Schenck.[18]
Apparently it did not catch on for the next record of its use is not until
1795, when Hendrick Van Mater in Holmdel, who had seen marl used in
England, persuaded his brother Cyrenius to try some on his land.
Marling had been a common practice in England during the High
Middle Ages, its long-lasting effects giving rise to the old English
saying: "A man doth sande for himself, lyme for his sonne and marle for
his grandchild."[19] During the upheavals of the fourteenth century
farming was so disrupted that men neglected and finally forgot how to
use both marl and lime.[20]

In the early seventeenth century both marl and lime were
introduced in England as new discoveries. Then the armies of
Parliament and of the King took away the able-bodied farmers and in
some places confiscated most of the agricultural produce that the
women, old men, and children could raise. Knowledge of good farming
methods and the incentive to produce to capacity were eroded. When the
English settled in the New World deterioration of farming methods was
accelerated by the abundance of good soil. Farmers could afford to
neglect the soil because when the fertility of their land was gone they just
moved on. Even after 1815 when several papers on marl were presented
to the Philadelphia Society for Promoting Agriculture and Mark Reeves
of Evesham gave an account of his success in tracing a deposit of marl
across the countryside, the farmers of New Jersey were reluctant to try
it.[21] Where there were outcroppings on their own land, however, men
gradually began to use it and to sell cartloads to their less fortunate
neighbors. By the time Rogers covered the territory he was able to list
some eighty farmers who were digging marl on their lands.[22]

Rogers dealt with several problems having to do with the marl, and
he mapped the beds more accurately than had been done before. Exact
geological knowledge of the various layers of clay, sand, and marl is
virtually impossible, as Kemble Widmer, present State Geologist of New
Jersey has pointed out in his *Geology and Geography of New Jersey*.[23]
There are between fourteen and twenty-four layers of clay, sand, and
marl lying from 3,800 to 6,400 feet below sea level. They vary in
thickness, composition, presence of fossils, and origin.

Relating New Jersey's marl beds to the marls found in England and
France was the second problem Rogers tackled. Marl occurs in different

colors. In England it is gray, blue, yellow, or red, whereas New Jersey marls tend toward the green. For this reason Rogers used the term "greensand" for the Jersey marl. However, another "greensand" is found near Le Havre and in Kent. Rogers pointed out that much work needed to be done before the geologists could be sure that all were the same. In his analyses of marl samples he found that percentages of the constituents silica, alumina, protoxide of iron, potash, lime, magnesia, and water were essentially the same in the New Jersey greensand as those which the French chemist M. P. Berthier had found in the Havre greensand.[24] In contrast, Dr. Edward Turner's analyses of the greensand of Kent contained a larger proportion of magnesia and only a trace of potash.[25]

A greater puzzle was the fact that of the approximately seventy-five varieties of fossils found in the New Jersey strata only one was found in similar strata in Europe.[26] Rogers's conclusion was that the marl group belonged somewhere among the secondary rocks (in one of the later deposits) dating back about 130 million years and probably in the same part of the series as the greensand and chalk formations of Europe. The fact that the fossil species were dissimilar convinced him that the greensand of New Jersey must have "originated during a somewhat different epoch from that which produced the European greensand formation."[27] At the time geologists and chemists were debating as to which ingredient in the marl was the fertilizing agent. Some held that gypsum was somehow produced by the action of water on marl. Others believed that lime in the marl was the active agent. Rogers maintained that it was the potash. He pointed out that several specimens had no lime at all.[28]

In an effort to encourage farmers to locate and use marl, Rogers gave detailed instructions.[29] First they would need a pocket magnifying glass in order to make an estimate of the proportion of the small round dark-green grains to the clay and sand. Then the suspected marl should be washed in a tumbler to wash off any clay that might be covering the greensand grains. If great accuracy was desired, the separated greensand and clay could be weighed on an apothecary's balance to determine the percentages. This crude analysis was necessary in order to determine whether or not there was enough greensand to bother about. An alternate method involved putting samples of the material on a hot shovel or a stove top. Particles of greensand would be identified when they turned red. If marl contained copperas or sulphate of alumina it was not beneficial to the soil. In that case it was helpful to taste the marl. An inky taste indicated that deleterious materials were present. In addition to these do-it-yourself tests, Rogers explained the method of analyzing the greensand chemically.[30]

Such practical advice to farmers was balanced by an equally solicitous concern for miners or would-be miners. Europeans may have known of mineral sources in New Jersey since the 1650s, when the Dutch were supposed to have built a road 140 miles long through the wilderness from Kingston on the Hudson to the Pahaquarry copper mine on the Delaware River.[31] Though evidence is scant, it is possible that ore from this mine was hauled back across the long miles to Kingston—or Esopus as it was then called—and thence to Holland. After the English acquired New Jersey any knowledge of such a mine was lost. Farther south an attempt was made as early as 1665 to establish an iron works to refine bog iron, and about ten years after that Colonel Lewis Morris bought 3,900 acres of land in Monmouth County with the same aim.[32]

Over the years various optimists had tried their hands at mining copper in Hunterdon, Middlesex, Somerset, and Essex counties with varying degrees of success. Rogers took some pains to emphasize the folly of such enterprises. He warned that there was no evidence that a true vein of copper ore existed in the state.[33] True, there was some copper, but it was interspersed irregularly in "strings and bunches" in the red shale and sandstone. As mine owners in New Brunswick, Griggstown, and Belleville had discovered, the copper obtained was very unlikely to cover the cost of getting it out.

On the other hand, iron mining in New Jersey was a flourishing industry until the discovery of the great iron ranges around Lake Superior about 1880. The early iron works of James Grover and Lewis Morris depended on bog iron or limonite, found mostly in the coastal plain, but the search began early for the iron ore magnetite which is found in pods in the Morris and Passaic county highland areas. By 1710 a forge was established at Whippany to work the ore mined at Succasunna.[34] In the 1840 survey, Rogers gave an account of the mines strung out in the hills from Ringwood to Dover with accompanying analyses of several ore samples and descriptions of the process used in analysis.

Ironically, although men had insisted on trying to get rich from the insufficient copper ore in the state, hardly anyone had attempted to open the great zinc deposits near Franklin and Sterling Hill in Sussex County. In the eighteenth century when the English colonists first became seriously interested in the area, they found evidence of ancient workings—perhaps by the Dutch.[35] Geologists and miners sensed unscientifically but correctly that the ores at Franklin were potentially profitable, but they misunderstood the nature of the ore. In the eighteenth century the area around Sterling Hill was known as the "copper tract," presumably because the red oxide was mistaken for copper oxide.[36] William Alexander, Lord Stirling, later made the same mistake and shipped a load to England for smelting as copper. He sent some of the black ore from the area to his furnace at Charlottesburg under the impression that it was the iron ore magnetite.[37] Such mistakes were understandable as neither of these ores had been discovered elsewhere in the world. When techniques proper for the extraction of copper or iron were used on the red and black zinc ores, the "iron" frustratingly went up the flue in white smoke.[38] Finally, in 1810, that enthusiastic mineralogist Dr. Archibald Bruce of New York City succeeded in analyzing the red ore and discovered its zinc content.[39] Appropriately enough, this was called zincite. Bruce, however, did not discover that the more plentiful black ore was also a zinc ore. Like others before him Bruce thought it was magnetite.[40]

About a year later, William Maclure became interested in the Franklin minerals and sent some samples to France where they were analyzed by M. Vauquelin who confirmed the presence of zinc.[41] The definitive analyses were done by M. P. Berthier of the French Royal Corps of Mines in his laboratory at the Royal School of Mines in Paris. He finally established the black ore as an association of "the oxid of iron, the oxid of manganese and the oxide of zinc" which he named "franklinite, in order to remind us that it was found, for the first time, in a place to which the Americans have given the name of a great man, whose memory is venerated equally in Europe as in the new world by all the friends of science and humanity."[42]

Although Berthier pointed out that franklinite could be a valuable source of iron, manganese, and zinc it took some time before the source was exploited profitably. A legendary figure in the early history of zinc at Franklin was Dr. Samuel Fowler who made strenuous efforts to get financial support to mine the zinc. He succeeded in arousing the interests of scientists and a regular procession, including Charles Thomas Jackson, William Keating, William Maclure, Thomas Nuttall, Henry Seybert, John Torrey, Gerard Troost, and Lardner Vanuxem, visited the Fowlers—some fairly frequently—to gather specimens.[43] Vanuxem and Keating discovered willemite, the third important zinc ore, a silicate of zinc which occurs in crystalline mass of various colors ranging from light greenish-yellow to pink. Troost described a less important zinc ore, jeffersonite, a greenish-blackish variety of pyroxene containing manganese and several other new minerals. But the enthusiasm of geologists did not help Fowler in his search for financial backing for mining operations. A major problem lay in the fact that the peculiar nature of the combination of manganese, iron, and zinc found in the New Jersey ores presented special problems in smelting even though the British had succeeded in refining zinc from other ores as early as 1730. It was not that the zinc could not be obtained. Ballou, one of Fowler's associates, made white zinc oxide from zincite, ground it in oil and used the resultant paint on Fowler's house several years before it was so used in Europe; and in 1838 enough metallic zinc was obtained by a Mr. Hitz, working under the direction of Ferdinand Hassler, Superintendent of the United States Coast Survey, to make a brass for the standard weights and measures then being produced for the United States Custom Houses. The difficulty was that no process practical for use in large-scale production had been discovered. Rogers, therefore, did not urge the opening of the zinc mines as enthusiastically as had Fowler or James Pierce, who, in an article in Silliman's *Journal* in 1822, had expressed his amazement that "no attempts had been made to furnish that very useful metal to the public from the New Jersey mines."[44] Rogers did point out, however, that the metallic ore deposit at Sterling could be excavated with considerable ease because it was exposed on the flank of the hill. He suggested that the pure red zinc oxide, zincite, found at Franklin would probably be better for smelting than the mixed ore found in the Sterling mine.[45]

Basic to the development of scientific geology was the observation, recording, and classification of observable geological phenomena. Rogers, with an interest in the structure of formations and the mineralogy of the region, worked with great pains from the inadequate evidence of surface outcroppings to trace deposits of limestone, gneiss, franklinite, and other rocks and minerals. He devoted the major part of his time to this necessary but tedious exploration, analysis, and classification but he was also interested in the formulation of theories of causation. An early version of his theory of mountain building is included in his explanation of the New Jersey landscape.

Theorizing was very popular among geologists and natural scientists until well into the nineteenth century. The magnitude and necessity of the job of classification and observation became clearer as the century progressed but for a long time the formulation of hypotheses on minimal evidence was universally accepted. The less reliable the data the more reason early theorists found for roaming in what William Mather called "the wild and ample region of pure theory."[46] One of the most popular areas for theorizing was the development of historical explanations for the landscapes that people saw around them. It had early become clear (as when men discovered sea shells on mountain tops) that, unless one wished to postulate (as many did) that the earth had not changed since its creation and that any observable anomalies were the work of a sometimes whimsical creator, explanations were needed to account for the changes the earth had experienced through its lifetime and the forces that had brought them about. Two popular schools of thought developed—the catastrophists and uniformitarians.[47] The labels oversimplified the varieties of opinion held by most scientists but they highlighted a fundamental conceptual divergence. Catastrophists tended to believe that change had been wrought by cataclysmic occurrences—floods were particularly favored and pious folk could identify these with the biblical flood. Uniformitarians followed the theories of James Hutton who ascribed changes to the slow effect of meteorological forces like wind, tide, and rain that were easily observable by all. In his most famous line, Hutton wrote, "We find no vestige of a beginning,—no prospect of an end." Charles Lyell, whose landmark *Principles of Geology* was published in England in 1830, re-examined and supported Hutton's theories. Until Lyell visited the United States in 1843, however, his ideas were not generally known there.

Geologists of the United States in the 1830s, Henry Rogers among them, favored great floods as the major causes of geological change. In his New Jersey report Rogers postulated the existence of a great body of water held back by the Appalachian Mountains and emptying into Raritan Bay. After a long period of time, the floor on the western side of the mountains rose, forcing the waters of this great sea to burst on to the plain to the east with a mighty rush, washing away and pulverizing the rock surface of the hills, exposing older rocks and depositing a sediment of sandstone and shale. Possibly because he thought the "mighty rush of waters" explained everything he did not write specifically of the strange occurrence on the northern New Jersey landscape of odd striations upon exposed rock surfaces, the existence of large boulders strewn far from rock of similar composition, and the mounds of gravel and sand piled in hills and ridges (all of which were to be later studied by George Cook).

Rogers's description of the stratigraphy of New Jersey were determined by the stage of development of that branch of geology. Geologists had not yet settled upon the broad terms to be used in designating the various layers of rock and mineral. Rogers's use of "Primary" for the oldest, "Tertiary" for the newest, and "Secondary" for the strata in between were totally inadequate to comprehend the vast variety of groups and subgroups. Rogers was well aware of the problem and in the Pennsylvania Geological Survey report he fashioned a neat and poetic system of classification using Greek terms for the various times of day. There were fifteen in all, beginning with "Primal" (dawn) and Auroral (daybreak) and progressing through Meridian (noon) and Cadent (declining day) to Ponent (sunset) and Seral (nightfall).[48] These never caught on and eventually names chosen for the geographical location where the formation was first identified were adopted. As for the task of determining the age of rock formations, William Smith in England made the task more manageable when he suggested that fossil remains could be used for the purpose—the more primitive life forms existing in the earlier rocks.

In later assessments of his position among American geologists Rogers comes off fairly well. George P. Merrill said he was "unquestionably the leading structural geologist of his time," although Joseph Barrell later wrote: "In ability to weigh facts and interpret them Edward Hitchcock showed much more insight . . . while in the philosophic and comprehensive aspects of the subject James Dwight Dana far outranks him."[49] But these men were considering Rogers as a leader in the development of geological theory. George Cook later wrote that Rogers

made every effort to make the location and mode of occurrence [of the strata] understood. This is especially true of the marl formation, on account of its usefulness in agriculture. He took great pains to get representative specimens from all parts of the marl region, analyzed them, and then discussed at length the fertilizing qualities of the marl, and described its remarkable effects upon the sandy and exhausted soils of the country. The earnestness and enthusiasm he shows in his description of the marl and its effects upon farm products was an attractive feature of the report.[50]

During most of the nineteenth century, people generally conceived of a geological survey as a limited operation which could be completed in a relatively short time and having been done well once would not have to be done again. In many states surveys were inaugurated just after the peak of an economic boom and were discontinued during the subsequent period of economic depression.[51] Fifteen state surveys were begun during the enthusiastic commercial and industrial expansion of the 1830s. By 1849, after the financial collapse of 1837 and the ensuing depression, only three states supported surveys. In 1854 another period of prosperity was about to crest. Governor Rodman Price in recommending a new survey used arguments that concentrated as much on economic benefits as had those of Governor Vroom twenty years earlier. Although a special committee of the legislature had reported in 1852 that the Rogers survey had been inaccurate and incomplete, the increased use of marl following publication of Rogers's report had brought larger crop yields to New Jersey farmers and Price argued that a more accurate knowledge of the marl strata would raise the value of agricultural lands even more. A weighty argument for the legislators was that this increased prosperity would result in more tax money for the state treasury.[52] Furthermore, said Price, a new survey would give Jerseymen a more accurate idea of the worth of their holdings and keep them from being bilked out of their valuable mineral lands by rapacious "foreigners" from other states. Convinced by Price's arguments, the legislators approved the survey, authorizing an expenditure of not more than $4,000 for the next year.[53]

William Kitchell, the director of the survey, was only twenty-seven years old at the time of his appointment.[54] His scientific credentials were impressive. After two years at Rutgers College he transferred to New York University where he earned an M.D. He never practiced medicine but taught natural science at the Newark Institute for a few years before going to Germany where he studied for a time at Werner's famous Mining School. At the time of his appointment as state geologist he was back at the Newark Institute teaching chemistry. Kitchell was an active member of the Natural History Society of Newark and had played a leading role in a revival of the New Jersey Agricultural Society. This background, plus recommendations from Congressman George Vail of Morristown and other influential friends persuaded Governor Price to appoint him.[55] Kitchell's closest rival for the appointment was Dr. Francis Moran of Sussex County, whose numerous friends wrote many letters urging his appointment. In his younger days Moran, who was a practicing country doctor, had had a lively interest in geology. His supporters wrote that he had always been a good Democrat and was now badly in need of money as his health did not allow him to drive around to visit the sick in bad weather.[56] One sympathizes with poor Dr. Moran but it was as well for the interests of the survey that the governor looked for a man with more substantial qualifications.

Kitchell took charge of the northern section of the state while George Cook was appointed assistant geologist with responsibility for the southern part. Lieutenant Egbert Viele, a recent graduate of West Point, was made topographical engineer and directed eighteen or twenty surveyors and field men.[57] Dr. Henry Wurtz was appointed chemist and mineralogist and two artists were hired to make woodcuts of significant landscapes. Original plans called for Timothy Conrad to be invertebrate paleontologist for the survey, but he became ill and had to resign. Kitchell asked James Hall to replace Conrad but Hall was so busy with other responsibilities that he was not able to accomplish much for New Jersey. Joseph Leidy, professor of anatomy at the University of Pennsylvania, was put in charge of the classification and identification of the vertebrate fossils.[58]

Kitchell's survey was more ambitious and more scientifically sophisticated than Rogers's. It reflected development in geology during the intervening years as well as Kitchell's European training. The great New York State Survey carried out by Hall, Lardner Vanuxem, Ebenezer Emmons, W. W. Mather, and T. A. Conrad had become a model for all subsequent American geological surveys. The strata identified in New York served as the standard for every part of the United States and were directly applicable to New Jersey because the formations of lower New York State extend into New Jersey.

The most striking feature of Kitchell's plans for the New Jersey Survey was a topographical survey and map. Although England had begun a topographical survey a hundred years before and other European countries were investing large sums of money in topographical work, very little had been done in the United States. No state survey had attempted one. When Kitchell started his survey there was not only no topographical map of New Jersey, there was no map which even showed accurately the locations of towns and cities and the distances between them. The best map available (which was the one Rogers had used) had been made on the scale of three miles per one inch by Thomas Gordon, a surveyor, in 1822. Gordon had done some new surveys at the time and had corrected older maps. The greatest error in latitude was three-quarters of a mile and in longitude was five-eighths of a mile. This was a considerable improvement over the best earlier maps, which had been off by as much as 2,415 feet in some instances.[59]

Kitchell decided that in order to make the most progress and consequently insure continued support from the legislature Lieutenant Viele should start his field parties working from the New Jersey-New York boundary instead of beginning with the two thousand square miles of primary and secondary triangulation along the New Jersey coast already completed by the United States Coast Survey. Viele might have begun on one side of the Coast Survey in the center of the state and sent working parties north and south simultaneously but both Kitchell and Viele thought it would be less expensive to work from the New Jersey-New York boundary line. Unfortunately, the northern boundary markers had long since disappeared and the line itself was in doubt because of a tendency of local surveyors to shift it one way or the other for the convenience of their clients. Repairing the effects of this neglect took more time, more equipment, and more men than had been expected.

Viele went into the field in Sussex County with three paid and four volunteer assistants.[60] As the tight budget did not allow the purchase of necessary instruments the surveyors used their own instruments. Alexander Dallas Bache, Superintendent of the U.S. Coast Survey, agreed to lend a theodolite and a plane table. When the New Jersey Franklinite Company also lent some equipment, Viele was able to put three more assistants in the field before the end of the first summer. The volunteers (recent college graduates eager to pay their own expenses for the training they would get) proved to be of doubtful value as they frequently tired of the work or ran out of money and had to go home. In spite of these difficulties, by the end of the first year Viele and his parties had gathered topographical data for three-quarters of Sussex County, finished seven hundred miles of leveling in preparations for the drawing of geological sections, and filled thirty-four boxes with specimens of rocks and minerals for the state collection.[61]

The next year the legislature with unprecedented generosity increased the appropriation to $20,000.[62] Viele began plane table operations in nine counties. The teams completed Sussex and Cape May Counties, made good progress in Salem, Morris, Monmouth, and Warren, and began work in Hudson and Atlantic. Kitchell expected the Morris County map to be finished by midsummer. In 1856 $25,000 was appropriated to take care of engraving maps of Sussex and Cape May, printing the report and map of Sussex and the report and map of Cape May. A revisory party was at work in Cape May, a plane table party in Cumberland, and draughtsmen and engravers were busy transferring the accumulated data to maps.

In southern New Jersey Cook spent his time tramping over the area and making notes for his report. The southern part of the state with its flat terrain, sandy or clayey soils, with hardly a rock or a hill and dating as it does from recent geological time, is less interesting geologically than the northern regions. In July 1854 Cook started out to update Rogers's treatment of the marl beds of Monmouth County and thus began what was to be thirty-five years of travel through the state on geological or agricultural missions of one kind or another. Riding on the state's extensive systems of railroads to a town, he would rent a horse

and buggy or wagon (or borrow one from a nearby friend) and drive off
to inspect the objective for the day. In a succession of small, tan, leather-
covered notebooks which he always carried (and which became a kind of
trademark) he recorded facts and observations which would be helpful
in writing his reports and lectures. Fortunately, his teaching tasks at
Rutgers allowed time for these geological journeys. In 1855, for example, he informed Kitchell that a new arrangement of the program had
relieved him from recitations or lectures on Tuesdays, "although I
design generally to be in my laboratory or study when anything is doing
in college," he added.[63] Winter vacation breaks gave him time to prepare
his reports, while during the spring recess and the summer vacation
more extensive travel was possible.

In his survey Rogers had outlined the various strata of the marl
formation but many openings exposing the marl deposits had been
made since then as more farmers opened pits in their fields. Because of
this increase in openings, Cook was able to delineate the layers more
precisely than had Rogers and roughly to measure the thickness of each.
He found the fossils *Exogyra costata, Gryphaea convexa, Ostrea falcata,
Terebratura sayii* and *Belemnites americanus* in most abundance in the
first thirty-foot-thick bed of marl.[64] This was the bed seen on the side of
the "Nevisink Hills" (Navesink Highlands) and on the shore of Sandy
Hook Bay. The second bed, which surfaced a short distance below New
Egypt near Eatonstown and Long Branch, contained the fossils
Terebratula harlani and the *Gryphaea convexa* (smaller and thinner
specimens than the same species found in the first bed).[65] The third bed
(about fifty-five feet thick) included three layers found in marl pits in
Deal and Shark River. Few fossils occurred in these beds and they were
entirely different from those found in the two lower beds. At the time of
Cook's report they had not been examined closely enough to determine
the species.[66]

During his second year in the field Cook traced the marl beds more
carefully and examined the beds of clay on the banks of the Delaware and
Raritan Rivers. His more detailed mapping and description led James
Hall to write:

I have read your description of the successive beds of marl and sand which throws
new light on this subject, and I am glad to see that you have set to work without
any preconceived opinions and think your elucidation clears up the difficulties I
experienced more than twenty years since in collecting fossils from Freehold,
New Egypt and Squankum to find that each locality—that of Salem not
dissimilar from Egypt furnished 5 peculiar fossils with no intermixture of

others—this certainly was inexplicable upon views of the formation then adopted.[67]

Well aware of the economic importance of the marl, Cook quoted acreage values from the census of 1850 and reported that in the fifteen years preceding, a great increase in profits from agricultural pursuits had been realized.[68] He felt this was attributable almost entirely to the use of marl. The identity of the effective fertilizing agent in the marl was still, as it had been in Rogers's day, an open question. Cook outlined a brief history of former studies which had attributed the fertilizing effect to everything from the shell and calcareous ingredients to iron pyrites and clay as well as lime and potash.[69] Comparing the practical experience of farmers with the analyses of Henry Wurtz, the chemist of the survey, he reported that the marl bed which tested highest for phosphate of lime was the one which farmers found to have the quickest and most powerful action.[70]

Although the mapping of the marl beds was perhaps the most important result of Cook's work in South Jersey, his imagination was especially captivated by evidence of subsidence in the coastal areas. In Lyell's reports of his investigations in the United States, Cook had read the reports of a partial subsidence of the land along the New Hampshire coast, the Bay of Fundy, and in North and South Carolina.[71] Others, including Dr. Charles Jackson in his *Report on the Geology of New Hampshire,* and professor John William Dawson of Canada, had written similar reports of subsidence elsewhere along the coast.[72] Now Cook saw for himself and heard reports from farmers and fishermen of some two dozen similar examples. He was told of cedar stumps found deep under swamp mud and of encroaching tides which had swallowed up as much as fifty acres of land on Stipson's Island in the past fifty years. The residents attributed the higher tides to local causes, but Cook was convinced that they were due to a subsidence of the lands, which at that time he estimated to be at the rate of two feet a century.[73] Furthermore, he concluded that because shells have been found in various locations above the present tide level, the same land had previously experienced a period of elevation.[74]

Cook wrote on subsidence in the New Jersey survey reports and read a paper, "On a Subsidence of the Lands on the Sea-Coast of New Jersey and Long Island," at the Montreal meeting of the American Association for the Advancement of Science in 1857 that was later published in the *American Journal of Science and the Arts.*[75] His report "On the Marls of New Jersey," published in the *Mining Magazine* for 1855, was a major step in the establishment of his reputation in geological circles.[76] An important result of his work on the Kitchell survey was the publication of Cook's survey of Cape May County.

The Geology of Cape May County, accompanied by Viele's large topographical map and woodcuts by H. Carmiencke, was instructive, economically helpful, and geologically significant. It had a useful index, a history of the county by Dr. Maurice Beesley, and catalogues of the birds, wild animals, fish, plants, and marine algae of the county. Quantitative tables included compared analyses of soil from different parts of the county with analyses of soil from other parts of the world; gave analyses of materials used for fertilizer including seaweed, ash, swamp earth, Cancerine (made of crushed crabs), dried menhaden and Peruvian guano; and showed the increase in agricultural production in New Jersey between 1850 and 1856. Because most men in the country earned their living by wood-chopping, lumbering, or "going by water," Cook included a table giving employment figures and income from fishing, clamming, oystering, and shipping.[77] He devoted several pages to the "mining" of cedar logs used for shingles, and the cutting of cedar trees for fence rails. For prospective farmers he pointed out that an earlier growing season provided a potential advantage in supplying the markets of Philadelphia and New York which would be realized when transportation was improved. One crop which he especially noted was cranberries, later to become a major source of income but at that time cultivated mostly in small plots.

One solution to economic problems seemed to be the bringing of as much land under cultivation as possible and Cook saw in the salt marshes a source of fertile land if it could be diked and the salt tidal water kept out.[78] In his search for areas of economic opportunity, he looked beyond the geological and agricultural and also recognized tourism as a likely source of income. By the 1850s the beaches of Cape May had been a favorite summering place for over a hundred years. As many as five thousand people at a time visited the town's twenty-four boarding houses and enjoyed the sea bathing, sailing, fishing, and hunting.[79]

In writing of the geology of the region Cook, using the terms to identify strata that were accepted at the time, described the geological formations as belonging to the Quaternary System and distinguished two separate formations: the Drift and the Alluvium.[80] He characterized all the material (sand, clay, gravel) which had originated in another location and had been brought in by some method not then clearly understood as Drift. The Alluvial formation, more recent than the Drift, included all the sands, clays, peat, and mud which had been deposited where they lay.[81]

Nothing was published on the geology of the northern part of the state where Kitchell supervised the work except in the annual reports to the legislature. Kitchell himself took to the field the first year but he became bogged down in administrative work thereafter. A large portion of his work was an updating of Rogers's descriptions of iron and zinc mines. Over fifty iron mines were named and described. Forty-five years after the Fowlers had urged their exploitation, Kitchell was able to report that zinc deposits were being mined by three companies organized since 1848. Edwin Post of Stanhope had developed a process using anthracite coal that enabled the zinc to be recovered for commercial use and at the same time produce a high grade of iron.[82]

Kitchell's stratigraphic work (confined to the Paleozoic and Precambrian areas of Sussex County) consisted in the tracing of the formations delineated by the New York survey as they penetrated into New Jersey. He found fourteen layers in four divisions, which, he pointed out, corresponded to the Silurian and Devonian of English usage and had been identified by Rogers as layers IV and V. In the Precambrian area the report focused to a large extent on geographical description, although Kitchell identified the various gneiss, hornblende, feldspathic, quartzose, schistose, and limestone deposits, giving the angle of dips and the directions of layers as well as the popular names of the hills they formed. He described the rock debris or drift (later identified as due to glacial action) which bounded and overlay the Precambrian rocks. These rocks, which Kitchell termed Azoic, he described as sedimentary and without organic remains. The white crystalline limestone found in the Vernon and Wallkill valleys he characterized as metamorphic, traversed by numerous dikes of granite and syenite with a great variety of rare minerals.[83]

Despite Kitchell's academic qualifications, his work has been criticized by George Merrill, who wrote that the important stratigraphic of the survey was that done by Cook. The evidence of letters in the Cook papers seems to indicate that Kitchell tended to be lazy. His ineptitude in working with people made him antagonize almost everyone connected with the survey although he kept the support of the Agricultural Society. Egbert Viele, who wrote to Cook with complaints about Kitchell's tardiness in paying him and his workers, also complained that Kitchell was trying "to make of me like Wurtz a fifth wheel in the concern."[84] Governor Price wrote to Cook, "I speak frankly to you. Your work is up to the mark. Viele has fallen short, and what Dr. Kitchell has done I have yet to see, and we shall show an expenditure of probably 12 or 14,000 dollars—the large expenditure, small amount of work and the embarrassed condition of the Treasury I fear will prove fatal to the survey . . . ."[85] It was largely Kitchell's insistence on the expensive though scientifically desirable topographical survey which brought the survey to an untimely end in 1857.

The newly elected governor, William A. Newell, stated in his message to the legislature that the financial affairs of the state made it impossible for him to ask for money for the geological survey. Outgoing Governor Price told Cook that the only financial emergency was in the new governor's mind, but nevertheless the survey was discontinued. The work straggled on in disarray as long as the men could hold out in hopes that the treasury would eventually receive the money to pay them. An unnamed friend of the survey contributed the necessary funds to complete the survey of Monmouth County. But only the Sussex and Cape May maps were finally engraved and published.

When the survey was discontinued it had in its possession a great accumulation of geological notes, preliminary topographical information, maps in various stages of completion, boxes of mineral and fossil specimens, and a sizable amount of equipment. All this belonged to the state, of course. No one knew quite what to do with it. Cook and Kitchell hoped that the survey might be continued in a more affluent future and therefore wanted to keep everything together. Governor Newell asked Cook to gather up the unfinished work, the minerals and fossils, and the apparatus, and store it in a room at Rutgers College.[86] This proved to be more difficult than it appeared. Kitchell wanted to continue the survey and after failing to borrow money from a bank he decided to continue on his own to whatever extent he could. Consequently, he wanted to retain all of his notes and some of the instruments and equipment. William H. Phelps, the principal of the State Normal School in Trenton, supported by L. D. Chandler (who was a state assemblyman as well as a trustee of the Normal School), requested that the possessions of the survey be transferred to the Normal School, where they could be used for educational purposes. This appeared to be a reasonable request as the school was a state-supported institution of higher education and Rutgers College was not. Cook's uncle, Dr. Munn, attempted to prevent such a disposition by suggesting to Chandler that he form a committee to make the decision, hoping that Cook would be able to persuade the committee to keep the property together at Rutgers.[87] Cook himself explained to Chandler that while the idea of giving the minerals and use of the apparatus to the Normal School was admirable because they would thus be put to use, most of the specimens had not been examined or named and they were labeled with reference numbers only.[88] He feared that if the specimens were laid out for exhibition, the information about their identity and original location would be lost and they would become mere curios—almost useless from a scientific point of view.

The influence of the trustees of the Normal School prevailed, however, and the legislature authorized the Normal School to take possession of the property of the survey.[89] In an effort to prevent the work of the survey from being completely scattered, Cook gently reminded Governor Newell that control had originally been placed in the hands of the governor and that it should perhaps remain there.[90] Shortly thereafter Cook invited Phelps to inspect the apparatus and specimens stored at Rutgers and suggested that a person with knowledge of the survey be appointed to put the collection in order before it was moved to the Normal School.[91] This struck the trustees of the Normal School as a reasonable request and they authorized the hiring of Cook and Kitchell to carry it out. At the same time Governor Newell, at Cook's suggestion, arranged for a representative selection from the mineral and fossil collections to be displayed in the State House.[92] This job fell to Cook also and caused him some difficulty. It was a year later before he managed to persuade a reluctant state treasurer to remove the documents which were stored in the room next to the Chancery Court so that he could set up shelves and arrange the specimens.[93]

Through the whole difficult business of terminating the survey and disposing of its property Cook was able to maintain the good will of all concerned—a masterful performance in view of the number of people involved and the number of toes that might have been stepped on. The fact that Newell saw fit to give him instead of Kitchell the responsibility for the winding-up operation was a clear recognition of Cook's conscientiousness and tact. Through the repetition of a variety of such encounters over many years Cook built up a reservoir of trust and good will throughout the state. His experience with the survey added to his understanding of the management of the complex relationships necessary for leaders of scientific state-supported enterprises.

Kitchell meanwhile had been busy trying to figure out a way in which the survey might be continued and had decided that it might succeed as a private venture. He asked Cook to join him in the endeavor, but Cook felt that it would be impossible either to do a good job or to make any money.[94] He was convinced that only state-financed support would insure sufficient resources to do justice to a survey. However, with the help of the New Jersey Agricultural Society, Kitchell engineered passage of an act which gave him the right to carry out the survey for private profit.[95] Cook turned over what remained in his possession of the survey property and discontinued his connection with it altogether.[96]

The Kitchell survey, though aborted before completion and unsuccessful in its attempt to complete the topographical mapping of the state, put New Jersey ahead of most states in mapping and provided some groundwork for future efforts. In other respects, because of Cook's stratigraphic work with the marl beds, his completed survey of Cape May County, and his articles and papers on the subsidence of the coast, the survey contributed to the sum total of geological knowledge of New Jersey. Cook's work on the Kitchell survey gained him a place of respect among his fellow geologists. James Dwight Dana cited Cook's study of subsidence in his *Manual of Geology* and Benjamin Silliman recognized the value of his work in the *American Journal of Science and Arts*.[97] Cook's later appointment as state geologist of New Jersey and his influence in state agricultural and legislative circles began with his work on the Kitchell survey. But for a few years he turned his energies to Rutgers College.

6

1860-1864

The Land-Grant College of New Jersey

In the early 1860s Rutgers College was in the doldrums. Although the general exodus of "old fogys" in 1859 and the ensuing new faculty appointments had brought a measure of new energy to the campus, an ailing and aging president, apathetic alumni, and lack of support from the Dutch Reformed Church community made the college an unlikely place for a dynamic change of direction and growth. Events on the national scene seemed certain to hasten its decline. After the outbreak of the Civil War in 1861 enrollments dropped from 164 students in 1861 to sixty-four in 1864. For George Cook, whose fortunes were now wholly dependent upon the prosperity of the college, the situation was one of great concern. Fortunately, two events in 1862 brought new vitality and a new commitment to the college. The first event was the selection of William Campbell as president. The second, partly a result of the war which was contributing to the college's plight, was the passage of the Morrill Act by the Congress of the United States.

Campbell was singularly well fitted for the presidency of the college at this crucial juncture. His former position as principal of the Albany Academy had given him experience in administration and he was already associated with the college as professor of belles lettres. His primary interest and responsibility was as professor in the New Brunswick Seminary, however, and he was not anxious to take up a different post. Through the spring and summer of 1862 he resisted the pleas of the trustees but he finally gave in and was formally named president in September. His inauguration as eighth president of Rutgers took place in June 1863. For nineteen years he served in the office, and, especially during the first ten, he led the college brilliantly and energetically. Under his guidance both the endowment and the number of buildings were increased; the academic program was expanded; and the morale and self-confidence of faculty, students, and alumni raised. He was by all odds the most effective president the college had ever had. His portrait shows a wise, kindly man with a sparkle of humor; his contemporaries knew him to be vigorous, fiery, and sometimes short-tempered as well. But his willingness to admit his mistakes endeared him to his colleagues. About some now long-forgotten altercation he wrote a note to Cook which shows this trait,

Prof. Reilley informs me that it is his own judgment and that of the other members of the Faculty, that I was wrong in making any allusion in the faculty meeting to the affair of Tuesday morning. I had reached the same conclusion before Prof. Reilley had spoken to me, and I write to make you the amend which as a Christian I feel bound to do. I am sorry I made any allusion to the subject at all. It ought to have been dropped by me altogether, and I should only have been on my guard lest by any means I might hurt anyone's feelings in the future by remark or deed. I hope this statement will be as satisfactory as I wish it to be. I have too few friends left me to be able to afford to lose any of them and it would afford my enemies a great triumph if they could have it to say that I had quarreled and broken with Dr. Cook after a friendship of twenty years. . . .[1]

Many years earlier Campbell's impatience and short temper had been the cause of a protest famous in the annals of the college because it led to a great improvement for both college and seminary. One July day in 1854, sweltering in a hot suit (for no gentleman ever removed his coat) Campbell found the third-floor classroom assigned to him for his seminary class so unbearable that he persuaded his students to meet at 5 A.M. for the remainder of the term.[2] The following year, again annoyed by the heat and also because he had to share his room with college classes, this uninhibited man of God incited his seminary students to write letters of protest to the faculty and to the Synod of the Church. The letters brought great sympathy and caused considerable consternation. A committee visited Mrs. Ann Hertzog of Philadelphia and convinced her that a new building for the seminary would be an admirable memorial to her husband. In a remarkably short time, Hertzog Hall, a great, high-ceilinged building, was constructed several hundred yards north of the college and the entire seminary (except for two professors who continued to live in Old Queens) was able to move in by September 1856.

Six years later Campbell's effect upon Rutgers College was equally dramatic. The faculty which he was called to head consisted of six full-time and three part-time professors with a heavy representation of ministers. In fact, except for George Cook and Gustavus Fischer, professor of modern languages (who was not a full-time professor as he did not receive a salary but had to depend upon individual tuitions from students for his livelihood) all were ministers. Four of the six professors taught languages and literature. Besides Fischer there were DeWitt TenBroeck Reilley and Howard Crosby (who taught Latin and Greek respectively) and the Reverend Dr. John Forsythe who taught English. The relative lack of importance in higher education and the early stages of development of mathematics and the sciences is clearly demonstrated by the fact that one professor, the Reverend Marshall Henshaw, taught all the mathematics and physics and that George Cook's teaching assigment included chemistry, botany, physical geography, geology, organic chemistry, heat and electricity, and political economy (the last, however, only because there was no one else to teach it). Cook did not teach all these subjects every term, of course. There was little freedom of choice in the curriculum. Freshmen studied no science; sophomores met with Cook once a week to study botany the first term while during their second term he taught them elementary chemistry twice a week. In the junior year students were given a selection of the other sciences (as, for example, physical geography, and heat and electricity) and the seniors studied geology and organic chemistry with him every day.[3] Although Cook's teaching duties were arduous, they were made lighter by the fact that classes at the college began at nine o'clock (right after daily prayers) and lasted only until one o'clock in the afternoon. He had many more courses to prepare than do present-day college professors, but the number of hours he taught was approximately the same as now taught in smaller colleges where personal individual research is not necessarily expected. However, Cook had an additional responsibility as librarian of the college from 1860 until 1863, when he became curator of the cabinet of the Natural History Society.

About the time Campbell assumed the presidency, there were three resignations which made possible the addition of several energetic and able men. Foremost among these new professors was David Murray, a colleague of both Cook's and Campbell's from the Albany Academy. Murray had succeeded Cook as principal of the academy and, like him, had been hoping to move into the ranks of college professors. With this in mind, he told Cook, he had been teaching conic sections, analytical geometry, differential and integral calculus, Jackson's mechanics, mathematical astronomy, optics, and surveying in addition to the usual algebra, geometry, and trigonometry.[4] He was appointed to the post of professor of mathematics, natural philosophy and astronomy and proved to be a man of industry and intelligence with great ad-

ministrative skills. These were later put to good use when he was
commissioned by the Japanese government to reorganize the Japanese
educational system. His respect for Cook and their common interest in
science made them especially congenial and allowed them to work
together in great harmony. Murray's regard for Cook is shown in a note
sent after he had visited New Brunswick before accepting the Rutgers
position, "For your kindness in this,—and indeed in everything I ever
had to do with you—my thanks is all that I can return."[5]

Campbell, Cook, and Murray were the leaders in setting the college
on a new track, but they had the support of other capable men. The
Reverend Theodore Sandford Doolittle was appointed in 1863 to a new
professorship of rhetoric, logic and mental philosophy endowed by the
Collegiate Church in New York City. George Atherton, later to become
president of Pennsylvania State College, joined the faculty in 1869 as
professor of history, political economy and constitutional law. Like
Murray, Doolittle had known Cook for some time. He had been a
student in the class of 1859 and was a great admirer and supporter of the
Natural History Society and its Cabinet. This interest was clearly
demonstrated on one occasion when the Society had been offered a
particularly desirable mineral collection. No money for its purchase was
available from college funds and consequently alumni who had been
interested in science while in college were "taxed" two dollars each.
Doolittle, then pastor of a rural church in Seneca County, New York,
wrote an enthusiastic response which not only indicates his generosity
but throws some light on the way the discoveries of scientists were
received by enlightened ministers of the period,

I fully recognize the right of the Society to lay a "tax" and the duty of the
graduate to pay it, and to show at once my loyalty to science and my gratitude for
being let off so easy I send you Five Dollars. I only wish it were within my ability
just now to send you more—for having just finished reading Hitchcock's
Religion of Geology I am more than ever convinced, of which indeed I knew
before, that the science of geology and all its kindred branches rightly
investigated and applied are powerful auxiliaries both to theological knowledge
and to Christian faith—and the day is speedily coming, when in the unanimous
opinion of the learned, Hebrew accounts and fossil remains will be found to
speak one language and that only in praise of the ever working and wonderful
God. In the meantime your efforts in Natural History and other departments are
calculated to aid greatly in bringing in the good day—as such I hail them.[6]

Doolittle was not an accurate prophet—having been unable to
calculate the long-term effect of Darwin's theories—but his response

shows why Cook was pleased to have him on the Rutgers faculty. Indeed, one of Doolittle's letters referring to Cook as his "strong friend at court" indicates that Cook was as instrumental in procuring the assignment for Doolittle as he had been for Murray.[7] Doolittle, Murray and Cook were the most scientifically minded members of the faculty, but others, including Fischer, Reilley (who was Campbell's son-in-law), the new Greek professor, David Cole, and Cornelius Crispell, the college's first history professor, offered no impediment to the opportunity for an increased emphasis on science that was soon to appear.

In the mid-nineteenth century the natural history cabinet which Doolittle supported so enthusiastically was the most visible manifestation of science at Rutgers. It took the place of later government- or industry-supported research grants, elaborate experimental laboratories, and publication of university or college scientific research. The cabinet provided a focus of interest for the public, the student body, and the alumni as well. Even in the period of the 1860s, when most alumni were reported to be apathetic if not hostile toward Rutgers, a goodly number sent in donations and some, like Peter Stryker, felt a deep loyalty to the college and wrote that he took great pleasure in doing all he could for the welfare of "our beloved college."[8] From "130 miles west of Fort Laramie, north side of the North Platte River" another alumnus, Abraham Ackerman, sent specimens of dried flowers, Indian peas, and Indian sage from the prairie; a missionary alumnus, the Reverend Alvin Ostrom, sent a box of specimens from China.[9] Many years later Doolittle told of another way in which the natural history collection was increased:

One day, while inspecting some remarkable fossil tracks, which were among the finest in the whole world . . . I asked Dr. Cook, "What did they cost?"

"Oh, I don't know: between one and two hundred dollars, I suppose."

"Where did you get the money?"

"Oh, I got it."

"Did the Trustees furnish it?"

"Not that I know of."

"Did you thrust your hand into the pocket of some alumnus?"

"I guess not," he replied with a characteristic shrug of his shoulders and shake of his head.

"Well, where did you find it?"

"Oh, no matter: I found it."

"Ah, I see," said I; "You have been playing another one of your tricks upon your own purse."

"Perhaps so," he replied, while his eyes were laughing and sparkling: "but you needn't say anything about it, though."[10]

   The collecting and gathering of specimens in cabinets or museums continued to be a major interest of geologists and paleontologists throughout the century. Unlike earlier random collections of curios brought together primarily for intellectual titillation, later collections were made for the purpose of analyzing and classifying specimens. Cook kept up a lively correspondence and exchange of specimens with several leading geologists. One of his most faithful correspondents was Fielding Bradford Meek, who had been on several scientific expeditions exploring the western territories. Even in the midst of the Civil War, Cook and Meek, who was at the Smithsonian Institution, wrote to each other about specimens and once Meek invited Cook to join him in a scientific expedition on the Potomac River. Meek had met a Navy surgeon with an interest in fossils who managed to get a leave of absence and the use of a steamer with as many men as he needed to sail up and down the Potomac for thirty days looking for fossils.[11] Unfortunately, Cook was not able to go, but Meek later reported that the finds had been disappointing anyway.

   Meek's associate, Ferdinand V. Hayden, who had been with him on several western expeditions, had curtailed his scientific activities to serve as a surgeon in the Union Army throughout the Civil War but was later instrumental in the creation of Yellowstone National Park. He and Meek visited New Jersey and were taken on a specimen-collecting tour of the marl pits by Cook.[12] Later Cook sent other specimens for identification and description. Rutgers profited by this association for it was put on the list of institutions which received specimens sent out periodically by the Smithsonian. In turn Cook sent specimens of New Jersey minerals for the collections at the Smithsonian.[13]

   Another close scientific associate was Joseph Leidy, probably the greatest naturalist in America in the nineteenth century. He taught anatomy at the University of Pennsylvania and was one of the first Americans to study vertebrate fossils. In the 1860s when he was in the midst of an extensive study of the extinct reptiles and fish of the marl formation, Cook sent him boxes of New Jersey fossils on loan for description and classification.[14] One specimen of a turtle skull pleased Leidy especially as it was the only well-characterized chelonian fossil taken from the greensand marl that he had seen.[15] Leidy gave Cook advice in preparation of specimens for the cabinet at Rutgers, telling him that ordinary beeswax would make the best cement for the restoration of a Misaursarus skull.[16]

As the acquisition of prized specimens for their college museum was an important achievement for many nineteenth-century scientists, they were not above a bit of skullduggery in the process. One such incident took place in New Jersey when Professor Othniel C. Marsh of Yale chartered a train in order to get to the railroad station in time to prevent Professor Arnold Guyot of Princeton from acquiring a fossil specimen the latter had arranged to buy from the farmer who had found it on his land.[17] Marsh arrived at the station where the farmer was waiting for Guyot and offered him a higher price. When poor Guyot arrived some time later he found only an empty station.

At Rutgers there is no indication of such shady dealings, but the cabinet was an important educational facility and its inspection was a highlight of the annual commencement celebration. Commencement in those days was a three-day affair and a highlight of the social season in New Brunswick. It included the baccalaureate service, the annual meeting of the alumni, the annual meeting of the Board of Trustees, various addresses before the literary societies of the college, a concert, exercises for the junior class and a meeting of the Natural History Society, in addition to the commencement exercises themselves.[18] In 1862 the local newspaper reported that new specimens were presented during the meeting of the Natural History Society to the accompaniment of a running commentary by Professor Cook and others. The meeting must have been fairly hilarious—the reporter referred to "the relation of curious, marvelous and good-natured anecdotes, which were certainly amusing to say the least, showing that even the devotees of science enjoy a good joke and laugh, as well as other people. . . ."[19]

There is no doubt that when Campbell took over the presidency of Rutgers the college was solid enough in all its departments and positively lively in Cook's. It was also blessed with an extraordinarily energetic, loyal, and intelligent group of trustees; those often dimly perceived men whose ability to raise endowment funds and make policy decisions played a determining role in the welfare and directions of the college. What the college lacked was money, a leader, and a sense of future direction. William Campbell was able to supply all three. Even before his formal inauguration he organized a fund-raising committee of twenty men prominent in the affairs of the college and the church. With an overall goal of $100,000, each visited a section of New Jersey or New York State to plead the cause of the college.[20] Ultimately almost $145,000 was subscribed—an enormous sum for any college of that day.[21] Important as the fund-raising effort was, however, Campbell's decision to support the effort to have Rutgers named land-grant college of New

Jersey had a much greater long-range effect on the college.

For many years men of vision from Benjamin Franklin and Thomas Jefferson to Jonathan Turner of Illinois and Justin Morrill of Vermont had realized that neither the apprentice system of training mechanics nor the classical and religious colleges' method of fashioning gentlemen and ministers could produce the trained scientists and technicians necessary to build the railroads, bridges, and factories and manage the efficient farms needed by an industrializing society.[22] Foresighted men also dreamed of providing through education a path by which sons of workers and farmers could achieve more comfortable lives and move into positions of power and influence. But the legislators who finally passed the Morrill Act, which established agricultural and mechanical colleges supported by grants from the vast western lands, at the time were more concerned with the pressures of war and politics. The law was passed partly because of the awareness of northern leaders of the importance of science, agriculture, and industry for the war effort, partly because the Eastern states were interested in getting a share of the public lands, and partly because land speculators hoped for personal profit.[23]

According to the Morrill Act (which was signed by Abraham Lincoln on July 2, 1862) funds derived from the sale of the public lands donated to the states were to be applied in each state:

to the endowment, support, and maintenance of at least one college where the leading object shall be, without excluding other scientific and classical studies, and including military tactics, to teach such branches of learning as are related to agriculture and the mechanic arts, in such manner as the legislature of the States may respectively prescribe, in order to promote the liberal and practical education of the industrial classes in the several pursuits and professions in life.[24]

The vague terms of the act and the individual responsibility of the various state legislatures produced a broad range of institutional solutions to fulfull the requirements. Experimentation was inevitable. From the manner in which the grant of land was turned into money to the way the student was prepared for the practice of agricultural or mechanical arts, the experiment was tried afresh in each state. Precedents were few and legislators and educators, for the most part, were not disposed to follow precedent anyway. Establishment of the land-grant colleges was a wasteful process of trial and error and the wonder is not that so many states fumbled badly at first, but that eventually they developed a system of education uniquely suited to the furtherance of the agricultural and mechanical arts and to the education of a democratic citizenry. In contrast to the European trade or mechanical institute where only specialized courses in engineering or agriculture were taught, the American land-grant college incorporated the liberal arts disciplines of the humanities and social sciences. The profound social and intellectual effects of this kind of curriculum can hardly be exaggerated.

The purpose of the Morrill Act, embodying as it did the philosophy that science should serve men, coincided precisely with Cook's beliefs. His own background made him sympathetic to the education of the sons of farmers and mechanics. But although New Jersey accepted the provisions of the act in March 1863, the first evidence of interest at Rutgers was not recorded until the minutes of the faculty meeting of December 8, 1863. Here it was noted that Cook and Murray had urged that the faculty "adopt a plan for securing the proceeds of [the land grant] as an endowment for Rutgers College by establishing a Scientific Department in connection with it on the plan of the Sheffield Scientific School of Yale."[25] They suggested that the long-established scientific course might be turned into such a scientific department. Such an upgrading of the science program would, they hoped, add weight to Rutgers' bid for the land-grant endowment.

The faculty (and later the Board of Trustees) approved Cook's and Murray's proposal.[26] The trustees formed a committee headed by ex-Governor Peter D. Vroom to lobby for Rutgers among the legislators. Jacob Wortendyke, a lawyer from Jersey City, was one of the most active of the committee members as was John Hopper, a lawyer from Paterson and Peter S. Duryee, a businessman from Newark.[27]

In Trenton, the legislature convened on the twelfth of January and appointed a joint committee from the General Assembly and the Senate to formulate a bill that would implement the provisions of the Morrill Act.[28] The committee was composed of three members from the Senate, Jonathan F. Leaming (Cape May), Edward W. Scudder (Mercer) and Theodore F. Randolph (Hudson), and five from the Assembly, John Y. Dater (Bergen), Edward W. Maylin (Cumberland), Abraham W. Duryea (Hudson), Rynier A. Staats (Somerset) and Michael Taylor (Monmouth).[29] Immediately advocates from Rutgers, Princeton, and the state Normal School at Trenton began dancing attendance on them. At the outset the Normal School seemed to have the inside track for the designation. The principal, William F. Phelps, with the support and approval of the State Agricultural Society, had started a course of instruction in agriculture in 1860.[30] Because the main purpose of the school was to prepare teachers for the grammar schools of the state, the agriculture course was not designed for farmers or scientists but for young women who would be instructing the children of farmers. A pamphlet from an anonymous Princeton supporter attacked this concept: "The idea that these young ladies . . . are to be successful teachers of Scientific Agriculture and the Mechanic Arts in the common schools of the State, we think, will hardly be entertained by any after other serious reflection upon it."[31]

Another argument against the Normal School appeared in an editorial in the New Brunswick *Fredonian* emphasizing the economic stability of Rutgers as evidenced in its successful fund-raising campaign as contrasted with the fragile existence of the Normal School, which was dependent upon yearly legislative appropriations and thus might cease operations any year.[32] The *Fredonian* and New Brunswick's other newspaper, the *Times,* also pointed out the advantages of having the college located in their city because it was the center of population in the state.[33] Though friends of the Normal School continued to work in its behalf, the united attack of the two colleges effectively put it out of the running. Rutgers and Princeton were left to battle it out.

Rutgers launched the first offensive in the form of a pamphlet printed at the suggestion of ex-Governor Vroom who directed the efforts of the Trustees' Committee. Based on notes made by Cook but largely written by Murray it was grandly titled: *Considerations in Regard to the Disposal to Be Made by the Legislature of New Jersey of the Lands Granted by Congress for Encouraging Education in Agriculture and the Mechanic Arts.*[34] In this statement, published in its entirety in the *Fredonian,* Murray drew attention to the Rutgers library, the botanical and geological collections, laboratories, and scientific course which could be readily adapted to give instruction in agriculture and the mechanical arts. The strongest arguments in the *Considerations* were clearly derived from Cook's special knowledge and stressed the advantage of locating an experimental farm near New Brunswick. Here, within a few miles, the greatest variety of soils in the state could be found: soils of red shale, red sandstone, clay, sand, salt marshes, peat, muck—even the tidal meadows and the marl pits were not far away. Because of Cook's experience as a consultant mining engineer and chemist for mining and industrial companies, Murray was able to draw attention to various New Jersey iron, copper, lead, and zinc mines which could be visited by students aspiring to become mining engineers. For those interested in industry, factories making India rubber, machinery, and woolen and cotton materials were located in or near the city. Future military engineers could profit by trips to canals, railroads, bridges, and the military installations of New York Harbor. Finally, the *Considerations* mentioned the presence of the headquarters of the New Jersey Geological Survey in New Brunswick. The work of the survey in economic geology would provide material for the program.

From the College of New Jersey at Princeton came two pamphlets. Only a part of the one quoted above has been found.[35] In flowery phrases the author urged that the most important decision to be made was "where this munificent bounty of Congress can be so placed as most effectively to accomplish the noble ends for which it was bestowed."[36] The writer stressed the age and reputation of Princeton as well as the existing buildings, collections, and laboratory equipment. His strongest argument was that friends of the college would guarantee to construct a building equal to that of the Sheffield Scientific School at Yale, "including lecture rooms, cabinets, apparatus, libraries, and fixtures and equipment for such a purpose unsurpassed in the land."[37] Cook's friends in Trenton reported that they often saw Professor Lyman H. Atwater and other representatives of Princeton in that city. Cook himself visited Trenton on another matter.

It was a fortunate coincidence for Rutgers' interests that Cook had come to the attention of leaders in the state legislature and agricultural community as director of the State Geological Survey then under the general supervision of the New Jersey Agricultural Society. He had been asked to read his 1863 report to the Society before the Senate during the same month that he was arguing Rutgers' cause on the land grant issue. The report, which centered on the condition of agriculture in New Jersey, helped to convince the legislators that at Rutgers there was a man with a genuine concern for agriculture and a real understanding of it. As Professor Atwater's field was mental and moral philosophy and his colleagues were purely academic men, Cook's experience in agriculture, added to his scientific competence and realistic approach, were persuasive.

Behind the scenes also, forces were working in Rutgers' behalf. Cook's correspondence for the first three months of 1864 indicates a considerable amount of visiting, writing, persuading, pressuring, and maneuvering—all concentrated on furthering the cause. Alumni and friends from all over the state rallied round. South Jersey legislators were approached in a roundabout way through the brother-in-law of a Rutgers partisan, James Bodine Thompson, Rutgers class of 1851, who was minister of the Dutch Reformed Church in Metuchen.[38] In Somerset County the Reverend Abraham Messler of Somerville, in answer to a query from Cook, reported that he had found that the best man to influence Daniel Corey, assemblyman from Somerset, was John T. Veghte.[39] Messler thought that the senator from Somerset, Joshua Doughty, would listen to Governor Vroom. The Reverend Samuel Lockwood, on the basis of his friendship with Senator Henry S. Little from Monmouth County, promised that Little would not oppose Rutgers, though as a Princeton graduate he did not want to work openly against his alma mater.[40] In another letter from J. B. Thompson, crammed with gossipy political tidbits, Cook learned that Senator Jonathan Leaming (a member of the Joint Committee) was rumored to favor Rutgers over Princeton if Rutgers would also promise to put up buildings. Thompson continued: "He has a *strong* feeling of regard for *you* personally."[41] The same letter reported that Amos Robbins of Middlesex County, president of the Senate, and Senator George D. Horner from Ocean County seemed to be going for Rutgers. The Reverend J. H. Frazee, member of the Agricultural Society, who also lobbied for Rutgers, remembered in later years with great satisfaction that he had been of "some help to our College when it was a very open question whether Princeton or Rutgers should be the 'Agricultural' School under State patronage."[42]

Cook himself was deeply involved in trying to gather votes. On the second of January in a letter to Governor Vroom he had suggested that the Rutgers College memorandum asking for the appropriation might be sent to Governor Joel Parker for transmission to the legislature. Later that month he solicited the support of Joseph P. Bradley, a Rutgers alumnus later to become an associate justice of the United States Supreme Court. To Bradley, Cook explained the rationale of the campaign:

I write to ask a little of your time and influence for Rutgers College. The land scrip granted by Congress to states which would endow Colleges for Instruction in Agriculture and the Mechanic Arts, had been received by New Jersey, and is to be appropriated. It amounts to 210,000 acres—worth from $100,000 to $160,000. *We* could make it useful to ourselves and to the cause for which it is designed. The Trustees have appointed a committee . . . to ask the Legislature for it and to guarantee the State that it shall be property used by them, that they will establish a scientific school in connection with the college where such subjects as are required shall be especially taught by Professors devoted to those departments of science. . . . The Principal of the Normal School and his Trenton friends are moving rapidly every influence they can bring to bear, to have the school located there, to have an experimental farm &c. Princeton is said to want it. . . . I have no doubt Rutgers College would be benefited by an extension of its course of scientific instruction and an enlargement of its corps of instructors . . . and on the other hand it is nearest to the center of population at the most accessible place—and has the greatest incidental advantages of any in the state.

Now *you* could do much by a letter to General Cook [William Cook, Chief Engineer of the Camden and Amboy Railroad] asking his influence actively in our favor, or in a more moderate way by his pointing out the impolicy of centering everything in Trenton, or by letter to other members who would be glad to carry out your wishes. What is especially needed is *votes.*"[43]

Toward the end of January and through the month of February the pace of the lobbying quickened. Jacob Wortendyke in Trenton notified Cook that a hearing would probably be held before the legislative committee during the first week in February. "Mr. Duryee must be here early in the week and as many others of our friends as can be induced to come—I am pretty confident now that the contest will be between us & Princeton and we will have to exert ourselves next week and show as much interest as we can in the matter."[44] In a letter written the following day, Wortendyke wrote: "After I left you last evening I had an opportunity to sound Randolph and Chandler [Theodore F. Randolph, Senator from Hudson County and Lyman C. Chandler, Senator from Morris County] upon the College question—I think I can say that they will not go for Princeton neither do I think that Randoph will under any circumstances favor the Normal School plan, and I am almost sure that Chandler will not."[45] Wortendyke suggested also that Cook call upon Dr. Thomas Dunn English, assemblyman from Bergen County, and talk to Chandler because this would please him and "make sure of his countenance to our wishes."

A particularly feverish note was struck by Charles D. Deshler, an editor of the *Newark Daily Advertiser* who had been given an honorary master's degree from Rutgers in 1848:

To make sure of the Agricultural project, don't let our folks think that talking and writing will accomplish much. Of course they are necessary but not primarily so. The main thing is to secure the *votes* of the members of the legislature: and this can only be done by personal and indefatigable effort. James [Bishop] must use his influence. Get Martin Howell and Garret Voorhees and John Van Dyke enlisted to work upon the Republicans. Get Bradley and Frelinghuysen and Courtlandt Parker (the latter may decline), all of whom are graduates of Rutgers, to go to work. Above all get Gus Newell [William Augustus Newell, governor of New Jersey from 1857-1860] at work, for if you do he is a powerful "team." And while you are getting agencies in operation among the Republicans don't overlook the Democrats, who are in the ascendancy in the legislature. Get Robbins [Amos Robbins, Democrat from Middlesex County, President of the Senate in 1864] interested. . . . Get all the Somerset members in the lower house interested. . . . If Doctor Campbell would go to Trenton, and present the case to the committee who will have the matter in charge, in his clear, forcible, candid and persuasive way, he will make a strong impression. So also with Professor Cook.[46]

The climax of the campaign to influence the committee came on the evening of February 23, when representatives of the three competing institutions presented their claims before a hearing of the Joint Special Committee of the legislature in the Senate chamber. Speaking in behalf of the Normal School were two prominent figures, Judge David Naar, editor of the *True American* of Trenton, the leading Democratic journal of New Jersey, and Joseph C. Potts. To plead Princeton's cause came President John Maclean, Professor Atwater, and Dr. John S. Schenck, professor of chemistry. Campbell, Cook and Vroom appeared for Rutgers. "The arguments," according to the *Fredonian*, "were very elaborate and able."[47] Apparently the arguments of the Rutgers contingent were more persuasive. When the bill emerged from committee, the name of the college proposed for the land-grant designation was Rutgers.

Some opposition still remained, however, and the bill had yet to be voted on in the legislature. A new threat appeared on March 5, when the Methodists in their Conference passed a resolution advising that the grant not be given to a denominational institution and that the whole matter be postponed. In presenting this protest to the Assembly, Paul C. Brinck, member from Camden County, pointed out that the Methodists had one-eighth of the religious population of the state, and that the Dutch Reformed Church had less than any other. He felt it improper to give an amount as large as this to a denomination that had no church south of New Brunswick. The friendship of Assemblyman Thomas Dunn English from Bergen County, with whom Cook had talked earlier, proved helpful. English replied to Brinck's charge that the denominational character of the college had nothing to do with the scientific department and that Rutgers was a most suitable college "to develop those sciences which shall elevate agriculture."[48]

On March 24 the bill passed in the Senate by a vote of 12 to 6, and on March 30 sailed triumphantly through the Assembly 50 to 1. The Rutgers people were amazed and jubilant. Garret Vroom wrote: "It certainly was a great triumph for our college, the manner in which we carried the House surpassed anything I have ever seen. As Judge Naar said, 'Your lobby works better and more successfully even than that of the Camden and Amboy.' Our opponents the Methodists were amazed. I don't wonder myself, for we polled some seven or eight more votes than even the most sanguine counted upon. . . ."[49]

An editorial in the *Newark Daily Advertiser* expressed the sentiments of some of Princeton's supporters:

Some disappointment and surprise has been expressed by the friends of science and learning . . . that the guardians of this ancient College . . . did not secure the use of the proceeds of the share of New Jersey in the Congressional land grant for the establishment of Agricultural Colleges. . . . Nassau Hall could not condescend from her high moral position to the questionable practices by which it seems necessary to engineer even meritorious applications through the legislature. She made her proposal and trusted in her superior merits. . . . It is left for that College, unaided by the State, which thus ignored her first-born and most illustrious child, to go on in her work,—This with no unkind wishes for her younger and more favored sister, she will do. . . .[50]

This attitude of condescending acceptance was not long maintained—President James McCosh of Princeton became the leader of the private colleges in violent opposition to the principle of federal aid to the land-grant colleges.[51] The legacy of animosity to Rutgers from friends of Princeton, the Normal School, and the Methodists may help to explain the difficulty the college had in getting financial support from the state in the years that followed.

The effect upon Cook's career of the establishment of Rutgers as a land-grant college was enormous. He was immediately made vice president of the college and, although he did not realize it at the time, for the remainder of his life was to be responsible for the college's agricultural program. In addition, his efforts in the legislature on behalf of the college and the geological survey had helped him to polish his skills as a man of science in the political area, a role he had begun while he was investigating the salt industry in New York State more than ten years earlier. Because, like most scientists, he never wielded direct political power, he became exceedingly adept at using the weapons of patience, persuasiveness, and a sense of timing in pursuit of his goals. He learned that arguing for the college or the geological survey among legislators meant that he had to inform and educate them in basic scientific knowledge as well as in agriculture and geology. Before he could expect success he had to persuade them that the projects for which they were being asked to vote public funds were desirable. Occasionally he had to compete for these funds with powerful private interests. He learned to harness such interests to his own causes when he could. Efforts to gain legislative support for worthwhile scientific projects that were too expensive or unprofitable to be financed by private capital required the use of a variety of subtle pressures, arguments, and friendships'of long standing. The citizens of New Jersey, like those of the rest of the country, were not unaccustomed to having public funds diverted to scientific study or projects intended for the public welfare. Scientific information had been gathered on the Lewis and Clark expedition and the Long expedition to the Rocky Mountains in 1819 as well as on subsequent expeditions, while Henry Clay's ideas on the "American System" which urged public support of agriculture and industry for the good of the country were familiar concepts. Equally important to Cook was the desire to put science and industry to work for the public welfare—a somewhat off-beat ambition in a period of rampant and ruthless industrial individualism. Cook's experience, his penchant for hard work, his dedication to the people of the state and the steadiness of his character made him peculiarly fitted to be this kind of public servant.

Cook's public spiritedness carried over also into his private life. He served on the New Brunswick Water Commission and the Board of Education of the city. In connection with the latter, he sometimes found the demands on his time to be excessive. C. M. Harrison, principal of the public school in 1862, relied heavily on Cook's advice for day-to-day problems—a teacher who stayed home from school for insufficient reasons or a textbook to be chosen for the following year.[52] The pressure on his time eventually became so onerous that Cook tried to resign but when he submitted his resignation, Harrison wrote imploring him to reconsider and promising that although he had bothered him frequently during the past years he was now used to the job and would not have to trouble him as often.[53] The Board of Education refused to accept Cook's resignation.[54]

Cook's deep involvement in the affairs of the Second Reformed Church also continued. He attended consistory meetings and Tuesday prayer meetings. He engineered the leveling of Hamilton Street behind the college for the Synod and as an elder became more deeply imbedded than he wished in an unpleasant episode wherein the minister resigned under pressure from some members of the congregation.[55] Cook, who was not among them, found himself acting as liaison between the minister and the elders.[56] After the eventual departure of the pastor,

Cook was saddled with the task of finding supply ministers until a new man could be called to the pulpit.[57] These responsibilities he discharged conscientiously but without much enthusiasm. In contrast, he felt deeply and undertook gladly and prayerfully the job of superintending the Sabbath School. Much to his children's delight he began the practice of monthly concerts at the school.[58] And because of his work with the Sabbath School, as with his work in other areas, letters of appreciation came for his help and friendship. William B. Merritt, who had stayed in New Brunswick for a time and worked with the Sabbath School, wrote, "I am. . . very thankful to you and the S.S. for the interest you have taken in me. You certainly have made my stay at New Brunswick very pleasant. I feel that you have contributed much to my happiness. True friendship is rare, but when it is manifest, it really elevates one's ideas of its value."[59]

Although he was deeply involved in the mundane work of the church, Cook's sincere commitment to his religion should not be underestimated. Originating in a profound personal experience of conversion, his participation in church life continued to be much more than the performance of unwanted or perfunctory duties. This sincere and complete commitment, however, did not preclude the honest acquisition of worldly goods and in this endeavor he continued to show a strong interest. His growing family made him increasingly unhappy about his financial situation. Robert Anderson Cook, youngest of the five children who lived to grow up, was born in 1861 when Cook's salary from the college and such small amounts as he had been able to invest in mortgages were insufficient to support his family.[60] Fortunately, his training as surveyor, geologist, and chemist enabled him to supplement his income. Cook's drive to attain financial security (if not affluence) was always in conflict with an equally strong inclination to perform scientific services as a favor or to contribute any money he might receive for his extracurricular scientific activities to the church or a worthy charity. The story has been handed down that he was not above adding a hundred dollar fee he had received on a Saturday to the collection plate on Sunday!

For a while, Cook tried his hand at being an inventor and even sold a patent for a product used to line rubber pipes for smoking tobacco.[61] This mixture of cement and plaster of Paris was useful because it could be worked on a lathe and did not crumble when moisture condensed in the stem and at the bottom of the pipe. Another patent, which he obtained with Theodore Porter, a friend from the days when he worked for the salt industry in New York State, provided a way of improving flue walls in salt blocks.[62] Cook was not much of an inventor, however, and he probably received more money and considerably more satisfaction from the delivery of two lectures in a series sponsored by the Young Men's Association of Albany on science and various cultural topics. Delivered in Tweedle Hall (which held 1,700 people) the other speakers included such notables as Henry Ward Beecher, Oliver Wendell Holmes, and James Russell Lowell.[63] Cook's friends who arranged the series promised him a large audience, as the citizens of Albany had not been treated to a lecture on science for several years.[64] Great preparations were made for Cook's lecture; a gas supply was piped to the lecturer's desk, the footlights put in and the area in front of the stage was boarded over so that the experiments could be better seen.[65] Cook's papers do not reveal how much he received for the lecture but presumably the citizens of Albany were much enlightened and entertained.

Another supplement to Cook's income, although it never amounted to as much as he hoped, was the placing of markers of the true meridian in all county seats to provide for greater accuracy for surveyors.[66] Cook hoped that this new state requirement would bring him enough money to pay expenses for his work on the geological survey. Unfortunately, few of the twenty-one counties' Boards of Chosen Freeholders recognized the value of meridian markers and most simply failed to appropriate the money to have it done.

Cook's most lucrative outside jobs came to him because of his extensive knowledge of geology. He was engaged to inspect and evaluate mining properties in several states and sometimes to provide expert testimony in court cases.[67] His fee for inspecting mines was $10 a day plus expenses and such inspections kept him fairly busy during college vacations. He inspected iron ore property near Dover and mines at Mt. Hope for the Lehigh Zinc Works. In April 1864 he undertook one of his more ambitious trips—the inspection of the lead, zinc, and silver ore in a mine at Eastport, Maine.[68] Getting there proved to be the most difficult part of the job. The first leg of the journey was a night voyage by the sailing vessel *Bay State* from New York to Newport, Rhode Island. The weather had been stormy that day and the boat traveled through rough seas. Cook spent most of the trip lying in his bunk trying to avoid seasickness. At Newport Cook expected to meet an accommodation train for Somerset where he wanted to inspect a rolling and rail mill. But the storm had delayed the boat and instead he traveled seven miles by wagon and a mile in a small sailboat which left him thoroughly wet from spray. The mill proved to be uninteresting and he went on by rail to Boston that afternoon. Not a whit dismayed by the ordeals of his journey he completed a round of sightseeing in Boston before leaving the next day for Portland and Eastport. Again he traveled by sea and again he suffered from seasickness. He wrote to his wife that he thought he would have got used to the seasickness if the trip had lasted a few hours longer. After his arrival in Eastport he had to wait for a snowstorm to subside and then for a favorable tide before he finally got up to see the mine.[69]

Thanks to the variety of moneymaking schemes Cook discovered, his family managed fairly well—at least William Gurley thought so, for he wrote, "I am glad to know you are busy and from your prompt payments [for a solar compass which Cook had purchased from Gurley's company] I infer that you are getting wise enough to charge something for your services, a kind of practical wisdom I am afraid you do not always practice."[70]

During the Civil War years, though the Cooks for the most part were personally uninvolved in the tragedy, they were every day surrounded by its effects—the· City of New Brunswick sent seven hundred young men to fight. The college, besides the drop in enrollments because young men who would have gone to college went instead to battle, saw twenty-two of its students join the Union armies while three young Texan brothers fought and died for the Confederate cause. Every day the lead story in the *Fredonian,* headlined "The Secession Rebellion," carried the latest news from the battlegrounds.

The beginning of the war with the firing on Fort Sumter on April 12, 1861, would undoubtedly have been the occasion for a great demonstration on the campus except that it happened during the spring recess.[71] After the college term resumed, students, faculty and townspeople gathered in front of Old Queens on May 23 where a large new flagpole towered more than forty feet above the building. The ladies of New Brunswick had made a flag which they presented to the college and which was soon hoisted up the pole. Congressman Garnet B. Adrain, Rutgers class of 1833, President Frelinghuysen, and Professor Henshaw made formal speeches while Professors Forsyth and Cook were persuaded to speak informally.[72]

The raising of flagpoles was a common means of displaying support for the Northern cause as the following letter from George's brother Henry attests:

There is not much talked about here but the war. It has produced some patriotic excitement which finds vent in tall poles, large flags, neighborhood military companies, and a great deal of talking. There have been some very nice poles raised in the vicinity, one in Columbia, one at East Madison, and another at Whippany Bridge. These are all considerable [sic] over 100 feet high. Besides there are several others from 60 to 80 feet. At most of these pole raisings Mr.

Johnson gives a patriotic speech. He has also given us a patriotic sermon for the times. . . .[73]

It was the draft riots in 1863 that brought the war nearest to the Cooks. George had taken Paul, then a sophomore at Rutgers, and John Smock, who had graduated in 1862, as his assistants on a job for the New Jersey Zinc Company in Sussex County. He was commissioned to survey the land and estimate the cost of building a railroad from Mine Hill and Stirling Hill to Andover.[74] Mary was left at home with the three girls and Robbie who had been born a month after the firing on Fort Sumter. Shortly after Cook and the two young men left, word arrived in New Brunswick of riots in the working sections of New York City. In July 1863 the working class, heavily Irish, Catholic, and Democrat, became angered by the first drawings for a military draft of civilians which allowed the middle-class and wealthy men to buy their way out. Illogically, they concentrated their wrath on the poor blacks instead of the rich whites who were benefiting by the inequity. Four days of pillaging, burning, and lynching of Negroes was stopped only by the arrival, fresh from the battle of Gettysburg, of regiments of General Meade's army. Outside New York City, wherever there was a large Irish immigrant working class population, fear spread. In Chatham, New York, Mary Cook's brother Elijah was warned that the Catholic Democrats were gathering firearms and planning to resist the draft by destroying the property of all Republicans.[75] Elijah heard that his house would be the first one burned. New Brunswick as well heard rumors that the Irish would take up arms. John Farley, the Cooks' gardener, told Mary, "They won't put up with it when the bigwigs can get off by paying $300 and a poor man must go."[76] The Negroes in New Brunswick were so frightened, wrote Mary to her absent husband, that, "I am sorry and ashamed to tell that Peter [probably an employee of the college or of the Cooks' neighbors, the Bishops] has fled—he sent his family off to a place of safety ten days ago and went himself Saturday—I am disgraced that the law will not protect citizens of any color."[77]

Mary urged George to return home as soon as possible for "you are needed here." But Anne wanted her father to know *she* was glad he was away and so would not be killed in the riots.[78] Fortunately, in a short while the apprehension of New Brunswick's citizens proved to be groundless and the people took up their customary business.

One of George Cook's foremost concerns was the continuation of the geological survey. After the state withdrew its financial support, he had rejected William Kitchell's offer to participate in the continuation of the survey as a private enterprise because he thought the product would not be worth the effort. But he continued to hope that the legislature would vote to fund the survey and that he could be involved in it again. In 1861 Kitchell died suddenly of an unidentified illness and Governor Charles S. Olden asked Cook if he would be interested in taking over Kitchell's position as unpaid director of the survey under the sponsorship of the New Jersey Agricultural Society. Cook wrote to ex-governor Rodman Price that the lack of funds was "poor encouragement from the state authorities but I should be ashamed to allow all that has been done to be lost when I am somewhat mixed up in the work."[79] For this reason, because it was a chance to continue with the kind of work that he enjoyed most and because he would have a chance to publish the results of his research in scientific journals, Cook accepted the appointment.

Shortly thereafter, he and William Force, secretary of the Society, set out to retrieve the survey's apparatus and materials from Kitchell's widow and father. This proved to be a difficult, frustrating, and time-consuming task and delayed the resumption of the work of the survey. Many instruments belonging to the survey could not be found at the Kitchell residence and the elder Kitchell was reluctant to relinquish much that was there.[80] He refused to turn over his son's notes and sketches on the grounds that the only written material that had to be turned over to the state was a finished report. All else the elder Kitchell considered to be private property.[81] It took Cook about six months to retrieve the equipment of the survey after which it was installed at Rutgers in a room provided by the trustees.[82] Cook's inability to get Kitchell's notes and the fact that Ketchell had written out neither a full account of the geology of the state nor of the northern mining area (his primary interest) meant that a considerable amount of the work had to be done over. Information on the mines would have had to be brought up to date in any event.

Although Cook had to wait for some of the necessary surveying tools he began as best he could during the summer of 1863. His pleasure at being in the field again is clearly evident in the following excerpt from a letter to his wife:

I don't think I ever before so fully appreciated the force of those descriptions of a land of hills and of brooks of water. Exhausted with heat there is nothing so much craved as cool water—why it seemed almost to give a new excellence to everything one can desire or relish. . . . The scenery on the route we have come is very fine. I think the most charming view we have had was on Tuesday evening when we came out of the mountains about Hampton and from the brow of the hill saw the long valley of the Musconetcong spread out before us and almost under our feet.[83]

In his tan notebook (number twenty of its kind) he made notes on the geological details of the state from the Shark River Inlet on the Atlantic Coast to the Delaware Water Gap. The entry for August 31, 1863, reads: "The beach at Shark River Inlet is only hillocks lying on the older post-diluvial—there are no old beaches. These are not more than 8 or 9 feet above high water and the upland projects from under them. The country from thence to Corlies Pond along the straight road is flat and of a coarse, gravelly soil—there is no part of the road more than 8 or 10 feet above tide."[84]

From his notes and two sketches he made of the Water Gap from the Pennsylvania side, he drew a detailed columnar section illustrating the state's various geological strata.

Although Cook was glad to be back in the field making geological observations, he realized that if the survey were to amount to anything the state would have to begin funding it again. He was not optimistic. He wrote to a young man who had inquired about employment on the survey, "I have been so often and so sorely disappointed . . . that I have not dared to place any very high expectations upon [a rumored state appropriation] and would not venture to do anything which would bring disappointment to others or to myself, deeming it only prudent to wait until the means and time allowed for completing the work are fairly in hand."[85] He had written earlier to James Jenkins of the Bethlehem Zinc Works giving an estimate of the cost of completing the survey and of his views as to the responsibility of the state.[86] He thought that the state should conduct the survey, pay all expenses, and publish the results so that the public could obtain as complete information as possible about the geology of the state. He estimated that $2,600 a year for three years—$7,800 in all—would enable him to complete the survey. As the appropriation for the last year of the Kitchell survey had been $25,000, the legislators found Cook's estimate most acceptable. For himself, he asked a salary of $1,000 with an extra $500 for expenses.

In January 1864, at the request of the Agricultural Society, he read a report of the work he had completed, showing a drawing of a geological section of the state outlining formations from Shark River Inlet to the Water Gap. Arguing the case for continuation and funding of the survey he said,

To the practical man it is of the first importance *to know* that the materials of the globe are not jumbled together in a confused mass where any particular substance can only be found by chance, but that there is an orderly arrangement of them, and each is to be found in its appropriate place. The soils upon each rock formation have their peculiar characteristics, and the farmer who wished to devote himself to dairying, to the raising of stock, or grass, or grain, or fruits or of garden vegetables, will look for the rock formation and soil upon which his special product is most profitably raised. Our iron need only be looked for in one kind of rock, and that rock is confined to a particular district of country. The limestones are all in regular layers, traversing the country in a northeast and southwest direction, and never in any other. Our greensand marls are only found in one favored portion of the state. The fire-clays are only in one belt of country, which crosses the middle of the state from northeast to southwest. It would be worse than useless to look for magnetic iron in southern New Jersey, marl in the northern part of the state, or coal-beds anywhere within our bounds. It is only by surveys of this kind, carefully carried out over the whole country, faithfully described and illustrated, that the results brought within the reach of all our citizens, that we can fully and profitably make this arrangement known and appreciated. Our abundant but undeveloped resources require from the State this kind of survey and publication.[87]

Outlining future plans for the survey, Cook explained that he expected to trace and describe the lines of meeting of the different formations and to collect and describe the soils, rocks, minerals, building materials, fertilizers, and other useful substances found in the state. He suggested that the Kitchell survey, incomplete though it was, had been partly responsible for the fact that cash value per acre of farmland in New Jersey had increased more rapidly than in six nearby states, that production of New Jersey iron mines had increased to over 200,000 tons by 1863, and that the transportation and sale of marl (just begun in 1855) was expected to reach more than 150,000 tons in 1864. In an era more attuned to individual private enterprise than social welfare, the Agricultural Society was also impressed by the fact that by using the findings of the Kitchell survey men had gained profits that equaled the total cost of the entire survey. Such economic advances during the period of depression following the panic of 1857 were especially appreciated and the Society decided to have Cook present his program to the legislature in the hopes that it would be persuaded to resume funding of the survey. Cook's report was well received and the legislature in March, 1864 (the same month that saw the passage of the bill making Rutgers a land-grant college) passed a bill providing for a $5,000-a-year appropriation for four years to complete and publish the survey.[88]

This action of the legislature immediately made Cook a leader in the task of putting science to the service of the citizen, a position he was to occupy with distinction for the next twenty-five years.

7

1864-1869

The Geology of New Jersey; Rutgers Scientific School

The course of American science in the post-Civil War period, especially in the last quarter of the century, was marked by a great advance both in the quality of basic research and in the application of scientific knowledge to the needs of industry. In applied science Americans were spectacularly successful. The ingenuity and inventiveness which had produced the cotton gin, the reaper, and the telegraph before the Civil War were followed by improvements in technology which, to a greater degree than in the earlier period, depended on basic research and the development of engineering techniques. Chemistry, where basic knowledge was well advanced, was the first science extensively applied in industry and agriculture. But geology flowered also, especially in the United States, and by the end of the century American geologists rivaled their European counterparts in the quality of their investigations and often assumed leadership in research and theory. With a background in both geology and chemistry, George Cook was able to put both to good use in the revitalized State Geological Survey, and as chief architect of the land-grant college at Rutgers.

Despite the fact that the land-grant colleges developed concurrently with advances in science and technology, their progress was not as universally accepted and well supported as might have been expected.[1] Politics and personal ambitions often got in the way. What seems in retrospect to have been a perfectly compatible and necessary educational development was, in its first decades, a trial-and-error process that in many states produced wasteful and sometimes disgraceful shenanigans. Eventually the land-grant colleges developed into a system of higher education uniquely suited to the furtherance of the agricultural and mechanical arts and to the education of a democratic citizenry. But first the states tried a variety of solutions to the problems of converting the land grants into money, finding students, setting up curricula, and training professors. In New Jersey the process of establishing the new college was not easy but because of the abilities and perseverance of George Cook the state was spared many of the excesses of ill feeling, ineptitude, and inadequacy that other states suffered. Cook's rare gifts for administration and public relations, added to his scientific background, made him uniquely qualified for the task. Like many scientists of his generation he saw no conflict between basic and applied science although his personal preference would have been a life devoted to geological research.[2]

When in the same month the legislature voted to resume the geological survey and named the Rutgers Scientific School the land-grant college of New Jersey, Cook realized that he would be involved to some extent in the planning and direction of both. But during that first year demands were made on his time and energy that exceeded his expectations and would certainly have defeated a lesser man. Cook managed them all and went on to accept even more demanding responsibilities. The resumption of the survey proved to be less difficult than gearing up the Rutgers Scientific School for its new role. No one at the college expected many problems. The future looked bright. The college was in the vanguard of the postwar swing away from a classical and religious emphasis toward a concentration on science and "practical" training in research and teaching. One recognition of this new direction was Cook's appointment as vice-president. The secularization of the college moved a step nearer when the General Synod of the Dutch Reformed Church in June of that year allowed the trustees of the college to repurchase Old Queens, the main college building which had been taken over by the Synod in 1827 to help the college out of its financial difficulties. As a secularizing step, this was somewhat negated by a provision that the president of the college and three-fourths of the trustees had to be members of the Dutch Reformed Church. Most of the students and faculty continued to belong to the church. Changes were so gradual that it cannot be said that the college was entirely removed from the influence of the church until well into the twentieth century.

In the spring of 1864 the first priority for the Rutgers trustees was to raise money from private sources to prepare the college to fulfill its new mission. Although still immersed in the fund-raising drive Campbell had initiated in 1862, the trustees began to look for new sources of support. Heretofore most contributions had come from church members who gave because of their religious loyalty or because their gifts entitled their sons to free tuition at the college. Now the trustees hoped to tap the resources of a broader public—the agricultural community—often the wealthiest class in mid-nineteenth century New Jersey communities. Seventeen trustees and friends of the college, most of whom had been active in the effort to have Rutgers made the land-grant college, gathered late in May in the Jersey City law offices of trustee Jacob R. Wortendyke. They selected Cook's neighbor, James Bishop, as their chairman and made Cook their secretary. The Board of Trustees had already officially approved the raising of money for the enlargement of the chemical laboratory; the furnishing of an astronomical laboratory; the equipment of rooms for the study of mechanical and civil engineering; the provision of a room for a geological, zoological, and botanical museum, and the establishment of an experimental farm.[3] In the weeks that followed the original committee enlisted the aid of another fifty prominent state leaders. A circular letter to which all these names were signed was sent out in the hope that it would elicit generous contributions. Subscription books were printed and when the central committee met again on June 2, $1,450 was subscribed at once. The committee prepared to carry their plea throughout the state.[4] In Somerville, Abraham Messler arranged to have Cook speak at a public meeting to explain the effect the new school and farm could have on the practice of agriculture in the state.[5]

Even before the money was raised the trustees, upon recommendation of the committee, bought a one-hundred-acre farm on the outskirts of New Brunswick. Originally cleared and farmed by Cornelius Longfield in 1681, the farm had passed through the hands of thirteen owners.[6] At one time it had been used as a racetrack. Known as the old Voorhees place (five of the previous owners having borne that name), it was part of the estate which James Neilson, a prominent and wealthy resident of New Brunswick, had left to his wife Catherine. The farm cost $15,000 and was in such a deplorable condition that it was pronounced most appropriate for experimental farming. Any improvement at all would provide a convincing demonstration of the effectiveness of scientific farming.

In addition to the special committee and the Rutgers Board of Trustees the Scientific School and farm had another board watching over its welfare. Formation of a Board of Visitors had been stipulated in the land-grant college law. Appointed by the governor, it was given general powers of supervision and control. One might have expected that the two boards, each with some degree of authority over the same school, would have been constantly in a state of conflict, confusion, and frustration. This does not appear to have been the case. There is no indication that the Board of Visitors was anything less than an enthusiastic admirer and supporter of the Board of Trustees and the Scientific School. Composed of two men from each congressional district, in its first years the Board of Visitors numbered among its members Seth Boyden of Newark, inventor of patent leather, manufacturer of locomotives, horticulturist, and developer of an improved strawberry; James Bishop of New Brunswick; William Parry of Cinnaminson in Burlington County, Quaker, leader of the Republican Party and owner of the Pomona Nursery, the most extensive establishment of its kind in the state; and Jonathan Ingham of Salem, manufacturer of the fertilizer "cancerine," also a Quaker and an old friend of Cook's from the days of the Kitchell survey. Ingham wrote Cook that he had accepted the governor's appointment although he had not known that such a board existed and "had it not been for *your* connection with the college I should have declined it."[7]

At the end of its first year the Board of Visitors reported the first of its many endorsements of the Board of Trustees because of the latter's willingness to invest in the new program before any of the expected funds had been received.[8] By the fall of 1864, having already purchased the farm, the college was making plans to receive the first scientific students the following September. Planning the curriculum for what was virtually a new academic field was a major challenge. Cook had earlier given some thought to a proper curriculum for agricultural education and had corresponded with Luther Henry Tucker of Albany on the matter.[9] Tucker, a graduate of Yale College, worked with his father, Luther Tucker, publisher of *Country Gentleman*. This popular periodical had long shown evidence of the Tuckers' interest in scientific agriculture. They regularly published articles by such leaders in science and agriculture as Samuel W. Johnson, professor of chemistry at Yale, and John Johnston, leading advocate of tile drainage. It was in the pages of the *Country Gentleman* in 1854 that the first test plot experiments with corn had been proposed. Cook and the younger Tucker, who, in addition to his publishing duties, was also a member of the Executive Board of the New York State Agricultural Society, agreed that the primary focus of agricultural education should be on the scientific principles underlying the practice of agriculture rather than on manual labor on a farm. This conclusion not only determined the character of the Rutgers Scientific School but shaped the future of Rutgers College. With help from Tucker and David Murray Cook worked out elaborate three-year programs for two curricula, one in civil engineering and mechanics and the other in chemistry and agriculture. Courses for the first four terms (each year was divided into three terms) were the same for both programs and most were taken with the students in the existing classical program.[10] Scientific students studied algebra, geometry, French, history, rhetoric, bookkeeping, draughting, zoology, mineralogy, botany, and line surveying. They were not required to study Latin or Greek. In the second term of the second year, the curriculum in chemistry and agriculture was split into three subject matter areas "Principles," "Processes," and "Products." "Principles" included the relationship of various sciences to agriculture, soils, and the theory of manures. "Processes" covered tillage, plowing, implements, machinery, drainage, irrigation, manuring, and farm buildings while in "Products," which extended over three terms, students would be taught about artificial fertilizers, dairy management, orchards, market gardens, and horticulture. Courses in general chemistry, qualitative and quantitative analytical chemistry, physics, mineralogy, geology, metallurgy and mining, and elements of technology were also included along with such liberal arts subjects as German, mental philosophy, moral philosophy, political economy, and English composition and declamation.

The second and third courses in civil engineering and mechanics included differential and integral calculus, topographical draughting, optics, astronomy, engineering construction of roads and bridges, machinery employed in engineering, hydraulic engineering; architecture, and designs for construction. The engineering students were also required to take English, German, mental philosophy, and so forth.

Cook believed that the curriculum compared favorably with the scientific and engineering program at the Rensselaer Polytechnic Institute, while Tucker wrote: "As compared with Yale, Rutgers seems to have omitted nothing that ought to be put in."[11] Their judgment has been upheld in recent years by Paul W. Gates, who commented in *Agriculture and the Civil War* that Rutgers College had "planned a well-designed and comprehensive program of studies which . . . might have been a model for faltering efforts elsewhere."[12] The fact that it was not was determined not by the faculty and trustees of the college but by the nature of student demand, as we shall see.

Although the curriculum was revised in future years, the philosophy that originally formulated the curriculum persisted and Rutgers students were always trained in basic scientific principles and the liberal arts. This was in contrast to many states where the faculties of land-grant colleges responded to the harsh criticism of farmers who scorned "book-farming." Farmers equated a college degree with the traditional, classical education (manifestly useless in running a farm) and faculties, to placate them, endorsed the teaching of practical skills. Some required that students endure hours of manual farm labor. In Kansas, for example, cabinetmaking, wagonmaking, engraving, and blacksmithing were among the artisans' skills which were appropriated for the college's curriculum in agriculture. At Cornell and Iowa, labor on the college farm was an integral part of the program and many other colleges followed their example.[13] Perhaps because of its close connection with a classical college, the Rutgers Scientific School never included manual labor or the teaching of simple skills in the agricultural curriculum. President Campbell vigorously defended this position in one of his yearly reports to the Governor, "The Trustees have considered it no part of their duty to turn the agricultural department into a school of manual labor. They have from the beginning proceeded upon the theory that while the practical applications of science should be kept carefully in view in a course of instruction, yet that the main business of a scientific school must be to teach scientific principles and the methods of scientific investigation."[14]

The curriculum had been planned and the farm purchased with the expectation that the income from the land grant—that "munificent gift"—would appear shortly in fairly large sums. By the terms of the Morrill Act each state was to receive scrip representing a donation of 30,000 acres of land for each member of their congressional delegation. States which still had areas of public land within their borders were able to convert the scrip to land which could be used by the college or kept as investment. Other states were forced to sell their scrip. At first it was expected that the scrip would sell for at least $1.25 an acre, but the market was soon flooded and the scrip often sold for much less.[15] In New Jersey the sale of scrip was the responsibility of a Board of Commissioners which postponed selling in the hope that they could get a good price. The enterprise appeared to move so slowly that Cook took it upon himself to write to John T. Blair, an expert in such matters, for his advice.[16] There is no indication that this helped matters. Eventually a part of the scrip for the 210,000 acres allotted to New Jersey was sold for seventy cents an acre and the remainder for fifty cents an acre.[17] By the end of 1865, $112,825 had been received and the total finally reached $116,000.[18] It was the interest on this amount that the college received. During the first years this amounted to $6,900 but the return began to dwindle and as it became more difficult to find the 5 percent return required by law, the fund was turned over to the state treasury which guaranteed the payment of the required interest. Payments eventually amounted to $5,800 a year.[19] By January 1, 1866, however, the trustees had received only $1,200 to pay all the salaries of professors who taught the Scientific School students. As this was not enough money to hire any new faculty members, Rutgers might have been justified in taking the course decided upon by Yale College whose Sheffield Scientific School had been named the land-grant college of Connecticut. Yale, which in any event was not required to provide an experimental farm, undertook no expansion of its regular program until after some funds had been received.[20] However, the Rutgers Board of Trustees, confidently expecting that the land grant would eventually prove to be a bonanza, went ahead with its plans. Cook had predicted that at least thirty students in the class would enter in September 1865. He expected that twenty would pay tuition and ten would receive tuition scholarships.[21] As the college's enrollment during these years had averaged seventy students, this would have been a substantial increase.[22] A faculty of five full-time and two part-time professors had been able to manage seventy students in the classical program but the new courses in the Scientific School meant that professors had to be hired to teach agriculture and engineering and carry out the required military drill and tactics. In addition tutors were needed to assist Cook and Murray with their added student load in chemistry and mathematics.

It was a year before the trustees found anyone to teach engineering and conduct military training. In 1866 Major Josiah Holcomb Kellogg, who had just retired from active service in the army and was teaching natural and experimental philosophy at West Point, joined the faculty as professor of civil engineering and superintendent of military instruction. John Conover Smock, a Rutgers alumnus, served one year as tutor in chemistry and was succeeded by Francis Cuyler Van Dyck who after graduation from Rutgers in 1865 studied in a postgraduate course in analytical chemistry in the Scientific School. No tutor in mathematics was hired the first year, but Isaac Hasbrouck, also a graduate in the class of 1865, took up the duties of tutor in mathematics in 1867.

Although the curriculum did not call for courses in agriculture to begin before the second term of the second year, the trustees were anxious to engage a professor to undertake management of the farm and begin delivery of the county lectures as soon as possible. Their natural choice was Luther Henry Tucker. Not only had he worked with Cook and Murray in planning the curriculum, he was highly recommended by Ezra Cornell, Colonel B. P. Johnson, Secretary of the New York State

Agricultural Society, and Yale's Samuel W. Johnson and James Dwight Dana.[23] For Cook the hiring of Tucker should have meant that his responsibilities in the Scientific School would be restricted to the teaching of chemistry and other sciences but unfortunately Tucker was never able to assume the full responsibilities of the professor of agriculture. Thus in the fall of 1864 Cook not only was scheduled to teach his customary classes and begin work on the geological survey but also was responsible for planning the agricultural curriculum and setting up the experimental farm. In addition, he and Murray were working with a Boundary Commission to establish the marine boundary between New York and New Jersey.[24] In view of all these responsibilities, that fall the faculty voted to reduce Cook's teaching duties and restrict both Cook's and Murray's classes to the first three days of the week.[25]

At first Tucker had been very enthusiastic about becoming professor of agriculture and, although the county lectures were not expected to begin until the winter of 1866, he agreed to be in New Brunswick for a few weeks in the spring of 1865 to deliver a series of public lectures. However, he never had planned to give up his editorial work and he soon began to have qualms about being able to keep it up if he had to spend a part of each year in New Brunswick. In addition, his father did not want him to be away from Albany for any extended period and so, even while promising to teach the first term of agricultural courses (scheduled to begin in 1867) Tucker suggested that the trustees begin to look for another professor of agriculture.[26] In the *Cultivator and Country Gentleman* he announced that he would "leave a . . . permanent acceptance to the test of its compatibility with other engagements."[27] Other engagements began to interfere immediately. On the day appointed for the first of the public lectures in the spring of 1866, Tucker found that his duties as treasurer of the New York State Agricultural Society made it necessary for him to attend the New York State Agricultural Fair. Appropriately enough, in the light of his future identification with agricultural education at Rutgers, the honor of presenting the first lecture under the auspices of New Jersey's land-grant college fell to Dr. Cook.

After noting the historical significance of this first lecture, Cook told his audience (mostly farmers from Middlesex and nearby counties) that although New Jersey farm land had a higher value per acre and a higher net yield than any other state, this yield could be improved by bringing undeveloped land under cultivation and managing the present farm land more efficiently.[28] "New Jersey," he said, in an early use of the word later adopted as the state's nickname, "should become the 'garden' of the United States."[29] Then, showing the influence of Amos Eaton's training in the giving of popular lectures, he performed several dramatic experiments to show how nutrients could be added to the soil.

The rest of the lectures in the series were delivered by Tucker, who talked about "Improved Agriculture and Its Promotion by Means of Agricultural Education." The following summer, before he had taught any courses in agriculture, Tucker resigned. During 1866 Cook, Campbell, and the trustees tried to find someone to fill the vacancy while in the meantime Cook supervised the farm and presented the county lectures. In June 1867 the search for a professor of agriculture was abandoned and Cook's title was changed to professor of chemistry, natural history and agriculture. He was not happy with his new appointment. Added to his regular teaching responsibilities and the direction of the survey it promised to be an unwanted burden. And indeed he found it, as he later wrote, "undefined, difficult, perplexing and wearing."[30] Professors of other subjects had only to instruct undergraduates—teaching agriculture included general planning and supervision of the work on the farm and delivery of the county lectures. Cook wrote to Gurley, "I have given a lecture on agriculture in every county of the State within the last year, and am somewhat familiar with its wants, and its means for improvement. But I have no desire to apply myself now to acquiring a new profession or to turn aside from those pursuits in which I have found most pleasure thus far."[31]

Rutgers was not alone in its difficulty in finding a professor of agriculture. All land-grant colleges had similar problems. The field was very new and instructors with any pretense to qualifications very scarce. Cornell in its first year engaged Joseph Harris, an agricultural journalist from Rochester, New York, who accepted the position on condition that he be allowed to fulfill his duties by visiting the campus only when he found it possible.[32]

The easiest part of Cook's "new profession" was the supervision of the remodeling of Old Queens to house the new laboratories, museum, and classrooms and of the construction of a gift from Daniel S. Schenck, a tidy little astronomical observatory. More difficult than fixing up classrooms and laboratories was the problem of getting students. In their desire to insure a maximum enrollment, the trustees had decided to accept one tuition-free student from each county even before the money from the sale of scrip began to come in. They were very much surprised when instead of the thirty they expected, only eight young men enrolled in the Scientific School. One of the eight was Francis Van Dyck, the postgraduate student who became a tutor in analytical chemistry the next year. Five were private students paying the $75 per year tuition and two, one from Union County and one from Sussex County, were scholarship students.[33] Two other young men had applied for scholarships but one was ill prepared and one was too young. The level of preparation required is evidenced in the "entrance examination" in which the candidates had to satisfy the faculty of a minimum acquaintance with arithmetic, English grammar, algebra, and geography by answering such questions as: "Extract the cube root of 77 to three places of decimals; State the difference between an adjective and an adverb; Divide 197 into two such parts that four times the greater exceeds five times the less by 50; Name the line of great lakes running across North America"; and, "How does the water of the Mediterranean Sea communicate with the ocean?"[34]

Enrollment increased somewhat the next year and by the time all three classes were matriculating, there were thirty-seven students in the Scientific School.[35] Still, this was nothing like what had been expected. The scholarship program provided for half the income from the land-grant money to be used for forty scholarships distributed among the counties according to the number of representatives each had in the State Assembly but these were never filled in the first years. In 1868, for example, there were only sixteen scholarship students. The southern counties consistently failed to send their quota of students, a situation which lasted up until the time the system was abolished in the mid-twentieth century. A number of tactics were attempted to attract more students: advertisements were placed in newspapers throughout the state and the cooperation of the state superintendent of schools was enlisted.[36] From the beginning there was no requirement that students had to study full time; special and part-time students were always accepted. In 1868 there were seventeen part-time students.

Not only were students scarce, but very few wanted to study agriculture; almost all were interested in civil engineering, mechanics, or chemistry. As students interested in chemistry had to enroll in the curriculum in chemistry and agriculture, they got a good dose of agricultural chemistry, but nevertheless the lack of interest in agriculture was frustrating for all concerned.

Cook's responsibilities in teaching the "scientifs" as they soon were known, included instruction in algebra and meteorology for the freshman, lectures in chemistry to the sophomores, and courses in geology and agriculture to the third (final) year students.[37] Even though few students at Rutgers studied agriculture, the Scientific School came to be known as the Agricultural College. This has been attributed to the printer who produced the first report of the Board of Visitors but more likely it was because the agricultural program had a visible and vocal constituency of farmers and the college farm was a prominent installation. It would have been better for public relations as well as nearer the truth if the school had become known as an engineering or scientific school. The scarcity of agricultural graduates from Rutgers and from all land-grant colleges was to provide a convenient justification for criticism in the years to come. The reluctance to study agriculture was as much of a problem in midwestern land-grant colleges as in New Jersey. In Illinois almost all students wanted to study engineering. The first three bachelor of science degrees in agriculture were not awarded until 1878.[38] That same year the University of Wisconsin turned out its first agricultural graduate—and it was several years before another was graduated.[39] As late as 1874, Cornell, out of a total enrollment of 506, had only seven students in agriculture.[40] A letter in the *Practical Farmer* a few years later further illustrates the universality of the problem: "It is announced that not one of the twenty-nine young men about to graduate from the Massachusetts Agricultural College, proposes to become a farmer, and that all of them look forward to engaging in business, or in the learned professions, just as [do] the graduates in academical departments of classical colleges."[41]

Reasons for the failure of young men to take advantage of the vocational education offered in the land-grant colleges were many and complicated. The confused condition of the society and the economy in the post-Civil War period were partly responsible but it is more likely that the causes were rooted in widespread traditions, the expectations of society, and certain flaws in the reasoning and planning of advocates of agricultural and mechanical education in the colleges. In the first place, no one in the nineteenth century believed that young men expecting to go into business, industry, or farming *needed* a college education for a successful career. Although some college-trained men went into business, they had matriculated because of family tradition or a desire for general liberal arts education, not for vocational training. The only "vocational" education colleges gave was for the ministry or the medical, legal, or scholarly professions. The need for special training for engineers was beginning to be recognized because mining and manufacturing companies and railroads needed men who knew geology, chemistry, or engineering. It was harder for young men and their parents to understand why farmers should go to college as many farmers were illiterate. In Cook's first lecture, when he urged education for farmers, he made it clear that he was primarily talking about the advantage of their learning to read and write so that they could benefit from advice given in newspapers and farm journals. Whatever farmers needed to know beyond the way to plough a straight furrow and milk a cow could be learned from the pages of the *Country Gentleman* or the local newspaper. If farmers were wealthy enough and willing to spare their sons at an age when they had reached their peak of usefulness on the farm and before they married and left home, they were more likely to want them to acquire an additional skill—that of the engineer or perhaps the chemist. Because free tuition at the land-grant college was not accompanied by free room and board, farmers who might have considered letting their boys go to college were seldom able to afford it. A further deterrent was the fact that while engineering was an easily marketable skill the would-be farmer had somehow to acquire a farm. Few young men had enough money to do that. Cook understood this well enough because it had been his own situation. His father could not have supported him for three or four years while he took advantage of the offerings of a scientific school. The Morrill Act had been conceived by well-meaning and intelligent men who realized that much farming was ill planned, wasteful of land and labor, and relatively unproductive. They theorized that the way to correct the situation was to offer young men free tuition at specialized colleges. They failed to realize that most of the young men could not come. Scientific agriculture was more successfully brought to the working farmer when experimental farms and agricultural experiment stations were acknowledged as the primary means of improving agriculture. But many years of frustration lay ahead for the colleges as they made heroic efforts to force the realities to conform to the dream. Not until agricultural business, research, and teaching provided outlets for a scientific agricultural education did enrollments in agricultural colleges increase. As long as the only place for a trained scientific farmer to go was back to the farm, the agricultural programs lagged.

At first George Cook had joined in the common expectation that the college classroom, aided by demonstrations on the experimental farm, was the best way of bringing a consciousness of the benefits of scientific agriculture to farmers. But very soon the scarcity of agricultural students and the favorable response of the state's leading practicing farmers to the work of the college farm convinced him that it was information and demonstrations at the experimental farm that were most effective. In April 1869 he wrote to Campbell:

The popular ideas of an Agricultural College are as yet vague and undefined. In the estimation of some it is a farm on which all the practical operations of tillage are to be taught,—others that it is a place where by means of chemistry and philosophy and the reading of books and papers the products of the farm may be obtained without hard work and the sound judgment which experience alone can give. Still others are of the opinion that it is the place where students can study a part of the day and work on a farm the remainder. All these delusions must be gradually overcome: they cannot be put down by authority or reasoning but will gradually yield to instruction and good examples.

There is no reason why practical agriculture should be taught more than carpentry or blacksmithing, or iron making or tanning,—and there is the same reason why there should be a regular apprenticeship to one as well as the others. There is a larger field for the exercise of intelligence in Agriculture than in any of the other arts, and so there is greater reason why farmers should be educated. This education, however, must be like that for other men, namely,—it must train their minds, teach them how to acquire knowledge,—and by opening to them the stores of knowledge treasured in the earth which is given them to subdue, show them in a somewhat enlarged measure, where their special knowledge is to be found. . . . The farm will be useful as a teacher but the most important contribution it can make is to the mature farmer. . . . We are now in communication with them through the medium of an Annual Report and Lecture which are published by the Legislature and distributed everywhere.[42]

Cook wanted to use the farm for experimentation, but because the trustees had guaranteed to provide the farm at no cost to the state, progress toward this goal was heartbreakingly slow even for such a patient man as Dr. Cook. The trustees, naturally enough, expected the farm to be self-supporting—an impossibility for an establishment devoted to experimentation. But this fact was not self-evident in 1865 and they embarked upon their venture confident that the appalling acres they had purchased would soon be a flourishing experimental farm.

In April 1865 John H. Knight, an expert farmer from Monroe, New York, was hired to manage the farm. For his services, which included the furnishing of his own pair of horses, Mr. Knight was given a salary of $1,400 and allowed to live in the somewhat ramshackle house on the farm. The trustees undertook to furnish seeds, extra labor when needed, and all farm implements and tools.[43] Acquisition of the needed implements was made easier by the efforts of Colonel N. Norris Halsted, president of the New Jersey Agricultural Society, and Isaac R. Cornell, a former president.[44] They persuaded various members of the society to donate wheelbarrows, wagons, harnesses, garden tools, and other necessary implements. Benjamin Haines of the Agricultural Supply Company of Haines and Pell in New York City was especially helpful, not only in promising to raise the money to pay the bill for shovels, a plow, and a harrow purchased from his company but also in rounding up gifts of plows, mowers, and hay cutters from six other agricultural supply houses.[45] Halsted worked willingly to get promises of gifts but found that "the promises are easily obtained but the performance very tardy."[46] Nevertheless, many gifts (duly noted in *Annual Reports*) were received and continued to come in every year.

The condition of the farm, which the Board of Visitors described poetically as "barren field and impassable morass" did provide Cook and Knight the means for a near-miraculous demonstration of scientific farming such as the trustees had promised.[47] If the farm had been prosperous, less money would have been spent in rehabilitation and more could have been used for experimentation. However, the primitive level of sophistication of agricultural experimentation meant that Cook was still able to make a modest contribution to the advance of agricultural science. At the same time, because of his emphasis on the concerns of the working farmer, the farm was able to be of real service in the state. Under Cook's guidance it was used as a testing ground for new farm implements and machinery as well as for new species of plants and varieties of seeds. Studies were made of the production of several breeds of milk cows, and, most important, analyses and trials of fertilizers were carried out. In his annual reports and lectures and by example in the farm journals he kept, Cook also emphasized the importance to the farmer of the keeping of businesslike records.

In 1865, however, the first priority was the rehabilitation of the soil. Thirty-five acres were full of bushes and stumps, twenty-five acres were too wet and swampy for cultivation, and fifteen were either covered with weeds or were bare of anything. Of the remainder, twenty-three acres were in grass but produced only one ton of hay per acre and that was so full of weeds that no one would buy it.[48] The two acres planted in wheat gave an average yield of only six bushels an acre.[49]

The first year John Knight took up his duties too late to put in any spring crops, but he did manage to raise a few acres of oats, corn, potatoes, carrots, and cabbages. Unfortunately, only the carrots and part of the cabbages were good enough to sell; the rest had to be fed to the teams. Before the next growing season, however, he had cut down all the scrubby underbrush and burned the grass to prepare the ground for cultivation and by the end of 1865 between twenty-five and thirty acres had been ploughed and were ready for the spring crops.[50] The remaining land was too wet and swampy for cultivation and required special treatment. During 1865 Knight, with one regular laborer and some part-time help, dug ditches and laid drain tile under six acres of the wettest land. The results were quickly seen. A few hours after a rain the ground that had been underdrained was dry and the vegetation grew more vigorously than before.[51] By 1868, 1,531 rods of drain tile had been laid and the drainage work was almost complete.

The barns, outbuildings, and farmhouse matched the soil in their state of decrepitude and neglect and the farm lacked stock as well; the first year the only cow on the place belonged to Knight. The Board of Trustees had already spent $3,000 over and above the $15,000 purchase price for the farm and in addition to the cash received for crops and the gifts of seeds and tools.[52] Having undertaken the commitment, however, they continued their financial support. The barns and sheds were repaired, the house was cleaned, painted, and papered, the roof was patched, and new fencing was put up. By 1869 the farm, while not self-supporting, was in fairly respectable shape: the grass crop had been improved so that as much as forty acres of hay might be expected in a good year; income crops like turnips, beets, asparagus, strawberries, raspberries, and blackberries had been successfully grown; and a dairy herd begun.

For several reasons, the development of a dairy herd was important. The sale of milk was the fastest and surest way to make money and the herd could be counted on to supply manure for fertilizer. Cook persuaded President Campbell and the trustees that the purchase of an Ayrshire bull and two cows for propagating a pure milking stock would be a wise investment.[53] By the end of 1868, the herd consisted of four full-blooded Ayrshire cows, two Shorthorns, a pure Alderney heifer and bull, a pure-blooded Ayrshire heifer and bull, and four native cows. Cook's plan was to "keep as large a stock of milk cows as is necessary to consume all the corn stalks and nutritious but unsalable fodder and to make as large a supply of manure as possible."[54]

During these years, the relative merits of various breeds were the subject of much controversy and speculation in agricultural circles. Owners of Alderneys, Ayrshires, Jersey, Devons, and Shorthorns became heated in defense of their favorite breed's excellence in supplying the largest quantities of milk, being the hardiest, or giving milk with the highest butter-fat content. (The latter was desirable so that any surplus farm milk could be used to make butter.) The pages of the *Cultivator, Country Gentleman, Scientific Farmer* and other farm journals were filled with enthusiastic letters supporting favorite breeds. The only way to end the controversy was by controlled testing and record-keeping. To this end Cook, on the modest scale that was possible to him, kept records of the production of the farm's herd.[55]

Most scientific investigation in agriculture in the late nineteenth century was concentrated on the study of fertilizers. A hundred years ago the principles and practices of fertilizing were not as clearly understood as they have since become and discoveries made about fertilizers were important and exciting. Partly because of its application to the needs of medicine and industry, chemistry made great advances in the nineteenth century. In Germany Justus von Liebig pioneered the application of the principles of chemistry to agriculture. At Giessen in Darmstadt, Liebig established the first school of chemistry to focus on research and about 1838 began to focus on the application of chemistry to agriculture. He continued these studies when he was persuaded by the Bavarian government to take the chair of chemistry at Munich University. The effect of his publications and the widespread teaching of his studies (Samuel W. Johnson of Yale's Sheffield Scientific School and Eben Horsford of Harvard's Lawrence Scientific School were two of his most famous American students) was "so overwhelmingly chemical that for the next half century after the publication of his book chemistry was assumed to be the whole of science in agriculture."[56] Not until late in the century did agriculturists turn their attention to entomology, botany, microbiology, and animal physiology for enlightenment on problems of agriculture.

Liebig's influence on Cook is clear. Cook was primarily a chemist anyway, and he eagerly began fertilizer analyses and experiments. No sooner had the first fields on the farm been readied for cultivation than field trials of various fertilizers began. In 1867 three trial plots of hay were planted; one was left untreated, one treated with four tons of marl to the acre, and the third with four hundred pounds of flour of raw bone.[57] The results, measured according to market value, showed that the increased value of the hay from the marled plot was more than twice that of the marl used, while from the raw bone plot the value was more than equal to the value of the bone. The trial of the greensand marl was the first that had been carried out in the New Brunswick area. The dramatic evidence of its effect prompted the Scientific School's Board of Visitors to approve the first of many annual resolutions commending the trustees of Rutgers for their support of the farm, "an important service to New Jersey Agriculture" with particular appreciation for the experiments in fertilizers.[58]

Of all the jobs Cook had to undertake for the Scientific School, he found the delivery of the required county lectures the most trying. It was not that he minded lecturing to groups of farmers—he had been doing that since he had first returned to New Jersey and in 1855 began helping William Kitchell to reorganize the New Jersey State Agricultural Association.[59] Nor did he mind having to travel around the state (although it took a great deal of his time). What bothered him was the frustration arising from his firm conviction that a single lecture every year was not the best way to teach the farmers. Furthermore it was irksome to have to concern himself with organizational details. No one at the county level had been given the task of arranging and publicizing the lectures. In the absence of any initiative from the county Board of Freeholders, the Board of Visitors or the New Jersey Agricultural Association, Cook himself was forced to write to friends and acquaintances, make arrangements through unrelated organizations (in Orange, the Library Association) or have John Smock plan meetings while on his travels for the geological survey.[60] Cook even had to pay for printing the handbills which advertised one lecture.[61] In the Board of Trustees' first report on the Scientific School, Campbell wrote,

It is not seemly or possible for the lecturer to prepare articles for the papers, or to set in motion those appliances or influences by which a proper audience is to be called together. The collection of fresh materials for the lecture, the making of analyses, the arrangement of farm experiments and trials, with the labor and time of getting from the College to each of the counties of the State, are enough to engross the whole attention and energies of the lecturer, and the work of providing a room and calling together an audience should be done by the energetic and public spirited friends of agriculture in the several counties.[62]

There was no response to this protest for several years. In some counties Cook felt the task of lecturing was worth the trouble and was pleasant. Someone in the community arranged the day and time and the farmers responded enthusiastically. In some cases, especially in the upsurge of interest during the first years, the farmers became so enthusiastic that they stayed for an hour or more asking questions and carrying on a lively discussion.

The subject of Cook's first lecture, delivered in all twenty-one counties during the winter and spring of 1866-67, was "The Conditions and Advantages of Agriculture in New Jersey and the Means for Its Improvement."[63] That condition, he told farmers, was much better than its reputation. Unfortunately, the oversimplified dictum of a geography published in 1789 had declared that in the north New Jersey was mountainous, in the center fertile and in the south barren and these ideas had been perpetuated even though as Cook told the farmers, "The barrenness is in the geographer and not in our soils."[64] Showing tables comparing production in New Jersey with six nearby states he pointed out that Jersey farm lands were worth much more per acre than the others.[65] He argued that the agricultural production of the state could be further increased by draining the more than 300,000 acres of tidal meadows and the swamp lands of the Passaic, Pequest, and Wallkill Rivers. If New Jersey wetlands were drained, Cook said, they could rival the reclaimed lands in Holland and the east of England.

Education too, said Cook, could insure the use of better agricultural methods. He pointed out that in the areas of the state that had been settled by Quakers (who were well known to place great value upon education) farms were more productive than in other parts of the state. He was not only arguing for college education but for primary and secondary education as well. The general census of 1860 had registered 23,081 illiterate adults in New Jersey. Cook urged the farmers to support basic education so that their sons could read agricultural reports in the newspapers and farm journals, understand farm machinery, and cope with complicated farm accounts. He continued his lecture by describing the courses of study available at the Rutgers Scientific School. He said that it was difficult to persuade young men of the value of agricultural education because merchants, mechanics, and other men with no farming experience thought that anyone could farm. If they themselves happened to try and fail, they blamed it on the weather or the soil or anything rather than their own lack of knowledge and skill. Among farmers themselves, the reluctance to send their sons to college to study agriculture was partly due to a doubt as to whether the young men would be able to plough any better for having studied chemistry, raise better fruit for having studied botany, or get more money for their crops after studying political economy.

Despite Cook's justifiable opposition to the lectures, they were not entirely unsuccessful in reaching the farmers. They followed the tradition of James J. Mapes whose pre-Civil War lectures had informed New Jersey farmers, and were a precursor of the Farmers' Institutes and extension courses of a later day. The county lectures frequently inspired the formation of farmers' clubs, as Cook urged such regular meetings as a forum for the discussion of common problems.

In his second annual lecture Cook talked about fertilizers and the following year about the New Jersey Geological Survey.[66] The discussion of fertilizers covered a wide assortment of those then available—ranging from such natural products as greensand marl, Peruvian guano, nightsoil, and seaweed through prepared or manufactured offerings like dry ox bones, cancerine (made from crushed crabs by the Beesleys of Salem County), potash, and a concoction made in Peter Cooper's Glue Factory by boiling, grinding, and drying the bones of horses. For their information, Cook also gave the farmers a chemical analysis of various fertilizers, an account of the methods used to obtain them, and a table from Boussingault's *Rural Economy* which showed the minerals needed by specific crops. In support of his theoretical advocacy of fertilizers he was able to point to the effect of the greensand marl on the fields of the college farm where by the second year two and a half times as much hay was being harvested.

Although Cook acknowledged his debt to James Dwight Dana and Samuel W. Johnson as leaders in the field of scientific agriculture, he did not hesitate to disagree with them. Both men, in company with many practical farmers, had recommended the addition of common salt to composts as a means of hastening decomposition. In disagreeing Cook rested his case on chemical principles which indicated that a mixture of salt and lime would be no more effective than lime alone.

Cook's lecture on the work of the geological survey focused on those aspects that related to agriculture, emphasizing especially the fact that soil analyses could indicate the best agricultural use and the best way to drain and fertilize each. Carl Woodward and Ingred Waller in *New Jersey's Agricultural Experiment Station* wrote of the lectures: "They were ably done, showing a remarkable grasp of the details of the agricultural situation in New Jersey and a vision of the service that could be rendered through the wise utilization of the facts of science. They were stimulating and advanced, and at the same time practical and popular."[67] Reading the lectures a hundred years later, one recognizes Cook's ability to make a discussion of agricultural problems interesting, comprehensive and practical—and the marvelous tact that enabled him to instruct farmers without talking down to them. But problems with the lectures continued as the following excerpt from the minutes of the Board of Visitors indicates:

The Professor of Agriculture in accordance with the requirements of the law delivered lectures on agriculture in the counties of the state during the past autumn, and with the exception of Hudson County . . . succeeded in securing a hearing. He stated to the Board his conviction that the requirement of a lecture in each county ought to be modified, so as to be imperative only in those cases where they desired a lecture. It was embarrassing and unpleasant to impose the delivery of a lecture in agriculture upon a community when it was not wanted.[68]

Busy as he was with the lectures, the farm, and his classes, Cook also had to fulfill his commitment to complete the geological survey by 1867. Work on the survey proceeded at a good pace—primarily because the assistant geologist, John Smock, was as hard-working and conscientious as his superior. Smock had worked with Cook and Paul Cook (then a freshman at Rutgers) in the summer of 1863 surveying the land for a railroad for the New Jersey Zinc Company and had also been a tutor in chemistry at the college for a short time. He had grown up in Holmdel in the greensand marl region of New Jersey and early acquired an interest in the fossils of the marl beds. This hobby had brought him to Cook's attention when he was a boy of thirteen.[69] In addition to Smock, Cook was assisted by G. Morgan Hopkins, Thomas Benton Brooks, and David Murray who surveyed and made maps, and Edwin H. Bogardus who made chemical analyses for the survey. Paul Cook worked for the survey for a while also, tracing lines of magnetic attraction and beds of iron ore.[70] Timothy Conrad contributed a list of invertebrate fossils, Charles C. Abbott was responsible for the list of vertebrate animals, and the Reverend E. Seymour of Bloomfield catalogued New Jersey minerals. Julius Bien, the most eminent engraver of maps of the period, produced all but one of the survey's maps. A German refugee from the revolutions of 1848, Bien, whom Henry Steele Commager called "one of the neglected artists of his generation," had brought to the United States technical skills that had been unknown here until his arrival.[71]

A lay Board of Managers was appointed to oversee the activities of the survey. Because the college had a Board of Trustees and the Scientific School a Board of Visitors, it no doubt seemed logical to New Jerseyans that a geological survey should also have a supervisory school but the arrangement was unique among geological surveys of the period, including the two previous New Jersey surveys. Of the thirty-two state surveys authorized by 1864, no evidence has been found to indicate that any others were provided with a board. In a way the Board of Managers was an added burden for Cook who had to attend meetings, explain what he was doing, and get approval. However, the board also provided a means of continuity and security for the survey. Its recommendations to the legislature carried more weight than they might have if presented by Cook or the governor alone. Like all such institutions the Board of Managers, once established, acquired a vested interest in its own survival and in the perpetuation of activities within its purview. This proved to be helpful to Cook as state geologist and director of the survey. Even more helpful was the fact that the first board (composed of two representatives from each of the five congressional districts and the governor [ex officio]) included a number of exceedingly able and influential men. Among them were John Augustus Roebling, the bridge builder from Trenton, William M. Force, secretary of the New Jersey Agricultural Association, Henry Aitkin of the New Jersey Zinc Company, William Parry, judge of the Court of Common Pleas and owner of the Pomona Nursery, largest fruit farm in the state, Selden Scranton, iron manufacturer of Oxford, N. J., Abram Hewitt of Ringwood, ironmaster, associate of Peter Cooper and later Mayor of New York, and Joseph P. Bradley, who later became a justice of the United States Supreme Court.

Cook's first job was to continue to salvage what he could from the defunct Kitchell survey. Unfortunately, Kitchell's notes at the time of his death were not sufficiently well prepared to be usable and only the information which had actually been published could be transferred to the new survey. In some instances the work done by Viele in triangulation and on the maps of Cape May, Sussex, Monmouth, Cumberland, Salem, Warren, and Morris counties was helpful but many of the triangulations were not exact enough to be of use and all the work that had been done upon them was wasted.[72] Descriptions of mines and analyses of marl beds had to be updated as some new mines and pits had been opened and others closed. Cook traveled through the state making his meticulous notes in the succession of small tan notebooks. The entries indicate the kind of information Cook felt to be important. In notebook #24, for example, an entry for Thursday, August 24, 1865, read: "Started from Milltown; on road 1 mile towards Petersburg came upon red shale in road—dipping E SE 35°—this shale grew coarser as I neared the mountain on left—On this mountain the dip of strata continued the same till very near the top when it changed to n.w. about 45° and so continued all along the crest of this hill. . . ."[73]

On August 17 the entry reads:

At Suffern. Rainy day, showers, went up to mine of Dater on top of Mt. E. of Ramapo River and 1½ or 2 miles n. of Sloatsbury. The mine is but recently opened and is not yet fully developed. It looks like the very crest of a fold and as if opened on the crest and a little to the left of n.w. and will probably descend on the n.w. slope in a "trued" vein or stratification. On the right the horizontal layer is not yet uncovered so as to show any curve downwards. The ore layer or vein is 10 or 12 ft. thick. . . . Rain drove me off before quite completing the observations. . . .

This description is accompanied by a sketch.[74]

Of a visit to Ringwood the notebook records: "Mr. Hewitt makes cold blast charcoal iron, using 325 bushels of charcoal for one ton of iron, another where the air is heated to about 300° requires but 255 bushels—and where the hot blast is used only 125 bushels of charcoal is required per ton."[75]

Smock also spent considerable time in the field and regularly wrote letters back describing his discoveries. In addition, mine and marl pit and railroad owners supplied information.

Published in 1868, the final report was a single volume of nine hundred pages with approximately one hundred photographic engravings and woodcuts. It was accompanied by a portfolio of eight maps: four general maps on a scale of two miles to an inch which covered the whole state and followed the geological divisions and four smaller maps which showed iron mines in Morris County, the Ringwood Iron Mine, the Oxford Furnace iron ore veins in Warren County, and the zinc mines in Sussex County. The limited time available and the size of the appropriation which made it impossible to continue the topographical mapping was as Cook wrote, ". . . a great disappointment to those engaged in the survey and a source of regret to all who know the absolute necessity for accurate and reliable maps on which to delineate geological results."[76]

In organizing the report, Cook abandoned the cumbersome county-by-county plan of the Kitchell survey and returned to Rogers's division of the state by geological formation. Cook listed them as: 1. Azoic and Paleozoic, 2. Triassic, 3. Cretaceous, and 4. Tertiary and Recent, and on Hopkins's maps they were shown more precisely than on any previous maps. The body of the report was divided into three parts, with most space given to the geological description of the state and Economic Geology. Historic geology was covered in about fifty pages. Cook was careful to give full credit in his preface to work done by Professor Henry Wurtz, Ernest Hauesser, E. D. Baldwin, Viele, and Kitchell of the 1854 survey but most of the preparation had been done by Cook and his staff and the report bore the stamp of his methodical, thorough mind and his penchant for statistics, charts, and figures. He included a table for each county showing the areas in each township which could be classified as beach, tide marsh, or wet meadow, a table on the population of New Jersey from 1737 to 1865, and one showing the population of the various geological areas. An appendix contained tables of latitude and longitude, heights of selected locations, and meteorological observations as well as catalogues of vertebrate animals, fossils, and minerals.

The work Cook had done on marl in 1854-57 was updated and included in the section on economic geology which also included material on soil analysis, limestones and limes, glassmaking, water supplies, and peat, with a large section on iron, copper, and zinc mines. Building stones, clay, cranberry culture, and water supplies were also dealt with. The generous attention given to details of economic interest was consistent with the expectations of the legislature and with Cook's conviction that these matters were of primary importance for a state-supported survey. Like Edward Hitchcock in Massachusetts and David Dale Owen in Indiana, Cook realized that the necessary attention to economic matters did not exclude the accumulation of "impractical" geological information and theorizing.

The marl beds were of particular interest and were illustrated with nine section drawings. Cook's description of the beds and layers of the formation included the average thickness of each bed, the dip, sketches of the most commonly found fossils, and the localities where various layers of marl could be found. In addition in his section on economic geology, sixty pages were devoted to chemical analyses of approximately one hundred marls, maps done by Julius Koch to accompany Cook's reports in 1855 and 1856 and others prepared by Smock especially for the 1868 report. In explaining the way in which the marl acted in the soil, Cook wrote that phosphoric acid was recognized as the most valuable constituent but the precise effects of the other components (potash, sulphuric acid, soluble silica, oxide of iron, magnesia, phosphate of lime) had not yet been determined.[77]

Cook placed the two lower marl beds in the Cretaceous formation but the Upper Marl Bed, which many geologists put in the same system, he characterized as belonging to the Eocene or earliest series of the Tertiary because of the fossils found in the bed.[78] His work with the stratigraphy of the marl beds has been superceded in recent years. Twentieth-century geologists have renamed the marl beds—using such designations as Manasquan, Shark River, Vincentown, Rancocas, and Hornerstown—but in his own time, Cook made a significant contribution. His careful explorations and synthesis of previous work on marls produced a stratigraphy sufficiently sophisticated to form the basis for later refinements.

The report on marls was useful for the period in which it was written because Cook included figures on the number of bushels produced at the various marl pits, the market price of marl, and statistics on the transportation of marl by New Jersey railroads.[79] In addition, he wrote detailed descriptions of the methods used by various companies to dig marl from their pits, a method of digging marl out of the bed of a stream, and a description of a track built by the West Jersey Marl Company which ran to the bottom of their pit and employed a "horse engine" which was kept running constantly to pump out the water.[80]

As in the case of the marl Cook identified as Cretaceous the beds of clay which like the marl ran across the state from the Raritan Bay to the Delaware River. The southeast border of the clay beds ran from Cheesequake Creek through Jamesburg, Cranbury, and Hightstown to the Delaware at Bordentown. The clay occurred in layers which could be traced only where there were outcroppings or where pits had been dug. At the East Trenton Porcelain Company, for example, the clay lay from two to eight feet below the topsoil in a layer four or five feet thick.[81] Cook gave locations and descriptions of many clay pits and included a columnar section of a typical arrangement of layers in each. The clay layers extended through the state, but pits had been dug only along the eastern and western boundaries because through the center of the state surface deposits of gravel and sand lay too deep over the clay. A chapter in the section on economic geology focused on the analysis, production, and use of the clays. Cook wrote:

It is to be regretted that these fine clays are not more fairly prized. They must yet come to be of great importance in our manufactures. There are clays about Woodbridge which, for crucibles and glass-pots, may be better than these very fine clays. They contain more silica and less alumnia. Wm. B. Dixon, of Woodbridge, has clay on his property in which the silica is 61.6 per cent, and the alumnia 28.4 per cent. When burnt it becomes very firm and solid. It is now being tried for making crucibles and glass-pots and promises well. There can be no doubt that these clays, when properly managed, will be found equal to the best foreign clays for these uses.[82]

As in previous surveys, much attention was given to mines. Iron and zinc mines were flourishing and reports on them included detailed descriptions, maps, and columnar sections, as a source of reliable information for all those interested. Like producers of clays, bricks, and other natural products, mine owners were pleased with the report for it provided them with free publicity. This was good for business in the state and was used to attract new people to settle there. When George Bancroft was about to take up his duties as United States Ambassador to Germany, he promised New Jersey Governor Marcus Ward that he would show the report and maps to leading men there in the hope that this might influence emigration to New Jersey.

As important as the chapter on economic geology was—and without the promise of commercial, mining, agricultural, or industrial benefits the legislature would not have authorized the survey—Cook was able to include a great deal of "useless" geological data. The scientific value of the *Geology* rested largely upon this painstaking accumulation of information.

While the *Geology* was superceded by later, more advanced work, measured against state surveys of the period it was the best one published. One reason for this was Cook's thoroughness and accuracy. Other state surveys sometimes tended to be superficial in their presentation of facts and given to unwonted theorizing. Ninety years before Edinburgh's John Walker had advised geologists to concentrate on establishing facts instead of formulating theories, but his words of caution were frequently ignored.[83]

This is not to say that Cook was not interested in the theoretical discussions and controversies. The 1860s were primarily years in which knowledge about the geographical boundaries of geological formation was extended but speculation about geological cause and effect continued. Major problems claiming the attention of geologists in the 1860s included subsidence, the origin of the erratic boulders and mounds of gravel (usually called "drift"), the question of whether or not there was a Taconic formation, the enormously intricate problems of determining stratigraphy, and establishing the geological time column and glacial action. The biggest controversy of all, that over evolution, was just getting underway but Cook appears never to have been concerned with that at all. On the matter of the Taconic question also he had nothing to say. He did participate in the discussions and investigations having to do with subsidence, drift, and stratigraphy and, especially in later years, on the time column. After his paper of 1857 and the section on subsidence in the 1855 survey were published, James Dwight Dana had quoted him in the 1864 and subsequent editions of the *Manual of Geology* in the section on changes of level on the earth's surface.[84]

Cook's most important stratigraphic work was done in the Cretaceous and Tertiary marl and clay strata although the *Geology* also described in detail the Precambrian (or Azoic as it was then called), Paleozoic, and Triassic formations which occurred in the state. On several points in dispute, such as the origin of the iron ores and the age of the crystalline limestones, Cook did not hesitate to state his own position. John Smock later characterized his description of the crystalline rock series as of first importance in the study of the structure of the whole crystalline rock series.[85] And while Frank Nason found Cook's treatment of the Archaean rocks to be outdated, it was his judgment that it represented a great advance over that of Rogers in 1840 and that both treatments were "landmarks which define most exactly progress in geological science."[86]

On the origin of the magnetic iron ores, Cook postulated:

The observed facts support the theory that these ores originated from chemical or mechanical deposits just as hematite or bog iron is formed; that they were then covered by strata of sand clay and carbonate of lime, that with them they have since been upheaved, pressed into folds, and under the influence of pressure and water for an immense length of time, they have undergone chemical and mechanical changes, which have brought them to their present condition.[87]

Cook regretted that the time allowed for the survey had made it necessary to cut short the studies on iron ore. Obviously Cook's explanations as to origin were always very much limited by the state of the science at the time. The present state geologist, Kemble Widmer, has pointed out that a great deal has been learned about metamorphic rocks and igneous intrusions in the twentieth century and the physical chemistry involved in both metamorphism and igneous activity has not been understood until recently. Widmer writes, "It is now recognized that during the intrusion of granitic bodies considerable volumes of material may move in a gaseous state through the space lattices or molecules of the rock-forming minerals and be precipitated as replacement minerals hundreds and perhaps even thousands of feet from the intrusion."[88]

Widmer explains the earlier theories,

The magnetite deposits have been studied since the earliest days of geology. As had been previously indicated, the gneissic banding in the rocks of the Highlands was at first believed to indicate sedimentary structures. Since the occurrence of most magnetite concentrations is parallel to and closely controlled by the metamorphic structures or foliation in the rock and since most, if not all, of the gneisses in which the magnetite is found were once sediments, the conclusion of early workers that the magnetite was originally concentrated in, and was part of, the sediments from which the gneisses were derived is not unreasonable. By about 1910 enough studies of the magnetite ore bodies had been made and enough learned about the characteristics of metamorphic rocks to indicate that the magnetite had been introduced into the host rocks by hot aqueous solutions from deep-seated igneous activity so that W. W. Bayley concluded, "They may be called, in short, igneous veins."[89]

It is not surprising that Cook raised as many questions as he tried to answer about the causes of observed phenomena. In his speculations about the traprock of Bergen and Rocky Hill and the First, Second, and Third Watchung mountains he asked whether these ridges of trap broke through the sandstone at once and after it was deposited or whether their fluid substance rose one after another while the sandstone was in the process of deposition.[90] He suggested that the "projection of the trap ridges above the general surface of the country must be looked at, not as an outpouring of fluid matter over the original surface, but as a layer of trap rock interposed between two layers of softer sandstone which . . . has resisted the action of abrading influences, while the sandstone has been worked away both in front and on the top of it."[91]

Cook's investigations on subsidence for the Kitchell survey were in support of Charles Lyell's theories but where Lyell used the phenomena of subsidence to explain the drift, maintaining that the subsidence and submergence of vast areas of land and the subsequent action of the sea explained the errant boulders and gravel, Cook did not agree. In the 1868 report, primarily because of time limitations, Cook did not pay as much attention to the drift as he was later to do. He wrote: "The phenomena connected with the formation and movement of the gravel and boulders are too varied and widespread to have been fully comprehended and arranged in the time devoted to the survey."[92] He did note the various occurrences of the drift on the western border of the Medina rocks and the Second Mountain and elsewhere. His comments in the *Geology* demonstrate clearly that he supported Louis Agassiz's theory that the drift was caused by glacial action and furthermore that there had once existed a continental ice sheet. The deposits of glaciers, the moraines, had been studied by Charpentier, Bernhardi, and others since before 1750 and Agassiz's publicizing of his observations had gained fairly widespread acceptance for the localized moraine effect of glacial action since about 1840. But the idea of a continental ice sheet was more difficult for scientists to accept. As late as 1893 the great Canadian geologist, J. W. Dawson, refused to accept the notion that a sheet of ice could be held responsible for the scattered boulders.[93]

Cook's 1868 report, after noting specific examples of gravel mounds and erratic boulders over many of the geological formations of New Jersey concluded, "They were taken from regular formations, torn off by the moving force of ice or water or [both]."[94] He described the regular and parallel scratches and furrows found upon rocks in the Highlands, the Paleozoic formation, and on the trap ridges. These he ascribed to "ice as the effective agent" and indicated his support of the theory of a continental ice sheet when he wrote: "It is only necessary to say that these all prove that some more rigid force than that of water had been operating *all over the country*. . . . These effects point to ice as the effective agent"[95] (my italics). Furthermore, Cook realized that such an ice sheet would have caused a marked change in the climate to the south of it and drew attention to two walrus skulls found in the gravel near Long Branch as evidence of a colder climate in an earlier period.

Earlier evaluations of Cook's work have emphasized his contributions in the realm of economic geology but it is clear that he was equally concerned with scientific investigation for its own sake. The 1868 *Geology of New Jersey* made a contribution to geological knowledge in general as well as to the knowledge of the geology of New Jersey.

No evaluation of the New Jersey survey can be made without some comparison with other surveys completed or attempted by other states during the period. Thirty-two states had undertaken some manner of geological survey by 1868—some had financed several with varying degrees of success. The great New York survey of 1840-43 which established a geological system using American nomenclature for the first time and the Pennsylvania survey in which Henry D. Rogers set forth his theories on the structure of the Appalachian mountains were perhaps the most outstanding. At the other end of the scale were such antic efforts as the Louisiana survey (written in French) which was afterward quoted only to point out its errors—or the Texas survey which was conducted by a gentlemanly newspaper editor with no recognizable knowledge or training in geology.[96]

Because of the exigencies of the Civil War, the depression of the late 1850s, or the disinclination of legislatures to support further surveys, during the 1860s there were only eleven state surveys underway. The California survey directed by J. D. Whitney failed to obtain support from the legislature because it concentrated on purely scientific objectives and neglected economic matters.[97] The first volume, published in 1864, had been eagerly awaited by Californians in general and the subcommittee on mines and mining in particular. They expected reports on the Monte Diablo coal region and detailed explanations of methods of extracting gold. When, instead, they were presented with a volume on carboniferous, Jurassic, Triassic, and Cretaceous fossils, they were not pleased. James Hall, director of the New York survey, managed to antagonize *two* state legislatures. At one time he undertook the direction of surveys in three states, adding Iowa and Wisconsin to his New York responsibilities. The Wisconsin legislature became convinced that he was not working hard enough in their state and not only would not pay him the salary they had promised but also refused to refund his expenses.[98]

George Cook was both too honest and too canny to commit such errors. The salary he asked for and received was only $1,000 a year as contrasted with Whitney's $6,000 in California and Hall's $2,000 from Iowa alone. Furthermore, Cook was fully aware of the importance of minimizing the burden on the taxpayers and recognized that the expensive topographical survey could not be resumed. The *Geology* was completed and published for the amount of money appropriated and, except for an extension to complete the writing and printing, within the time allotted. This meant, of course, that many worthwhile investigations had to be left out. The analysis of the subsoil in the limestone valleys of Warren and Sussex counties indicated that the rich amounts of phosphoric acid, potash, and soda might warrant its addition to other soils for their enrichment much as the greensand marl was used, but the discovery of these soils had come too late in the survey for an adequate examination of the possibility.[99] A discovery of new marl beds in Salem County needed further examination; a new process · for the manufacture of wrought iron was expected to increase the demand for iron and Cook recommended that the search for new deposits of iron ore be expanded; an investigation of possible ways to reclaim the tide meadows was desirable and there was a possibility that the Cranberry Inlet at Toms River might be opened again. Cook suggested that such necessary investigations warranted continuation of the survey and with the support of the Board of Managers a supplement to the "Act to complete the geological survey of the state" was passed by the legislature on April 1, 1869, authorizing continuation of the survey for four years with an annual appropriation of not more than $5,000.[100]

The favorable response from the public and other scientists to the *Geology* undoubtedly weighed heavily in the legislature's decision to continue finding the survey. A German language edition was published. Isaac R. Cornell, James Jenkins, and John Roebling expressed their pleasure with the report. Jenkins wrote, "Congratulations. . . . You have placed the people of our state under a debt of great obligation to you, and for all time. It is a monument to your promptitude and fidelity in the discharge of public duty, to your talent and skill in its preparation and to your zeal and industry in thus presenting in so brief a period a work of such magnitude . . ."[101] Cornell's comment was: "I, as well as every Jerseyman, am under infinite obligations for your zeal, patience and perseverance in the work. . . ."[102]

Praise came from all quarters for the mere fact of having produced that rare bird among geological surveys, a "completed final report."[103] S. W. Johnson wrote from Yale: "New Jersey should feel a just pride in possessing one of the least pretentious but most valuable of the many works of this kind which have been produced in this country during the last 25 years."[104]

Especially welcome was the generous praise from fellow geologists. From F. Sterry Hunt in Montreal: "I am well aware what a precious work you have been doing for American Geology."[105] From W. C. Kerr, the state geologist of North Carolina, came a statement of his intention of making Cook's marl report his standard reference, while the state geologist of Tennessee, after commenting on the excellence of the survey wrote, "I only regret that mine is not as good."[106] Othniel C. Marsh of Yale, who wrote a laudatory review in Silliman's *Journal*, expressed his regret at not having had more space to "express his appreciation of Cook's labors much more fully."[107] Joseph B. Lyman at the *New York Tribune* regarded the volume as a model. "Sufficiently technical, it has what no other geological report made in this country has—popular and strongly practical features."[108]

The maps accompanying the survey were also well received. Among others, Egbert L. Viele, who had directed the ill-fated topographical survey under William Kitchell, wrote, "I have received with a great deal of pleasure your superb report. I had not anticipated anything so very complete. I congratulate you most warmly and feel that I have a most invaluable accession to my stock of New Jersey information. The maps are exceedingly fine."[109]

Time did not diminish the original evaluations of the survey. Cook's reputation for excellence was firmly established, especially in New Jersey. In later years, George Perkins Merrill in *The First One Hundred Years of American Geology* cited Cook's *Geology of New Jersey* as one of the three most important American geological developments of the 1860s, the other two being the first edition of James Dwight Dana's *Manual of Geology* and William Logan's summation of the geology of Canada.[110]

As may be readily understood, Cook's professional activities were so pressing during this period that he was able to spend less time with his family and community activities than he might have wished. The time he had to take to travel around the state to give the county agricultural lectures was particularly irksome and he spent periods of days or weeks away from New Brunswick during the college spring and summer vacations. Except for some problems with housing, however, the Cook family continued to lead a pleasant and rather uneventful life.

Until 1866 the Cooks had lived in the house on the corner of College Avenue and Bartlett Street which Cook had built soon after their move to New Brunswick in 1854. Mary was perfectly content to stay there but for some time George had been thinking of selling the house and building a finer one. When two maiden ladies, the Misses Bucknall, wanted to buy the house to use as a girls' boarding school he gladly sold it to them. Mary was dismayed at being moved out of her home. She tried to dissuade her husband by quoting her brother Elijah, whose advice was that a man should not sell himself out of house and home—at least not unless he could get a better place than he owned for less money—"but it must be a great deal better and for much less money or the trouble and expense of moving will not be paid for."[111] But Cook did sell his family out of house and home. The Misses Bucknall took possession in April before the Cooks had another house. George, Paul, who was a Rutgers student, and Edward Thomas, a nephew of Mary's who had been living with them while he studied at the college, moved into rooms at the Misses Dumont's boarding house on Albany Street where Cook had stayed when he first came to New Brunswick. Mary with the other four children went to stay with Cook's family in East Hanover. After one visit to the three boarders Mary wrote, "My conscience almost reproaches me for leaving you all in such a state—tho' you know my freewill had nothing to do with your getting into it. Grandma feels very badly at your selling and I think no one here approves of it."[112] Later she wrote that although the people in East Hanover were all very kind and she was enjoying spring on the farm, "I feel a very bitter something in my heart . . . when I think of my lost home."[113]

George eventually built a much grander house on the corner of George Street and Seminary Place but it was many months before that house was finished. In the interim he bought a small house on French Street at the head of Paterson Street (which he sold later that year) and brought the exiles back to wait the completion of their new house. Cook himself designed the floor plan and, wishing to have the house built as inexpensively as possible, specified that there be no ornamental features except for projecting eaves "to give it character." Riverstede, as the Cooks called it, is a handsome building of stone with a slate roof and at the time it was built there was nothing between it and the Delaware-Raritan Canal and the Raritan River. The family greatly enjoyed watching the canal boats go by from the time the ice broke in the spring until it closed the canal the next winter.[114] However, they did not live there long. Cook had borrowed quite a large sum to build the house and the burden of the interest payments worried him. Therefore, when the manager of the college farm left in 1868 and Cook took over the job himself, he decided to move his family out to the farm for a few years. Riverstede was sold to the New Brunswick Seminary for one of its professors—though not without a disagreement about whether or not the bookcases went with the house or were to be sold separately.[115] The matter led to some sharp words between Cook and the seminary's George A. Sage, an episode which seems uncharacteristic of Cook, who was usually so obliging and willing to make sacrifices. But the fact is that along with his generosity he had an eagerness to make money. In a period without social security or pension plans when each man had to "lay some by" for his family and himself in his old age, the need to accumulate a nest egg was compelling. For some time Cook had been buying property in order to build up an estate. He probably did not make much from the Riverstede sale. It had cost him about $18,000 to build the house and Mary wrote to her brother that she thought the money which he received from the seminary would about cover the building costs. For financial reasons, she was glad the house had been sold, but Paul was the only member of the family who really wanted to move to the farm. Cook expected to live there for three years by which time "Mr. C." (as Mary always referred to her husband) thought the farm could be taken care of by another superintendent and they could make other plans.[116] In this, as in all financial matters, George made the decisions without consulting Mary though he seems to have discussed problems at the college, the survey, and many other things with her and respected her intelligence and good sense. But when it came to major financial decisions, in the most approved Victorian manner he made them himself.

In the spring of 1870, after the Board of Trustees had financed various repairs to the farm house, including a new roof, the Cooks moved in. Later that year Cook bought a farm near the college farm as an investment and source of income and put a tenant farmer on it.[117]

Aside from these housing disruptions, the Cooks' family life was happy and orderly. A few years later, Mary's nephew Edward, writing to tell them of the birth of a son said, "If . . . he wants to . . . go to college will you do him the favor you did me and let him live with you? I could desire but few things for him more than this."[118] Another visitor wrote that of the many homes he had visited the Cooks seemed the model one.[119] In spite of all Cook's absences and his habit of working from 5:30 in the morning until 10 or 11 o'clock at night, Mary managed to achieve the order, serenity, and purposefulness that she desired. Her training at the Troy Female Seminary and her love of botany and modern languages gave her a broader intellectual outlook than was possible for many women of the period and with her teaching experience enabled her to teach her daughters at home in this period when children were not required by law to attend public school. When Sarah and Emma eventually followed their mother's example and went to the Troy Female Seminary themselves they found that they had been well prepared by their mother. Mary's interests were not limited to her home and family. She was one of the earliest supporters of the Free Circulating Library of New Brunswick and her many years of service, particularly in the selection of books, contributed to its excellence.[120] Because Mary Cook lived in a period when women's talents were seldom put to use outside the home, most of her energies were directed toward the capable management of the household and the loving care of her husband and children. In this restricted society she was more fortunate than most women because she was not only able to teach her daughters and work for the library and church but she also could help her husband by translating scientific works or copying his lectures. She almost never accompanied Cook on his trips, preferring to stay at home or visit relatives. Once she was persuaded to go with him to a meeting of the American Association for the Advancement of Science in Salem, Massachusetts, but unfortunately was ill for most of the trip.[121] Even so, she wrote her sister Patty that she thought it had done her good by giving her something new to think about. But she really did not enjoy traveling and the experience was not repeated.

The Cooks were great letter-writers. When George was away or Mary and the children visiting in East Hanover or Chatham they wrote even if they were to be separated for only a few days. Mary's letters, reflecting her fondness for French usually began, "Mon Mari" and ended "Your Marie"; she never addressed her husband as "George."

When Cook became vice-president of the college in 1864 and the same year was named state geologist, the increase in his income enabled him to send Sarah to the Troy Female Seminary. She proved to be a good student and particularly conscientious and diligent in obeying all rules. She studied German, Italian, geometry, and drawing and received special credits for keeping her bureau drawers in order.[122] Described as of a "retiring nature, with a comprehensive mind, engaging manners and lovely character," she quickly became a close friend of Clara Gurley, William Gurley's daughter.[123] Gurley found her to be a good influence on Clara—perhaps because she was so conscientious. Like her father at about the same age, she kept a diary in which she recorded the high points of her first experience away at school and her resolutions for self-improvement. She was determined to "take time by the forelock" while at the seminary and extract the very most from her stay there. The diary recorded the year's excitements—a visit from her father on his way to a meeting in Elmira, and the scandalous behavior of two of the girls who flirted with some young men while attending evening church services. The wrath of the administration was visited upon all the students for that lapse and none of the girls were allowed to attend evening church services for a time! For Sarah's sixteenth birthday she listed her birthday presents—*The Vision of Sir Launfal* from her mother, a Roman scarf from her father, and a bottle of tooth powder from her brother Paul. A few months later she confided to her diary that she had received her first Valentine—an event so exciting that it caused her to break into French— "reçu mon premier Valentine ce soir—tres bien satisfait. . . ."[124]

Like her mother, Sarah loved the seminary but the next winter, probably influenced by his friend Abram Hewitt (a trustee of the Cooper Union Art School which had been founded by his father-in-law), Sarah commuted to New York City to study art at that institution.[125] In September 1867, however, she returned to the Troy seminary for another year, this time accompanied by her sister Emma.[126] Gurley wrote that he hoped Emma would be as good an influence on his daughter Hettie as Sarah had been for Clara.[127] And, indeed, Emma was as conscientious a student as Sarah. The Cooks heard from the school that their daughters were making good use of their time and privileges.[128] The next year the Willards asked that Emma be permitted to stay at the seminary— apparently on a kind of teaching fellowship—"Her fine character and scholarship have attached my parents [Emma and John Willard] warmly to her," wrote Emma Scudder, "and they would like to have her here for the school year with the opportunity of continuing her studies."[129]

Paul, too, had become the kind of hard-working, steady young man that his parents hoped for. At the age of nineteen he graduated from Rutgers fifth in the class of 1866 and the following year was enrolled as a special student in chemistry at the college.[130] After working for his father on the geological survey that summer, he got a job with Abram Hewitt, first taking orders for steel and iron products in the New York office and later moving to Peter Cooper's glue works. But he did not seem to be moving beyond a clerking position and Cook wrote to Gurley of his concern for his son's future. Gurley replied that he judged that Paul had the ability to do well at whatever he undertook and that "his integrity and purity of mind will preserve him from the temptations that lead away so many young men"—a fortunate and fitting opinion as Paul later married Hettie Gurley and became the manager of Gurley's instrument factory.[131]

It was through Gurley that George Cook received an inquiry as to whether he would be interested in returning to the Rensselaer Polytechnic Institute as its president—the trustees, wrote Gurley, felt that the man who was then president suffered from "lack of heart."[132] Other tokens of recognition of his position in the scientific world came from Union College which awarded him an honorary LL.D. in 1866 and from James Hall who nominated him to the National Academy of Sciences and wanted to suggest him for the chair of geology at Cornell.[133] But Cook decided that he wanted to remain at Rutgers and continue his work with the geological survey for a time at least. He was just beginning to see at Rutgers and in the survey the result of his efforts to set both upon a new track.

8

1870-1876
Applied Geology and Experimental Agriculture

For several years after the publication of the *Geology of New Jersey* and the legislature's decision to extend the survey, Cook concentrated its work on drainage, natural fertilizers, soils and iron ore, and other very practical matters. In company with earlier state geologists Edward Hitchcock in Massachusetts and David Dale Owen in Indiana, he recognized that attention to the economic aspects of geology would not only persuade legislators to continue their support of the state survey but were also the legitimate expectation of the taxpayers and in the long run could be combined with a pursuit of "impractical" geological knowledge.[1] But in postponing all projects that were solely analytical, exploratory, or theoretical he also postponed any significant advance of his professional reputation and denied to himself the kind of geological work he preferred to do.

The funding of surveys depended upon the support of farmers, industrialists, and businessmen who hoped to benefit from them, while the scientific reputation of the directors of surveys rested upon their contributions to the body of scientific knowledge and theory. Thus there was often a very real conflict between "pure versus applied science." Partisans of each frequently failed to realize that basic research often produces data applicable to commercial or industrial goals while practical research may uncover useful basic knowledge. In the nineteenth century directors of state surveys had to decide how much they should concentrate on geological sources of wealth and how much on the cataloguing of apparently unprofitable geological details or the formulating of exciting but not money-making theories. Some directors, like Josiah Whitney in California and James Hall in New York, concerned themselves almost exclusively with basic research. Hall, with an overpowering interest in fossils, was able to persuade the New York legislators (though with great difficulty at times) that failure to support his monumental and unending paleontological research would disgrace them forever. So convincing was he that one year, without quite knowing why, they voted to appropriate $83,000 for his paleontological work.[2]

Arguments supporting most state surveys had at least given lip service to the public welfare aspect of the survey with glowing sentences about the way in which the discovery of natural resources would help people by creating more jobs or about the educational benefits that would ensue as everyone grew to know more about the nature of the earth's crust. The only people to benefit directly, however, were those rich enough to invest money to exploit ores and minerals in the earth. While Cook, too, appreciated the educational benefits he brought a new dimension to the concept of the survey—that of public service. A pioneer in studies of water sources and drainage, he became a nationally and internationally known authority on both. He was as eager as any other geologist to pursue his scientific interests but he realized that the continuation of the New Jersey survey depended upon achieving maximum economic and welfare benefits at minimum cost. He was not cynical about this; he firmly believed that the people of the state deserved their money's worth and he knew that his practical projects would contribute more to the welfare of the general public than to the coffers of rich men. He also recognized (though the legislators probably did not) that growing demands from agricultural, industrial, and community interests, along with the constant advances in the sciences, made an indefinite continuation of the survey desirable.[3] Throughout his lifetime, the survey was kept alive by a series of four- or five-year extensions. Each time it was scheduled to end, Cook had to spend a considerable amount of time in Trenton convincing the legislators that it should be continued.

In 1869, when Cook announced his intention of "putting the results of the survey in form for practical use" he outlined the following five categories of concentration:

(1) Fertilizers found in the State and the means of making them more quickly and generally useful, (2) On the Marshes, and Tracts of Land subject to Protracted Freshets, (3) On the soils of the State, their origin, chemical and physical properties, distribution, and suggestions for their more productive management, (4) On the Iron and Zinc Ores of the State, and (5) Additions to the Scientific and Economical Geology of the State.[4]

These objectives were pursued with a small staff and a very limited budget. John Smock, named professor of mining and metallurgy at Rutgers in 1869, continued as assistant geologist and Edwin H. Bogardus as chemist. Edward A. Bowser did most of the surveying for the maps while George W. Howell and James K. Barton were engaged occasionally for surveying and mapping assignments. When necessary students in the engineering program of the Scientific School were hired as assistants. After 1871 the survey received help from the United States Coastal Survey under the terms of a new law.[5]

Bowser was a native of New Brunswick, Canada, who had studied at the normal school in Albany and graduated from the Brooklyn Polytechnic Institute. While an instructor there he wrote to David Murray about a mathematical problem and the resulting correspondence persuaded him to enroll in the Rutgers Scientific School. He graduated with the first class and was immediately hired as a tutor in mathematics and engineering. When Smock went to Europe to study for a year Cook put Bowser to work on the survey. He was soon promoted to adjunct professor at Rutgers and in 1872 after Major Josiah Kellogg left, he was made professor of mathematics and civil engineering.

In the years after 1868, drainage of the state's wetlands and flood control along the rivers became major concerns for the survey. The extensive tidal marshes and inland swamps held out the tantalizing possibility that they could be transformed into profitable lands for farming, while flooding, as Cook knew from his boyhood on the Passaic River, was a constant source of anxiety for farmers whose lands lay along the riverbanks. In addition, the permanent swampy condition of large areas of land along the Hackensack, Passaic, Pequest, and Wallkill rivers kept otherwise usable land from any cultivation whatever. Like others before and since, Cook could not understand why no one had drained and diked these marshes. He found this especially incomprehensible because in the southern part of the state over 15,000 acres of marshland had been reclaimed and were producing crops as early as 1700. A public health concern was involved as well. Not only did flooding destroy thousands of dollars worth of crops every year but malaria, always endemic along the rivers, increased during years of heavy floods.

Bowser was assigned to study the marshes around Elizabeth and Newark, the Passaic River above Little Falls, and the reclaimed marshes in Salem County. As a result of his findings and Cook's recommendations, a few acres in the area between the Passaic and the Hackensack rivers near the head of Newark Bay were drained. Tidewater was shut off and a large plot was ploughed and crops successfully raised.[6] This was an impressive demonstration of what could be done but it soon became obvious that the undertaking was an enormous one and would require large capital investments. At this juncture the Board of Managers of the survey decided that an investigation of drainage projects would be helpful and in 1870 Cook was sent to Europe to inspect the extensive and famous drainage and reclamation operations in England and the Netherlands and bring back up-to-date information and recommendations for similar projects in New Jersey.

During the trip, which lasted four and a half months, Cook not only examined drainage operations but also visited farms and agricultural schools in England and the Netherlands and in Norway, Sweden, and Germany and accumulated information on a number of industrial plants. Accompanying him were his daughter Sarah and her friend Clara Gurley, Francis Van Dyck, the chemistry tutor at Rutgers on his way to study in Germany for a year, James Neilson (a classmate of Paul Cook's) and Sheriff and Mrs. John D. Buckelew of Middlesex County. Mrs. M. A. Woodbury and her daughter Mary of Norwalk, Connecticut, who sailed on the same ship, later joined the party.[7] A romantic attachment soon developed between Miss Woodbury and young Neilson.

Cook managed Sarah's expenses only because he had a commission to write a series of articles on the trip for the *Cultivator and Country Gentleman*. His passage and some expenses were paid for by the state and in addition Seldon Scranton had persuaded fellow members of the survey's Board of Managers to contribute an extra amount of money so that Cook could stay longer. Cook's Rutgers colleagues helped by volunteering to take over his classes during his absence.[8]

The travelers had hoped to visit France first, but because the French under Napoleon III had just embarked upon their ill-fated war with Prussia, they visited Scandinavia instead. At a disadvantage because he did not speak Norwegian or Swedish, Cook nevertheless managed to steer his friends around the peninsula where he observed farming practices and inspected agricultural colleges. The visit was a great success in spite of the fact that they had to travel by horseback part of the time and occasionally wound up eating the coarse rye bread of the country for their supper and sleeping in the barn of a friendly farmer.[9] Fortunately they were an adventurous group—their pleasure not even dimmed by the "rather warm reception they received from the Norwegian fleas!"[10] A visit to the Norway Agricultural College at Aas left Cook marveling at the "vastly greater amount of work necessary to raise and secure their scanty crops."[11] In the northern latitudes the sun gave such little warmth that potatoes were killed by frost before the end of August and farmers could not make hay on the ground but had to cut it while still green and hang it on drying racks. In an experiment at the college designed to make the most of the meager supply of solar heat the fields were cleared of stones and underdrained with tiles made on the farm.[12] This raised the temperature of the soil sufficiently so that good crops of grains could be grown on soil which had formerly only produced birch trees and sour grass. For the most part farming conditions in the colder climate were so different from those in the temperate United States that Cook could not find much useful information to bring to the farmers back home. Nor did he find any hints on how to increase the small enrollments in the Rutgers agriculture program. The Norwegian school had the same problems in attracting students as did the American colleges. Only fifteen students were enrolled in the two-year course although it was designed for thirty-two students.

Cook found Germany to be a better source of transferable techniques and practices. At Halle he inspected the great sugar beet factory (a visit that doubtless had some influence on New Jersey's venture into the sugar beet business a few years later) while at the University of Bonn he saw the chemical laboratory and the university's two model farms at Poppelsdorf. One of these farms was easily cultivated because it was situated on very fertile soil. But even on the other, where the soil was so astringent that it had formerly been used for making alum, the agriculturists had been able to make a profit by extensive underdraining and a high level of manuring with the street dirt and night soil of the city of Bonn (which paid for the service of having it removed).[13] While in Germany Cook also visited brick kilns near Berlin where he found a new process of burning bricks that used one-quarter to one-third less fuel than traditional methods. Sketches and a detailed explanation were included in the 1870 survey report so that New Jersey brickmakers could adopt the new technique.[14] (It was in Berlin, also, that James Neilson and Mary Woodbury were married, he having proposed during the tour of Norway one afternoon when they had taken a little calash out for a drive.)[15]

In England Cook visited the famous experiment station at Rothamsted where he established connections which were to prove long lasting and of great benefit to Rutgers. At Rothamsted John Bennet Lawes, assisted by Dr. J. H. Gilbert, had been carrying on experiments with soils, crops, and fertilizers. Gilbert showed Cook the trial plots where wheat had been raised on the same plots for twenty-six years.[16] Some plots had been left unfertilized during the entire period while on others either farm dung, superphosphate of lime, or a mixture of alkalies, superphosphates, and ammonia salts had been consistently used. The completely unmanured plot yielded only fifteen bushels an acre compared with a thirty-nine and a half bushels or more per acre yield from the fertilized plots.

Cook found the Royal Agricultural College of Cirencester particularly valuable because of the thoroughness of its agricultural educational program and its farm where the students were required to observe but did not have to participate in the actual labor. In addition to visiting government supported experimental farms and colleges, Cook also made a habit of ferreting out the best privately owned farms in any area. In this way, in addition to the farms in Norway, Sweden, and Germany, he inspected dairy farms in Holland, vegetable farms in the east of England, and a farm near Exbridge where he saw a demonstration of a steam plough. His visits convinced him that the United States could learn much from European practices in the study and teaching of agriculture. In Europe, where for many centuries limited areas of land had been intensively cultivated, the need for conservation, enrichment, and scientific management of farm lands was firmly ingrained. In contrast, the United States farmers, deceived by an apparently inexhaustible supply of new land, had developed lazy and wasteful habits. When older farms were worn out they moved on to virgin soil, forgetting what their European forebears had passed on from generation to generation and not yet aware of what European scientists were discovering in experiment stations and model farms.

Useful and valuable as was his exploration of European agriculture, Cook's primary reason for visiting Europe was the study of drainage projects. In England he visited the Fens, the large marshy area on the east coast some eighty miles north of London. Here for centuries farmers had tried to protect their land from the tides of the North Sea and the floods of the rivers Nene, Ouse, and Witham, which drained 5,000 square miles of higher country to the west.[17] At the "Bedford Level" (named for Francis Russell, fourth Earl of Bedford, who had begun the drainage of thousands of acres between the Nene and the Ouse in the 1630s) Cook saw farms lying from five to fifteen feet below the normal high-water mark. Near Lynn he was impressed by a large drain in the Middle Bedford Level where problems with sluices had necessitated rebuilding in 1862. To cope with the nineteen-foot tide, the engineers had built a dam across the drainage ditch which kept out the tidal water altogether. The fresh water thus shut off from the sea was carried off by sixteen siphons, each three and a half feet in diameter, which lifted the fresh water twenty feet above low tide and spilled it out into a ditch below the dam.

In the Netherlands, Cook inspected the latest techniques of the Dutch engineers. The Dutch had been struggling with problems of flooding and drainage since prehistoric times. Their land had always been doubly imperiled by the great Rhine River which carried a burden of waters from inland rivers and streams to the sea and by the tides and storms of the North Sea which constantly eroded the low-lying coastal plain. At the time of Cook's visit 6,000 square miles of the Netherlands were below sea level and required protection from the seawaters. In some places tidal sluices built into man-made dikes were opened at low tide to allow surface rainwater to run out and closed on the incoming tides to keep out the seawater. In other locations ground water had to be pumped up (sometimes more than twenty feet) before it could run off into the sea. The effort to keep the sea out was so great that an entire department of the government and a special corps of engineers was maintained for the purpose. Only fifteen years earlier the Dutch had finished reclaiming thousands of acres lying between Amsterdam and Leyden. This land had been lost to the sea three centuries before in a great storm that burst the dikes and dams and flooded a large part of North Holland.

In Cook's survey report on the engineering marvels of the pumps, dams, and dikes in England and the Netherlands, he included descriptions of farms and dairies that were flourishing on lands reclaimed from sea or swamp. His report persuaded New Jersey legislators that their own swamps might become as productive as the English or Dutch and they passed an act providing for the drainage of marshy lands.[18] With customary caution, the legislature did not go so far as to provide for any public money to underwrite the effort. All financing and initiative were to be left to private landowners along the river banks and in the marshlands. On petition from owners of these lands, the Board of Managers of the Geological Survey was to decide if the project was in the public interest and if so would authorize drainage surveys and plans. The plans then had to be approved by the State Supreme Court and three commissioners appointed to superintend and carry out the proposal and collect money to pay expenses. Using this procedure the Great Meadow along the Pequest River in Warren County was successfully drained. In 1871 landowners along the Passaic River between Chatham and Little Falls and between Chatham and

Amos Eaton in 1841.
Rensselaer Polytechnic Institute

Albany Academy.   *From* Semi-Centennial Albany Academy (*1863*)

The Cook family home in East Hanover, New Jersey.   *Wynkoop Kiersted, Jr.*

Rutgers College, circa 1859.   *Rutgers University*

George H. Cook, circa 1860.
Rutgers University

William Campbell. *Rutgers University*   David Murray. *Rutgers University*

Water Works, Westons Mills, New Brunswick, circa 1870.
From New Historical Atlas of Middlesex County, *1876*

Marl pits near Mullica Hill, Gloucester County, New Jersey.
From Annual Report of the New Jersey Geological Survey for 1854

Raising or mining buried cedar timber.

Geology of Cape May, New Jersey, 1857

New Brunswick, 1870.

Rutgers University

Van Nest Hall as it was when Cook was teaching at Rutgers.   *Rutgers University*

Old Queens, Rutgers College, 1862.   *Rutgers University*

"Riverstede," now known as Demarest House.   *Rutgers University*

The College farmhouse and pond as they were when the Cooks lived there.
Rutgers University

Paul Cook, 1865. *Rutgers University*

Robert Cook, 1881. *Rutgers University*

Anne B. Cook (left) with two
friends, 1880.   *Rutgers University*

Sarah Cook Williamson, circa 1875.
Rutgers University

Geological Hall.   *Rutgers University*

The Mannington mastodon obtained for the Museum by Cook in 1870.
Rutgers University

Edward Bowser. *Rutgers University*

Cornelius Clarkson Vermeule.
Rutgers University

John Smock. *Rutgers University*

George Cook, 1868. *Rutgers University*

A portion of the original Atlas Sheet #3, issued by the New Jersey Geological Survey in 1884, an early product of the topographic survey. The area near Newfoundland is shown, with 20′ contours, place names, all streets, and occasional marked elevations. Full size.

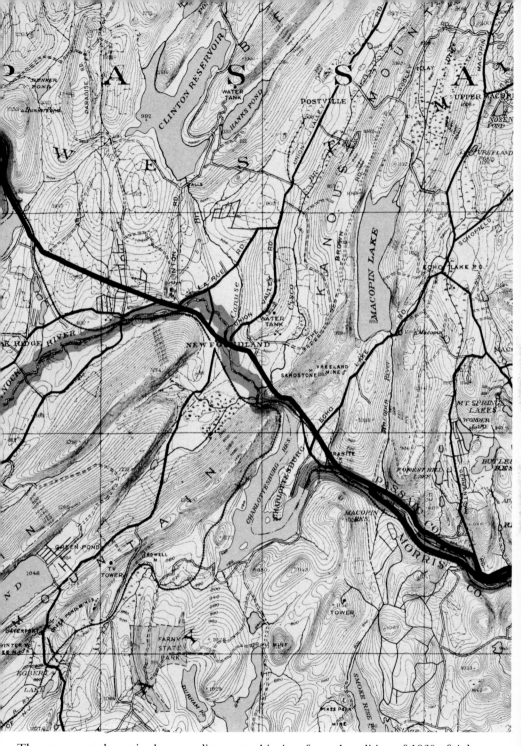

The same area shown in the preceding map, this time from the edition of 1960 of Atlas Sheet #22. Although culture has been updated, the old contour lines are still considered accurate. The scale of each map is 1 mi./inch.

New Jersey Bureau of Geology and Topography

New Jersey Hall. *Rutgers University*

A laboratory in New Jersey Hall. *Rutgers University*

George Cook about 1875.
Rutgers University

Mary Thomas Cook in later life.
Margaret Cook Thomson

The Cook house on Bleeker place.   *Rutgers University*

Queens campus from Hamilton Street as it looked in the 1880s.
Rutgers University

Millington began proceedings and plans were later developed for the drainage of Bear Swamp near Trenton.[19] But these later schemes did not materialize. Along the Hackensack and Passaic rivers the land was divided into small tracts and few landowners or groups of owners were wealthy enough to undertake the project. Some did not even want their tidal meadows drained and there was in addition considerable opposition from millowners.[20] Four dams on the Passaic within three miles of the town of Chatham provided water power for several mills. But they backed up the flow of water for twelve miles upstream and caused recurrent flooding problems for the farmers. These dams would have had to be destroyed or altered if the drainage proposals were approved. An editorial in the *New Jersey Journal* explained that the failure to support drainage was "partly traditional prejudice, partly Jersey fogyism, but mostly an apprehension that undue advantage would be taken by the proprietors of a general franchise for improving the meadows. . . ."[21]

In the years that followed a great deal of Cook's time was spent in the promotion, survey, and planning for the drainage of wetlands. He had little success; and difficulties with tidal marshes and rivers in flood continued to plague the state. Cook's knowledge of drainage, however, established him as an expert and led to increased demands on his time. Requests for advice meant more letters to be answered or talks to be given. One group interested in drainage of wetlands was the American Public Health Association, which concentrated on the relationship between wetlands and disease. One year Cook presented a paper to the group on how drainage would affect the wetlands of Orange County, New York, and Sussex County, New Jersey.[22]

While efforts to initiate drainage projects were for the most part unsuccessful, another of Cook's attempts to improve the economy was more enthusiastically received. In 1869 he reported that the clays of Woodbridge, South Amboy, and Trenton had been misused; the beds depleted to manufacture crude and coarse products that could have been made of a lower grade of clay. Cook feared that the fine clay was in danger of disappearing before its rare qualities were understood while at the same time imported clays of lesser purity were being sold for four times as much. Thanks to the survey's investigations the true worth of the New Jersey clays was recognized.

In 1872 Cook recommended that the northern boundary of the state be resurveyed. First established in 1772 as a straight line from a point at 41° north latitude on the west bank of the Hudson River to the point where the Machockermack (or Neversink) River empties into the

Delaware, and marked by a series of stone monuments, the line had been neglected over the years and many monuments had disappeared. The task of resurveying had been undertaken by the Kitchell survey but had not been carried through.

Bowser, with two Rutgers engineering students, began the new survey in 1872. The previous year the western terminus and the direction and length of the line had been determined by the United States Coast Survey whose engineers found the old border to be inaccurate, especially through the center of the state. The deviation, due to deficiencies in the old instruments, was 2,415 feet south of the Great Circle Arc at the 26th milestone at Greenwood Lake. There was a variation of two degrees in the old surveyor's instruments and the magnetic iron ore in the Highlands upset the surveyor's magnetic compasses.[23] Bowser was able to borrow an excellent theodolite from the U. S. Coast Survey which insured a much greater degree of accuracy. After the survey of the border was complete Cook recommended that joint action with New York State be taken to find the true line, set new monuments, and establish legal control over them.[24] In 1882, however, after further study by a commission of which Cook was a member, the two states decided to accept the 1774 line officially and set up new markers.[25]

One of the most important of the survey's public services was the investigation of water supply. Cook's interest in water sources had begun soon after his arrival in New Brunswick when he made analyses of the water of local wells. Later he was instrumental in the establishment of a municipal water works. The 1868 *Geology of New Jersey* included a short chapter on water supply with analyses of various river and well waters and the observation that river waters were purer than wells in most cities and towns. Cook wrote at that time that the resources of the survey were not then sufficient to carry out this important investigation. By the 1870s anxiety about the purity of private wells in towns and cities had increased. Contaminated by the filth absorbed by rainwater as it sank into the ground, the inability of cesspools to dispose of waste, and the lack of adequate garbage disposal, impure wells developed offensive smells, sometimes caused sickness and death, and eventually had to be abandoned.[26] Shore communities and the northern towns and cities faced the biggest problems. Along the coast people had traditionally made crude wells by sinking a barrel in the sand and then removing the sand from the inside of the cask. This allowed water to seep into the barrel. No bucket or pump was necessary and no cover was customarily used. As long as the population remained small this worked well enough but as more people moved in to the shore areas illness and death from contaminated water had been increasing and a new source of water was obviously needed. The alternatives were cisterns, pumping water from inland sources, or artesian wells. Seventeen years before in Atlantic City a 185-foot artesian well had been sunk but it reached salt water and had to be abandoned. In 1874 the Atlantic City Gas and Water Company had more luck, hitting fresh water in one well at ninety feet and at 118 feet in another. Cook was eventually to make possible extensive use of artesian wells because of his work on the geological strata of shore areas, but in 1875, although he cautiously advised the use of artesian wells for fighting fires, he advocated that for drinking purposes Atlantic City make greater use of cisterns or water piped from Absecon Creek.[27]

Water for Newark and Jersey City was drawn from the Passaic River only thirteen miles below where Paterson discharged all its sewage into the river. The Passaic also received all the drainage from the thickly settled region south of Paterson. A large section of the 1876 survey report concentrated on the exploration of new water sources for the state's northeastern cities and it was accompanied by a map of the Passaic drainage basin showing lakes and sites which could be developed for storage reservoirs.

Another task was allotted to the survey when plans were begun for the great 1876 Centennial Exposition in Philadelphia. The New Jersey commissioners decided that a special exhibit of New Jersey geology should be prepared. Accordingly, in the summer of 1875 John Smock, with two student helpers, Edward Reiley and Robert Meeker, set out to collect specimens. They visited more than five hundred localities, including more than one hundred iron mines. By the time they finished late that fall they had collected more than two hundred specimens of rocks, ores, minerals, soils, fertilizers, building stones, clays, and sands.[28]

Their collecting expeditions were beset with many difficulties, principally because of the weight of the boxes of rocks and minerals. They had started out with a wagon and one horse, but Smock, a kind-hearted man, was worried: "Our horse is too light for these hills. We walk much of the way," he wrote to Cook. "Everyone tells us that we shall injure him by this work . . . he looks thin and somewhat jaded out. And I hate to see so nice a horse worn out by this kind of work."[29] Fortunately, Cook approved a change and they were soon speeding through the hills behind a team of two horses.[30] Then Smock became concerned because the rapid pace made it difficult for him properly to observe the geological characteristics of the landscape.[31]

Although the problem of the tired horse had been taken care of, the weight of the rocks were often too heavy for the wagon. One day the hub of the back wheel split and two or three times the irons about the tongue gave way. In addition, the harness was worn and kept breaking. Much time had to be taken for repairs.[32] Smock hoped that the Centennial Commission would pay him for the collecting because he thought that it might pay more than the survey but, he wrote: "I don't want to embarrass you in any way or cause extravagance."[33] (Extravagance was a cardinal sin and always to be avoided so as to insure continued support for the survey from the legislature.)

As the boxes of minerals were collected, Smock took them to the nearest railroad station and shipped them back to Cook. Thirty-seven boxes of zinc ores and other rocks and minerals were sent from Franklin and Ogdensburg, three from Warwick, and three from Newfoundland.[34] Cook also persuaded various mine, marl pit, and clay bed owners to send samples of their products. Thhe owners were glad to oblige as this would insure free advertising for them when the specimens were identified in the exhibit.

The survey not only collected specimens for its own exhibit but also contributed to the displays of the Smithsonian Institution, the New Jersey Agricultural Society, and the United States Department of Agriculture. The packing and shipping of all these collections meant a considerable amount of tedious work for Cook that became particularly frustrating the day he found that he had sent the specimens for the Department of Agriculture to Philadelphia just before instructions arrived directing him to send them to Washington.

For the survey exhibit Cook had silk for the display cases especially made in the Paterson silk mills and he went down to Philadelphia himself to arrange the specimens. His efforts were rewarded when the Centennial Exhibition opened and awards were given out. The survey exhibit received a first place award.[35] The critique read:

Large, well selected and well arranged collection showing (1) all the rocks of the various formations known in New Jersey, including the potters clay and the green sand; (2) the ores of iron and zinc, and the products of their metallurgical treatment; (3) the building stones; (4) a fine collection of rare crystalline minerals of the State; (5) plans illustrating the mode of occurrence of the magnetic iron ores, a model of the Franklin Furnace zinc mine, and the geological maps published by the State Survey: the whole giving a very complete and most instructive view of the scientific and economic geology of New Jersey.[36]

The New Jersey Commissioners were delighted. Their report declared, "The Geological Survey alone contained enough of representative wealth to impart distinction to this state enjoyed by no other in that specialty. Our wonderful mineral resources, fertilizers, soils and so forth are displayed by the distinguished state geologist, Professor George H. Cook, in a manner that elicited highest praise from every quarter."[37] After the exhibit the specimens from the survey and the New Jersey agricultural displays were given to the New Jersey State Museum on the third floor of the State House in Trenton. Other specimen collections were sent to Princeton, the Trenton Normal School, and Rutgers.

Although the preparation of an exhibit for the Centennial slowed up the regular work of the survey, during the years 1869 to 1871 the reports included information on soils, zinc and iron ores, peat, fertilizers, infusorial earth, brickmaking, the movement of sand dunes, limestone, road-building materials, building stones, marble quarries, slate, and graphite. The survey's work on fertilizers dealt primarily with the greensand marls. Much of the time of the chemist, Edwin Bogardus, was spent in analyzing samples of marl sent in by owners of marl pits and soil and ore samples.

The survey continually produced maps of various kinds. In 1873 Cook began a resurvey of the northern boundary line and a map illustrating this accompanied the report of 1874. In 1873 a geological map of the iron ore and limestone districts was published and some work was begun in Warren County in surveying and leveling for the purpose of making a topographic map of the county in which elevation and outline of hills and mountains and lines of drainage would be shown by contour lines. A topographical survey of the Middlesex clay beds was also begun in 1874. In 1876 a map of the Passaic watershed was made on a scale of two miles to an inch. A map prepared especially for the Centennial on a scale of six miles to the inch showed the townships of the state, canals, railroads, and nearly all the county roads.

Cook found that more and more of his time had to be spent in administrative duties—arranging and directing the work on the clay beds, mines, surveys, and maps or in answering letters of inquiry. He wrote: "Much valuable time in laboratory and office was necessarily consumed in this way—such is the proper consequence of attempting to answer inquiries of intelligent and interested men."[38]

At the same time that Cook had to spend so much time with the work of the survey, the development of the college farm also made excessive demands. In 1870 he returned to New Brunswick from his trip to Europe convinced that the farm should eventually become an agricultural experiment station like those he had seen in Europe. He knew this could not be done in a short time, but he had learned from his experience with the geological survey that patience and perseverance might eventually enable him to achieve the goals he sought. As a student yearbook later recognized, "If baffled one year and in one way, he tries another year and in another way . . . and at the arrival of some opportune moment for which he had patiently waited and helped to create, he comes smiling to the surface with the favorite project, long after some others supposed they were abandoned. . . ."[39]

Some conservative citizens of New Jersey became suspicious that their tax money was being used for improvements at the farm and Campbell found it necessary to allay their suspicions by assuring them that no state or federal money had been used by the college or farm for anything but professors' salaries.[40] The lack of state support was not due to a lack of desire on the part of the trustees, however, and the Scientific School report for 1876 included a plea for state money introduced by a brief note on the successful experiment stations in Europe as well as the one in Connecticut. Cook argued that experiment stations were necessary for studies of fertilizers, feeding of stock, and field trials of special crops like sugar beets. Many states, including Maryland, Maine, Massachusetts, Pennsylvania, Delaware, Virginia, and Connecticut had given money to support their land-grant schools and farms—it was time for New Jersey to do likewise.[41] He managed to have a bill introduced in the legislature which would provide for the establishment of an experiment station but, he reported at a meeting of the Horticultural Society of New Jersey, "the legislators fairly laughed at the idea."[42]

While Cook waited and took every opportunity to argue the need for an experimental station, he concentrated on bringing the college farm up to the standards of an average well-run farm. It was 1874 before the scrub undergrowth had been cleared off, tile drains installed in the swampy field, fences and a farm road built, and some farm buildings repaired. No sooner had these improvements been carried out than it became apparent that the hundred-year-old Dutch style barn would have to be torn down. The roof was so leaky that rain damaged the hay and grain and so rickety that no one could get up on it to make repairs. The Board of Trustees had already spent $50,000 from its income and endowment and no extra money could be expected from the state.[43] Even though times were bad, the only hope was to appeal to the friends of the farm for help. This brought in $3,323 (Cook himself subscribed $250); enough to build a new barn and move and repair the plough house, the piggery, a carriage house, poultry houses, and a few other out-buildings.[44]

Without support from government funds it was impossible for the farm to operate as a full-fledged experimental farm. Within the limits set by poverty, however, Cook was able to begin some useful experiments and field trials and make the farm a practical, flexible, and effective means of encouraging scientific farming in New Jersey. Except for the annual reports of the school and farm and Cook's county lectures (no longer mandated in every county after 1873 but delivered only where requested), everything was done informally. The Board of Visitors of the Scientific School and the State Board of Agriculture (after its formation in 1872) visited the farm twice a year; the State Grange periodically sent a committee of inspection; and county and local farmers' clubs turned up now and then. In addition, individual farmers and other interested people came to see what was going on. Theodore West, manager of the farm from 1874 to 1886, was there to welcome visitors at any time and Cook, who by that time had moved his family to a house on Bleecker Street (now Voorhees Mall) arranged to be at the farm every Wednesday afternoon.

One of the visitors was Professor Alexander Hogg of the Alabama Agricultural College. Cook did not happen to be there when Hogg arrived and Bogardus and West took the visitor around. "The Professor," reported Bogardus, "was much pleased and full of questions relative to the details of the farm. He says they regard you south as the Father of Agriculture in America. . . ."[45]

Written queries sometimes came from out of state. O. H. Gallup from Greeley, Colorado, wrote to ask for details on Cook's experiments with artificial fertilizers on corn which he had read about in the *Fruit Recorder*.[46] Most of the questions came from New Jersey farmers who asked advice on whether the application of Paris green to plants in blossom would poison the fruit, how to raise sugar beets, applying lime to a stiff clay soil, scald on cranberries, the performance of a reciprocating screw mower, new varieties of seeds and crops, breeds of cattle, crop rotation, and a hundred other things.[47] To a much greater extent than the college classroom, this kind of educational procedure used the farm and later the experiment station for direct education of working farmers as well as for the development of a professional coterie of trained agriculturists and substantive material for textbooks and monographs. In a sense it was true "extension" education and embodied the same philosophy and kind of subject matter that was later to become formalized as extension.

Fertilizer trials with greensand marl started in 1866 and field trials of the effects of fertilizers on "Indian corn" begun in 1872 were two of the early studies made at the farm.[48] The annual reports provided analyses of fertilizers and recommendations for its use. More extensive fertilizer analyses began in 1872 under the aegis of the State Board of Agriculture.[49] Unexciting as it now seems, the initiation of fertilizer analysis in the 1870s was the first and a most important contribution of chemistry to the farmer. For years unregulated and unscrupulous merchants had offered completely worthless or highly adulterated fertilizers accompanied by extravagant claims of miraculous results. The credulous farmer bought, and when he did not achieve favorable results he became disillusioned with all fertilizers. In 1853 Samuel Johnson, a pioneer in the analysis of fertilizers in the United States, had published an article on the value of specific fertilizers. One of the farmers' principal problems was the lack of a standard of comparison which could be used to determine the relative value of different fertilizers. Johnson adopted a method developed by Julius Stoeckhardt of Darmstadt in which fertilizers were evaluated in the same way as mineral ores—by giving monetary values to each ingredient. Cook enthusiastically approved of this system and praised Johnson for his "full and fearless reports on the worthless manures which are so common in the market."[50] During the same period in the 1850s, Cook's studies on the greensand marl had contributed to the accumulation of information about fertilizers.

Fertilizer testing and field trials were the best known experiments taking place on the college farm, but Cook also carried on important studies with the dairy herd which had been acquired primarily for economic reasons. In 1871 Cook signed a contract with Patrick Healy of New Brunswick and in 1872 with Alexander S. Conover to sell them milk from the college farm for distribution and resale.[51] Production records were published in Cook's report for 1871 and sporadically thereafter.[52]

Over the many years that Cook was involved with the farmers in New Jersey, there was remarkably little resentment of him or his advice. Even the Grange, so much against agricultural colleges in other states, seems to have refrained from attack in New Jersey. One reason for Cook's acceptance was undoubtedly the fact that he was identified so clearly with the farming community. He had been raised on a New Jersey farm and his brothers, Henry, Matthias, and David, continued to farm in Hanover. In 1854, soon after he returned to New Jersey, he had become involved in an effort to establish a state agricultural society and he had kept up his friendships with farmers as he traveled around the state studying soils and natural fertilizers for the Geological Survey. But most of all it was his unassuming personality and his genuine respect for the working farmer that made him so popular. His academic honors and advancement did not make him a snob—unlike Henry McCandless who served for a time as professor of agriculture at Cornell. Professor McCandless roused the ire and disgust of the farmers because of his habit of wearing kid gloves when visiting farms and his refusal to dirty his hands or gloves by touching farm implements.[53]

The farmers' acceptance of Cook and his work, however, was not translated into financial support by the state government and the hopelessness of getting more support from the state led Cook to look to the federal government for help. At the same time, leaders in agricultural education across the country were beginning to organize. In 1871 a group calling itself the Friends of Agricultural Education had met in Chicago. Rutgers was not represented but out of the meeting came the decision to form a committee for the purpose of persuading Congress and the state legislatures to establish experiment stations and Cook was named to the committee as the representative for New Jersey. The next year he led a New Jersey delegation to a National Agricultural Convention in Washington called by Frederick Watts, U. S. Commissioner of Agriculture. With him went General N. N. Halsted and Amos Clark from the State Agricultural Society and former Governor Theodore Randolph. For Cook it was the beginning of a lifelong involvement with agricultural education at the national level.

The convention turned out to be a forum for the unleashing of grievances by leaders of agricultural education throughout the nation.[54] Many felt that the terms of the Morrill Act of 1862 had done their states an injustice. Southerners complained that the five-year limitation for acceptance of the land-grant colleges caused problems because many had not sufficiently recovered from the effects of the Civil War to take the required actions within the five-year limit.[55] Others complained that Congress had refused to recognize some legislatures that had accepted the terms immediately after the surrender. Easterners had complaints also—their states contained no public land and they felt cheated because of the loss they incurred when they had to sell their scrip on the market at fifty to eighty cents an acre while more fortunate western or midwestern states that still had large acres of public land were able to get five or six dollars an acre. Some of the midwestern colleges were unhappy because they had chosen to keep some of the choice public land available to them in their states only to find that it was subject to a high rate of taxation.[56] So great was the dissension that a friend of Cook's, John H. Klippart, corresponding secretary of the Ohio State Board of Agriculture wrote, "I suspect that of his own accord Mr. Watts will never call another convention."[57] Klippart went on to say that he was nevertheless glad that one had been called because men who were involved in agricultural education throughout the nation had been given a chance to get to know one another and exchange opinions. It led to the formation of the American Association of Agriculture and Cook was named vice-president for New Jersey.

The Convention adopted a resolution encouraging all states to set up boards of agriculture and one calling for federally supported experiment stations. It was fifteen years before legislation supporting the latter was adopted. As soon as Cook returned to New Jersey he wrote a letter to Governor Joel Parker outlining the duties of state boards of agriculture in the eight states that already had them and urging the governor to recommend one for New Jersey.[58] He pointed out that agricultural societies, the Board of Managers of the Geological Survey, the state geologist, the Board of Visitors of the Scientific School or the trustees of Rutgers College had traditionally carried out the functions proper to such a board. Cook urged that the "large and growing interests of farming" receive more systematic and extensive attention.[59] Several times in the previous fifteen years animal epidemics of pleuropneumonia, glanders, and rinderpest had threatened the state's livestock. The absence of a state agency to deal with them had thrown the burden upon the State Agricultural Society and consequently there was general recognition that a state agency was necessary. Within three months—in an unprecedented burst of speed—the legislature had authorized the formation of a State Board of Agriculture. Unfortunately, the willingness to fund the Board did not match the prompt acceptance. As the secretary of the Connecticut Board commented: "While I congratulate you on the establishment of your board, I notice that you have limited the salary of the secretary at a sum below just compensation for efficient service."[60] This was mild criticism in view of the fact that New Jersey allowed $200 for the secretary of the Board and $100 for a clerk in comparison with Ohio which paid a full time secretary $2,500 and allowed $600 for a clerk.[61]

The miserly funding kept the Board from striking out toward any innovative or original goals; the most it could do was follow patterns set in other states. Like the Connecticut Board, the New Jersey Board directed its attention to administering controls on fertilizers. A law provided that all fertilizer sold in lots of over one hundred pounds had to be analyzed by the chemist of the Board. Edwin Bogardus was named to the post and received $15 for each analysis. He performed seventy-two between 1874 and 1880 when the Board relinquished this responsibility.[62] In comparison, the Connecticut legislature had appropriated $4,600 for the period 1875-76 and its Board had analyzed 160 samples during those years alone.[63]

Although the lack of financial support kept the New Jersey Board from achieving its greatest usefulness, those fertilizer analyses which were made were enthusiastically received by the farmers. As Carl Woodward pointed out in the *Development of Agriculture in New Jersey*, the Board also served to dignify the role of the farmer and provided farmers with a voice by which their ideas and needs could be made known, enabling them to increase their influence in the state.[64] The Board served as a clearing house for farmers' questions, arranged annual meetings at which lectures on agricultural subjects were delivered, and distributed information on farm matters.

The first Board, organized in September 1872 at the college farm, had fourteen members including the governor of New Jersey; Campbell; Smock, Cook, and George Atherton from Rutgers; William M. Force from the Board of Managers of the Geological Survey and Joseph Thompson from the Board of Visitors of the Scientific School.[65] Governor Joel Parker was elected president and George Cook secretary. He continued in this position until 1877. In 1875 Gus Newell made a strenuous but unsuccessful effort to get him a full-time assistant. Cook frequently addressed the annual meeting of the Board, speaking primarily on fertilizers and soils.[66]

The 1872 Washington National Agricultural Convention that had provided such an admirable springboard for the formation of the New Jersey State Board of Agriculture was less successful in the case of two other agricultural causes which it espoused: the establishment of federally supported experiment stations and the making of additional land grants to the original land-grant colleges. A bill drafted by a committee of the convention and introduced by Senator Morrill called for more public land or an equivalent in value to support the "National" colleges, as the land-grant schools were then called.[67] Unfortunately, Morrill's bill soon became entangled with a movement to supply federal aid to elementary schools in states with the highest rates of illiteracy. Because both plans depended upon public land for financial backing the two groups supporting them became rivals. Considerable opposition to any more grants of the public land developed in the 1870s because of the corruption and abuses of the speculators who had grabbed up the land scrip from original recipients. Many farmers' groups, especially in the Midwest, opposed further grants to the colleges for this reason.[68] They were joined by representatives of the old established classical and sectarian colleges. Much to the annoyance and surprise of Rutgers people, the president of Princeton College, James McCosh, led the effort to discredit the land-grant colleges.

In a speech to the National Education Association in 1873, McCosh proclaimed that the allotment of public land to the agricultural colleges gave them an unfair edge in competition with private institutions.[69] He urged that money from the sale of such lands be given only to elementary and secondary schools. President Charles W. Eliot of Harvard went further and opposed all federal grants for education on the grounds that such dependence upon federal handouts would demoralize and weaken the independence of the schools. When McCosh attacked the land-grant colleges for their failure to enroll a large number of students in their agricultural programs, he stirred up a flurry of agitation and debate. Because Cook had been active in Washington early in 1873 (spending a tiresome stint working for the passage of Morrill's bill), Regent John B. Bowman of Kentucky suggested that he should take up the gauntlet with McCosh. But that task fell to George Atherton, Rutgers professor of history, political economy, and constitutional law and the superintendent of the military program. Atherton was a much more abrasive and authoritative personality than Cook, whose method always was one of reason and pleasant persistence. At the 1873 meeting of the National Education Association McCosh, pursuing the attack, referred to Rutgers as the "excellent college at New Brunswick managed by a few Dutchmen."[70] He was joined by President Eliot of Harvard, who managed to see something humiliating in the spectacle of the supporters of the land-grant colleges asking for increased public support but not in his attempts to thwart them. Atherton, Read of Mississippi, Patterson of Kentucky, White of Cornell, and Orton of Ohio denied that the land-grant colleges should maintain a narrow scope and partisan purpose; insisted that they were training independent leaders and that therefore the number of practicing farmers among their graduates was irrelevant. Atherton emphasized the fact that agricultural courses in the colleges were but a part of the total program, which incorporated broad educational aims in engineering, mechanical arts, and the sciences related to them.

Ironically, at about the same time McCosh was opposing Rutgers, he was asking Cook to favor Princeton with a series of lectures on the geology of New Jersey.[71] After the series was completed, he told Cook that they were so pleased with his lectures that they would like to have him give two or three more. Little wonder that Campbell told the Board of Visitors that he was "surprised by the unexpected opposition" from Dr. McCosh.[72]

As a result of the accusations of McCosh and Eliot, Professor James Monroe of Oberlin, also questioning the educational worth of the land-grant colleges, persuaded Congress to launch an investigation. Cook appeared before the investigating committee on behalf of Rutgers. After a full investigation the committee concluded that the land-grant colleges should be commended and not vilified for their efforts.[73] "The committee," stated the report, "noted a sincere purpose and well-considered plan for meeting the letter and spirit of the law and an appropriate and highly effective development of applied science instruction and of public service contacts."[74] But further land grants were held up for many years. More effective than the opposition of the classical colleges in discontinuing land grants for the agricultural and mechanical colleges were the claims of such rivals as the freedmen, the backward states, the elementary schools, and the railroads.

Despite the fact that Rutgers was chronically underfunded and could have benefited by an injection of government aid for the Scientific School, the college showed substantial signs of strength and growth during the early seventies. In 1870 the college celebrated the centennial of its founding under the mistaken impression that a charter dated 1770 was the original. Actually, a charter had been granted in 1766, but the original had been lost and its existence had faded from memory. To commemorate the centennial, President Campbell and the trustees embarked upon another money-raising venture which eventually netted more than $120,000.[75] The disposition of the fund clearly demonstrated the commitment of the college to the support of the Scientific School. Most of the money was used for the construction of Geological Hall and for the establishment of two new professorships in science. Geological Hall opened in 1872. Its most dramatic feature was a museum, a high-ceilinged room on the second floor with a balcony around four sides. Here was space for the ever-growing collections of the Natural History Society, including a seventy-four-pound mass of native copper from Somerville, New Jersey, a collection of 1,400 species of shells, mounted and catalogued by G. W. Tryon of the Academy of Natural Sciences in Philadelphia, and the bones of the Mannington Mastodon.[76] Several years earlier the tusks of the mastodon had been found by a farmer digging in his field near Mannington in Salem County, but they had disintegrated after exposure to the air. The next owner of the farm found the skull, vertebrae, shoulder blades, and pelvis buried under six to eight feet of earth. For several years Cook made an effort to find funds to mount the skeleton but this was not done until after his death. In the meantime the bones had to be kept from disintegrating and Joseph Leidy advised him that he had found that soaking the bones in linseed oil did well although he thought paraffin would prevent decomposition. Other exhibits continued to come in from alumni and friends. Mary Cook's cousin, John Halsey, working for the U. S. State Department in China, promised to send geological specimens from there; farmers in the marl country were always on the lookout for fossils for Rutgers; and Cook and other European travelers brought back specimens.

The two new professorships were established in mining and metallurgy and in analytic chemistry. The addition of a professor of analytic chemistry was necessary in order to relieve Cook of some of his duties. He was beginning to find it impossible to give the necessary time to the training of students in the analytical laboratory. John Smock was appointed professor of mining and metallurgy and given leave to spend two years in Germany at his own expense to prepare himself while the post in analytic chemistry went to Francis Cuyler Van Dyck, also a Rutgers College graduate, who had done postgraduate work in the Scientific School and had served at the college as a tutor in chemistry. He too was given permission to study in Europe at his own expense.

Thus for a time, following Cook's example and doubtless at his urging, a significant portion of the science faculty of the college was traveling and studying in Europe. Isaac Hasbrouck of the class of 1865, who had been a tutor in mathematics and was to become professor of mathematics, and T. Sandford Doolittle, professor of rhetoric, logic, and mental philosophy also made the trip. They all engaged in a variety of pursuits—from informal visits to laboratories of great repute to examine equipment and methods to formal matriculation in a European university. Hasbrouck wrote Cook that he had arrived in Vienna when the university was closed and all the professors off to the country with their families. The only person there was a janitor who had a blue coat with brass buttons but no key. After waiting around for two days Hasbrouck finally located a private assistant of one of the professors who let him into the drafting rooms where he learned something of the style of teaching, inspected some fine topographical drawings, and saw a "set of instruments for field work which cracked the tenth commandment."[77] After visiting universities in Dresden, Zurich, Munich, and Berlin, Hasbrouck settled down in Paris for the remainder of the winter to study mathematics at the Sorbonne.[78] His studies convinced him that the engineering schools in the United States were as good as those in Europe and that mechanical and topographical drawing were not well taught at the Sorbonne. Van Dyck visited universities and laboratories in twelve cities looking for "peculiarities that may be useful to us." He wrote, "There is no difficulty in getting the opinion of people over here. They run down each other, and bewail the backwardness of America in science without reserve. . . . The only American book I have heard heartily praised were your report [*The Geology of New Jersey*] and Johnson's 'How Crops Grow.'"[79] The European trips and studies of Rutgers faculty members followed a pattern common to most of the outstanding scientists and scholars of the nineteenth century. It insured Rutgers College of a faculty that was in the mainstream of scientific education.

In 1870 student enrollment at Rutgers reached a new high. While Cook was in Europe, David Murray wrote him a cheerful letter reporting that the entering class had about forty-five classical and twenty-six or twenty-seven scientific students—"a greater number than were in all the classes six years ago."[80] In addition to the full-time students, the college encouraged part-time and postgraduate students who were given certificates upon completion of a course.[81] This kind of practical instruction to college graduates had been provided upon demand since the Scientific School opened with Van Dyck as its first postgraduate student in chemistry. The instruction, however, was not necessarily more advanced than what was taught in undergraduate courses, but rather a new subject which the student had not had time to include during his regular course.

In 1871 an effort was made to raise admissions standards for students in the Scientific School. Campbell took the position that scientific education could not achieve its full potential until entrance requirements were the same for Scientific School students as they were for those in the classical course of study. In the years before general testing of educational aptitude or achievement, standards for admission were based solely on the courses applicants had studied in secondary school. At Rutgers Scientific School the faculty first required courses in geography, arithmetic, algebra to quadratics, geography and English grammar.[82] A few years later spelling, three books in plane geometry, and physical geography were added, then United States history, more algebra, and the whole of plane geometry. More important for the strengthening of the Scientific School curriculum was the lengthening in 1871 of the course to four years. This provided more time for laboratory work, for field work in surveying and engineering, and for general courses.[83] Thus the faculty and trustees reinforced their original insistence that a land-grant college should include broad basic courses in both sciences and the liberal arts. Student demand for the engineering and chemistry programs continued to exceed that for agriculture. In 1873, possibly in response to the pressure from President McCosh and the other opponents of the land-grant colleges, Rutgers added a course entitled "Lectures on Agriculture at the Farm" to the junior year and included a section on the care and management of domestic animals to the senior course in animal physiology.[84]

Emboldened by the increase in students and the improvement in the Scientific School curriculum, the trustees improved and renovated portions of Old Queens, building a new stairway, laying new floors, painting the woodwork and the outside of the buildings, and making three new recitation rooms in the east wing. A bequest from Sophia Astley Kirkpatrick added a fine chapel to the college buildings.[85]

In 1876 Cook was given permission by the Board of Trustees to hire an assistant in the teaching of chemistry on condition that he paid the man's salary himself. Cook had been severely ill with a respiratory infection earlier that year and had written to the Board of Trustees reminding them that his original appointment had been as professor of chemistry and natural history only. He had undertaken the professorship of agriculture because no one else could be found. "The duties of that Professorship," he wrote, "were undefined, difficult, perplexing and wearing, but I have discharged them to the best of my ability, and while they have not satisfied me I trust they have kept the College from unfriendly criticism."[86]

Cook hired Henry Prentiss Armsby, a graduate of the Worcester Industrial Institute and the Sheffield Scientific Institute, who came with enthusiastic recommendations from Samuel W. Johnson, "He is a good student, analyst and a most excellent man," wrote Johnson.[87] Armsby had spent a year in Germany where he concentrated on agricultural chemistry and Cook had been favorably impressed by a paper he had read at the Hartford meeting of the American Association for the Advancement of Science. Cook wrote to Armsby, "the trial still to be made is whether you will like the teaching of college classes. There is a good deal of difference in this respect, some liking it very much while it is distasteful to others. The teaching required will be mainly in chemistry—possibly a class in physiology. The pay would be $1,000."[88] In the absence of any evidence to the contrary, we must assume that the $1,000 came out of Cook's Rutgers salary, by that time up to $3,000. He was, of course, also earning $1,000 as state geologist and various extra sums from consultation fees. With Cook's responsibilities to the state in connection with the Geological Survey, the Scientific School and college farm, it may have been difficult for him to draw the line as to what he should include in the responsibilities of the state related positions and what services he could legitimately charge for. Most people who worked with him felt that he erred considerably on the side of not receiving or seeking enough money for his various services. For example, a farmer with a bull whose stud fees were falling below expectations wrote that he would appreciate it if Cook would let the situation be known and, "if I can make anything out of the matter, I will see that you are paid for acting on these suggestions or proposing any better ones. You can't work for the glory of the Country only. . . ."[89] There is no indication that Cook took him up on his offer and it would be surprising if he had; his tendency was to lean over backwards in such situations. He apparently never sent bills for his analyses of ores—his clients sent him what they wanted to. Many thought that he was being insufficiently paid for his services as state geologist. In 1874, when Augustus W. Cutler was a New Jersey state senator from Morris County, he tried to raise the salary of the state geologist to $3,000 and wrote to Cook ahead of time to caution him not to try to prevent it: "[Several senators] said they would favor it as it was simply a matter of justice to you. I expect, of course, you will shake your head and my object in writing you *now* is to apprise you of my intention in order that if you hear of it in any way you will not attempt to stop it."[90]

Some of Cook's consultant work was done for the New Jersey Zinc Company and for the Ringwood Mines of Abram Hewitt. He continued to seek improved methods for mining and industry and patented a process for the manufacture of zinc which he hoped to sell to some one for a good price.[91] None of this extra income was sufficient to make him independently wealthy and he had the reputation of putting the money he earned for consultations into the collection plate at church the following Sunday.[92] He also tended to be very generous in his charitable donations, subscribing $400 for a new parsonage at the Second Reformed Church in 1871 as well as the $250 to the fund to build and renovate barns and outbuildings on the college farm.[93] Cook also continued to buy specimens for the college museum when they were offered. Sometimes he was reimbursed for these expenditures by the trustees or alumni. It was not that he did not appreciate the advantages of having money to spare. Especially as he got older he began to look for an investment in a mine or some other enterprise that would bring him enough money to retire from teaching and concentrate on the survey and his geological research.

In 1875 he went to Colorado with William Gurley to inspect a silver mine.[94] They traveled by train to Denver and fifty miles beyond Denver to the mine by various kinds of horse-drawn vehicles. Cook was fascinated crossing the plains where he saw buffalo, antelopes, prairie dogs, owls, and where the train passed near a place where they told him twenty-seven Indians had shortly before been killed. In one of the telegraph offices on the route he saw the skull and crossbones of an Indian nailed over his door—an Indian killed by the operator during an attack on the telegraph office. As the train traveled through the plains, the passengers could see the campfires of emigrant camps and the emigrant wagons as they crossed the plains. One day they had the company of a young man who was said to have killed more men than he had fingers and toes. For Cook, these things all gave a reality to the stories of western life that he had not fully appreciated before. He thought that he could tell where northerners had settled because the houses were all painted, there were schoolhouses and churches and "everything shows an attempt to be comfortable," whereas where southerners settled all was very slovenly.[95] One reason that a fortune would have been welcome was that by 1876 it was fairly clear that Anne and Emma were not going to marry and thus he would have to find a way to provide for them. Sarah had been married in 1874 to Dr. Nicholas Williamson, the son of Rutgers trustee James Williamson of New Brunswick who was a partner of James Bishop in his importing business. Sarah and Nicholas settled in a house on George Street. Paul Cook continued to work for Peter Cooper in Brrooklyn until he announced his engagement to Hettie (Esther) Gurley, the younger daughter of William Gurley. The union pleased the two old friends immeasurably. Paul was just the upstanding, steady kind of young man to whom a fond father would like to entrust his daughter. After the engagement was announced Gurley wrote that he hoped that Paul would come to work in his company as he was fifty-three years old, had a large property, and thought that Hettie's interests should be represented. Besides, he would like to have her live nearby.[96]

Cook continued his many interests in the church and community.[97] His piety, probity and incredible capacity for work, far from intimidating people, seems to have encouraged friends of all ages and conditions. Clara Gurley, having been exposed to his work habits during the European trip in 1870, wrote with affection the following year, "I have been wishing to write to you for ever so long. . . . You cannot appreciate what a very good effect your example has had upon me, not in the matter of early rising—but in being constantly busy about something. I want a good talk with you on various subjects, and when I come to visit I do hope you will be able to make a little time to give me a short lecture at least."[98]

Although his remaining years were to bring more honors, the years between 1870 and 1876 were in many ways very happy ones for Cook. His family was growing up; he had achieved the respect and support of the state legislature for the geological survey; and he was beginning to see faint signs that more support would be forthcoming for the Scientific School and the experimental farm.

9

1876-1880
Glacial Geology and
Applied Agriculture

"My dear Anne," wrote Cook to his daughter on Sunday, July 14, in the year 1878,

I am here with the Rhone glacier, which is a great ice falls, right in front of my window and not more than a mile away. It is two or three times as wide as the Raritan and as high as the Bound Brook Mountain. It looks white like snow, but it is full of deep cracks which are wide open and you can see into them—the ice there is a delicate blue. The upper half of the glacier is too steep for anyone to think of climbing . . . but the lower half is more sloping and smooth so that it can be walked on by being careful. It is not smooth and slippery like winter ice but is dirty or else covered with stones.[1]

Cook's trip to see the glacier became possible when he was appointed an official commissioner from New Jersey for the Paris Exposition of 1878.[2] As a commissioner (an appointment his friends in Congress Augustus Cutler, Abram Hewitt, and Thomas Dudley had helped him to get) he had to set up the geological exhibition in the United States section, but once this was done he was free to visit the glaciers in Switzerland. For some time he had been wanting to inspect them in person. After his brief consideration of the drift in the 1868 *Geology of New Jersey* he had made a few sporadic investigations in New Jersey and Long Island but his decision to concentrate on economic geology during the early 1870s kept him from doing any extensive field work until 1877.[3]

The years of the 1860s and 1870s were important ones in the development of theories of glaciation. Thomas Jamieson and Archibald Geikie published studies of the drift in Scotland which supported Agassiz's theory of a continental ice sheet; and in 1871 Grove Karl

Gilbert recognized that when the pattern of distribution of the hills and ridges of gravel and rocks in Illinois was traced on a map, the resultant line represented the southernmost extension of the terminal moraine of a continental ice sheet in North America. Within the next twelve years geologists in all northern states were out in the field mapping the moraine lines. Warren Upham in New England, Henry Carvill Lewis and George Frederick Wright in Ohio, Indiana, and Illinois, Thomas C. Chamberlin in Wisconsin, and Cook and Smock in New Jersey were among the best known of the geologists who worked on the problem. The tracing of the terminal moraine exemplifies the manner in which the patient work of many geologists in several places over a number of years may contribute to the advance of geological knowledge.[4] By 1883 Chamberlin was able to gather together the results of all the work and set forth the general outline of the moraine border in North America. Although much basic investigation of problems of glacial geology remained to be done by 1900 most geologists agreed about the chief characteristics of the moraine and the way had been cleared for stratigraphic studies of the Pleistocene.[5]

Cook and Smock began their work in April of 1877. Smock had anticipated that it would be a fairly simple task to map the banks and ridges of tumbled boulders and grooved rocks, but after four months of effort he was not so sure.[6] He had spent the summer following the roads which traversed the area. Sometimes his wife drove the horse and wagon while he walked over the fields or examined ledges well back from the road. He wrote back reports to Cook once or twice a week detailing his findings, asking advice and noting particular spots which he thought Cook should visit. They soon recognized that the New Jersey moraine represented the effects of more than one ice sheet. While they could trace one fairly well-defined moraine line, the boulders and gravel of the outwash which had been deposited south of the ice sheet as it melted were so ill defined that Smock wondered if it could be drawn at all except as a vaguely defined belt.[7] The condition of the surface gave the clues for the location of the moraine line. South of it, the rock surface had disintegrated and decomposed, forming a thick bed of soil composed of the same ingredients at the rock beneath, while north of the line the earth was very much mixed and one could not be sure of the source of soils and the miscellaneous and dissimilar rocks. But in some places the dividing line was hard to find.

Cook also went to Staten Island, Long Island, and Pennsylvania and subsequently read a paper on the terminal moraine in those localities at the Wilkes Barre meeting of the American Institute of

Mining Engineers.[8] Entitled "On the Southern Limit of the Last Glacial Drift Across New Jersey and the Adjacent Parts of New York and Pennsylvania," the report was also included in the annual reports of the Geological Survey for 1877 and 1878. The 1877 report also included a map showing the line of the terminal moraine. Beginning on the north bank of the Raritan River at Perth Amboy the moraine ridge passes north of Metuchen, Plainfield, and Scotch Plains to the First Watchung Mountain, continues over the mountain to the north and west to Summit and Morristown. From Morristown westward, the deposit was not as regular and easy to find but was seen easily at Dover, where it reaches a height of some three hundred feet. From there it crosses the valley of the Musconetcong River about a mile northeast of Hackettstown and then over the hills in an irregular line to the valley of the Pequest River. It follows the southwest end of Jenny Jump Mountain and ends on the Delaware River below Belvidere.[9] In 1878 and again in 1880 Cook published refinements of the description in survey reports.

In addition to leaving a moraine, the ice sheets left lakes, ponds, marshes, and hillocks when they retreated. In the 1877 report Cook noted some of these which were scattered over the northern part of the state. Marks of glacial origin were noted as well as a list of scratches made by the ice on mountain ledges. Cook wrote that the land south of the moraine included stones of an appearance so different from those of the mapped moraine that "they must belong to some older drift deposit of which we have not yet sufficient facts to furnish any connected account."[10] He pointed out that to make a satisfactory study of all the details of the glacial drift it would be necessary to have a topographical map and to carry on a great deal more field work.[11]

When the chance came to go to Paris for the Exposition Cook was eager to visit Switzerland so that he could inspect the effects of existing glaciers and understand better the effects of the ice which had long disappeared from New Jersey. He was also able to attend a meeting of the International Geological Congress planned for that summer. After leaving Paris he went first to visit Professor Alphonse Favre in Geneva who was then the foremost student of glacial phenomena in this country.[12] Favre took him out to see the old glacial deposits near Geneva and gave him careful directions about the glaciers he should see and what he should look for. From Geneva Cook went to see the glacier at Chamonix and then by tortuous mountain roads to Zermatt. The travel on the eight- to nine-foot-wide wagon roads made him somewhat nervous but the bridle paths were even more fearful and he expected to fall into the valleys, be bruised against the rock wall on the other side, or at the very least to have his clothes torn on the rocks. But, as he wrote home, he supposed the horses were probably just as afraid of getting hurt as he was and so he tried not to worry too much.[13] At Zermatt he went to see the Pindelen, Gorner, and Mutt glaciers and then traveled on to the Rhone Glacier and the Aar glacier. Here he put in his hardest day's work, traveling up the Aar glacier to Abschuring. He visited four or five more glaciers and then, thankful to have done his mountain climbing without accident or sickness, he went on to St. Moritz which he thought was the most delightful summer resort he had ever seen.[14]

In the 1878 geological survey report Cook wrote in some detail of the habits of glaciers as he had observed them, the composition of two layers commonly found in glacial moraines and the distinction between stones worn by water and those worn by glacial action and he explained various theories about the causes of the movement of glaciers.[15]

John Smock was particularly interested in the thickness of the ice and made studies in the Catskills as well as in New Jersey. In 1882 he read a paper at the Saratoga Springs meeting of the American Association for the Advancement of Science, "On the Surface Limit or Thickness of the Continental Glacier in New Jersey and Adjacent States," and a year later reported the results of further studies at the Montreal meeting of the Association.[16] He concluded that the great ice sheet had filled the Hudson Valley to a depth of 3,000 feet and, becoming less deep toward the south, probably covered northern New Jersey to a depth of 1,200 to 1,300 feet at its highest.

In the geological survey report for 1880 Cook and Smock again returned to the effects of glacial action in New Jersey, tracing the extent of two lakes which had covered a large area of the state when the ice was in retreat: Glacial Lake Pequest in the Great Meadows area in Warren County which had been eight miles long and two miles wide and Glacial Lake Passaic which had stretched for thirty miles between the Watchung Mountain and the Highland range from Basking Ridge in the south to Paterson in the north. From six to eight miles wide and as deep as two hundred feet in some places, the lake covered the areas where Madison, Chatham, New Providence, Hanover, and Whippany now stand.[17] The Great Swamp in Morris and Somerset counties is all that now remains of this once great lake.

Cook would have liked to continue with the scientific study of glacial formations but, as Smock wrote later, "his intense loyalty. . . to the practical interests of the people for whom and by whom the survey was authorized, prevented him from following the subject where its application would have been of little real value, although it would have given him honor and gratified a natural thirst for additional knowledge.[18]

In addition to studies of glacial geology, survey reports after 1877 contained information on a wide variety of subjects, among the most important of which were stone quarries, clays, fossils, chemical soil analyses, iron and zinc mines, and climate. Work was begun on a topographical map and special studies on the fossils of the Triassic, Cretaceous, and Tertiary formations; a special volume on the clay industry was published in 1878 and problems of water supply became an increasingly important part of survey investigations. In 1880 the legislature extended the survey for five more years with an appropriation of $8,000 a year.

Cook had always recognized the value of accurate maps and the fact that the maps of New Jersey, while better than those of other states, were unreliable. But the high cost of mapping, which had defeated Kitchell's efforts to complete a topographical map, persuaded him at first to make new topographical maps only of specific areas under study by the survey such as the iron ore region or the Passaic and Hackensack meadowlands. When necessary, maps of the whole state were put together using data from Kitchell's efforts, existing local maps, and surveys. But by 1875 Cook decided that he had to try to complete topographical maps for the entire state. He wrote:

It is everywhere recognized. . . that the best interests of any country require an accurate map of all its territory. It should have a map which will show, not only the outlines of its civil divisions, and the location of its rivers and mountains, but which shall also show the height of every part of its surface above the level of the sea. Such a map is indispensable for the accurate description and exhibition of its geology. It is of the highest importance for showing areas of drainage and sources of water supply. It furnishes at once the information needed for the judicious location of roads and railroads; and it offers to every citizen, old and young, that practical information regarding geography of which they have heretofore felt the want.[19]

The 1871 federal law providing for triangulations to be made by the United States Coast Survey (later the United States Coast and Geodetic Survey) in states which were conducting their own geological surveys made the new mapping possible. During the Kitchell survey, the USCS had supplied the triangulations completed at that time. Following 1871 a closer link was possible—in effect the Coast and Geodetic Survey worked in the state at the direction of the state geologist. In 1875 Edward Bowser, who had been working for the State Geological Survey, was appointed an assistant in the USCGS and directed to extend the triangulation grid over the entire state. While the federal government thus bore the cost of triangulations, the state through its appropriation to the survey financed the topographical survey until 1884 when the new U. S. Geological Survey took over the financing. Cook continued to direct the project.[20] When the triangulations were completed and the latitude and longitude of a large number of points had been accurately determined, the topographical teams went in to establish the height above sea level of approximately twenty points in each square mile. With these sets of data and sketches made on the scene, contour lines could be drawn. In the *Annual Report of the State Geologist for 1885,* Cook included a very detailed explanation of the manner in which the topographers (using levels, transits, compasses, protractors, road sketches, aneroid barometers, and clinometers) measured elevations and sketched the physical characteristics of every part of the state.[21]

While Bowser continued the triangulations, George W. Howell, who like Bowser had graduated with the first class of the Rutgers Scientific School, began the topographical survey of the area between Orange Mountain and the Hudson River. In 1879 a young civil engineer, Cornelius Clarkson Vermeule, was engaged as topographer and surveyor. Twenty-one years old at the time, Vermeule proved to be as excellent, loyal, and hardworking an assistant as John Smock. He had assisted Howell in 1878, the year in which he graduated from Rutgers. For ten years he worked with the New Jersey Geological Survey as topographer and then became consulting engineer to the survey and the state—a position which he held for the next thirty years.[22] Vermeule designed the concrete jetties for the regulation of the Shark River Inlet, prepared the report on the New Jersey water supply for the 1894 survey report and maintained engineering consulting offices in New York City until 1943. In 1901 he received the prize from the Newark Board of Trade for the best plan for reclaiming the Newark meadows.

Some idea of Vermeule's activities in the field is gathered from one of his frequent letters to Cook,

We come here [Ogdensburgh] to spend Sunday as I had previously arranged to meet Mr. Staats [Peter D. Staats, a Scientific School graduate] here. We have been unable to work since Thursday morning as it has rained steadily. The prospects are not encouraging for a clear up, but I am in hopes that it will come by Monday morning and if so we shall work between here and Sparta next week. I am sorry that the work is kept back so as by this time last year I had 70 sq. miles or more done. I have had little opportunity as yet to judge of the character of the country but so far as I can judge I think you are right and I shall put Mr. Bevier [Philip H. Bevier] in the country between Sparta and Andover to work when he comes out. Mr. Staats is to work about Vernon and Wawayanda for the next week or two, and will use rainy days to plot his work as much as he can so that we can have it for sketching. I have been at work at sketch maps and everything that will conduce to our progress when the weather improves.[23]

After the coming of winter made it impossible for the teams to continue their work in the field, they settled down in their offices where the maps were carefully plotted on a scale of three inches to a mile. These original maps were then reduced by photographs to a scale of one inch to a mile and the map engraved and printed.[24] The first section of the great map was published in 1882 and covered 847 square miles of northern New Jersey on the one inch to a mile scale. The plan called for seventeen maps each 24 by 24 inches.[25]

During these years a great part of the appropriation for the survey was used for the expenses of the topographical map.[26] When it became necessary to pay for having the New Jersey fossils drawn and described it began to look as though the topographical work would suffer. But so dedicated were Cook and Smock to the map that they both put a portion of their salaries into the expense budget and worked for the Census Office for a part of the year to make up the amount. More funds were added to the topographical account in 1880. When Cook was made director of the New Jersey Agricultural Experiment Station, he decided that he would have to spend a considerable amount of time setting up the experiment station and accordingly reduced his work load with the survey and returned part of his salary which was added to the topographical account.[27] In 1882 Cook reported that neither he nor Smock had drawn pay for full service.[28] Other work was sacrificed to the map as well; the analysis of soils, marls and ores was discontinued; the geological field work was diminished.

Although most of the resources of the survey were concentrated on the topographical maps, many people in the state considered the survey's efforts to insure a pure and adequate water supply to be its most important service. In 1875 the mayors of Jersey City, Newark, and the other northeastern cities had asked that the survey study their water supply and a map was drawn of the drainage basin of the Passaic above Little Falls showing that enough lakes and reservoir sites were available to insure pure and plentiful water.[29] Interest in water supply continued to build; in 1880 Cook noted that more people wrote to the survey about questions of water supply than anything else.[30] Many people asked whether dug or driven wells were better; others sent samples of their well water or city water in for analysis and some wanted information about artesian wells.[31] Cook included a list of the state's principal artesian wells in the 1880 report but cautioned that results had not been encouraging.[32] One attempt had been made to dig an artesian well through the red sandstone at Paterson but after 2,100 feet they found only saline water and the attempt was abandoned. Cook wrote to other states to inquire about their experiences with artesian wells. Bishop P. N. Lynch of Charleston, S. C., who had served on the committee supervising the drilling of artesian wells in that city, replied that they had found water at 1,975 feet in the Cretaceous formation and suggested that similar formations along the Jersey Coast might hold water. The suggestions came at a particularly appropriate time. Atlantic City, Asbury Park, Ocean Grove, and other shore communities were increasingly concerned with problems of water supply. Following Lynch's advice Cook calculated the depth at which pure water could be found. He noted that the marl beds at Kirkwood, forty-five miles northwest of Atlantic City, were seventy feet above tide level. The marl beds dipped toward the southeast at a rate of approximately twenty-five feet per mile (except that the angle lessened near the ocean). Between Atlantic City and Kirkwood water had been found at a depth of 343 feet at the Winslow farm of A. K. Hay, a member of the survey's Board of Managers. Cook estimated that the marl beds at the shore should be approximately 1,055 feet below tide level and that water should be found at a depth of between 1,055 feet and 1,125 feet.[33]

To the north where the marl layers were not as far under the surface, water was found at higher levels.[34] Some shore landowners featured that wells drilled near the ocean would be infiltrated by salt water but Cook reassured them that the water would enter into the strata at their outcrop many miles inland to the northwest and the layers of clay and marl overlying the water bearing sand should effectively shut out the seawater. To enable landowners to estimate more accurately the depth at which water would be found, Cook prepared maps of the state with lines indicating the depth at which he estimated water-bearing strata would be found.[35] In 1882, seventy-eight pages of the annual report were devoted to water supply. Cook warned of the danger of drinking water from questionable sources; included information on the availability of potable water from the existing sources—lakes, ponds, streams, springs, artesian wells, driven, dug and bored wells, rainwater cisterns, and waterworks. He again strongly urged the use of artesian wells for seashore towns. In 1884 he was able to report that water had been found at Ocean Grove, Asbury Park, Red Bank, Ocean Beach, May's Landing, and Lakewood at the depths he had estimated. In this instance, as in so many others, Cook's awareness of the needs of the state, his search for solutions to the problems, and his willingness to follow through with meticulous study and analysis, earned him the lasting gratitude and respect of his fellow citizens. In a later comprehensive report on water supply, John Smock paid tribute to Cook's far-sighted and comprehensive views and the practical work which he started. "The subterranean as well as the surface-waters," writes Smock, "were studied in their accessibility, volume and character; and the artesian wells along the Atlantic Coast belt of the State are demonstrations of the accuracy of his studies."[36]

Cook's studies on subsidence, although they did not have the immediate applicability of his work on water supply, because they had to do with the beaches, were of interest to shore communities whose livelihood depended in large measure on vacationers. But they were inspired primarily by Cook's long-time interest in the phenomenon rather than by any expectation of practical benefit. Since the publication of the papers on coastal subsidence in the 1850s, he had continued to study and collect information about signs of subsidence. In 1881 he updated his former findings in the annual report and the following year presented a paper on the subject to a meeting of the American Association for the Advancement of Science in Montreal, the city where he had presented his first paper. Tradition has it that when he rose before Section E and read his opening sentence, "At a former meeting of this Association in this place, in 1857, I read a paper upon this subject," his audience broke into spontaneous applause in tribute to the perseverance and faithfulness of the scientist who had continued his research so patiently for such a long time.[37]

In the paper, entitled "The Change of Relative Level of the Ocean and Uplands on the Eastern Coast of North America," Cook presented new evidence of subsidence along the Atlantic Coast from Florida to Disco Bay in Greenland.[38] These widespread indications of subsidence persuaded him that it was a general rather than a local phenomenon but he felt that there were insufficient facts to decide whether it was due to local or universal causes. Estimating that the subsidence had taken place during very recent geological time—not more than five hundred to one thousand years ago, he speculated that an accumulation of ice in northern polar regions might have moved the center of gravity of the earth slightly to the north with a consequent disturbance to the relative level of the ocean and uplands resulting in apparent subsidence. In 1857 the accumulated evidence had seemed to point to a rate of one-quarter inch a year or two feet a century. In the years that followed other geologists had estimated the rate to be one-eighth inch a year and by 1882 Cook had decided that there was no way to determine the rate accurately. He hoped that bench marks to be set up across the state by the Geological Survey indicating the elevation above sea level of a number of points would settle all questions on the rate of subsidence. Unfortunately, the bench marks were not as helpful as he had hoped. Coastal subsidence was much more complex and variable than Cook had supposed. A recent definition describes subsidence as

a form of diastrophism which includes various processes such as faulting, folding and warping which deform the earth's crust. . . the land may sink or rise independently over large or small areas . . . a number of . . . influences may be operating at any one place so that the exact causes of emergence or submergence may be difficult to determine. The fact remains, however, that shorelines fluctuate, that these fluctuations can be measured and that they have produced many remarkable effects.[39]

Coastal subsidence has always been particularly interesting to press and public. Cook's early estimate of two feet per century has reappeared periodically for refutation or support. In 1929 a headline declared, "New Research Throws Doubt on Theory of Dr. George H. Cook . . . that New Jersey Was Slowly Slipping Into Sea."[40] Three geologists, Nevin M. Fenneman of the University of Cincinnati, Douglas Johnson of Columbia, and Captain R. S. Patton of the United States Coast and Geodetic Survey, citing Cook as the first American to support Lyell's theories of subsidence, took issue with his theory of subsidence on the grounds that mean sea level was not an absolutely level plane but irregularly distorted and varied in altitude with changes in the form of the shore.

In 1932 Henry B. Kummel, then New Jersey state geologist, read a paper at a meeting of the American Association for the Advancement of Science entitled "New Jersey Coast—the Two Feet Per Century Myth" in which he stated that the estimate appeared in geology textbooks without qualification even after Cook had stated that the exact rate could not be determined.[41] Kemble Widmer, present state geologist of New Jersey, put it succinctly and vividly:

Sea level during the Pleistocene has gone up and down like a yo-yo. As a result of these many changes, the present New Jersey shore is classed as a compound shore line. The Cape May terraces at about 30 feet indicate an emergent condition; the flooded estuaries of the Delaware, Mullica, Hudson, and other rivers a submergence; and the offshore bars that form our famous beaches indicate an emergence.[42]

A recent study by the National Geodetic Survey indicates that much of the continental United States crust is either falling or rising every year and that New Jersey appears to be sinking at a rate of about .2 to .4 inches a year.[43] Thus Cook's estimates were essentially in agreement with those of contemporary geologists and his careful investigations and keeping of records provided a basis for later studies.

The same kind of careful data-gathering was carried on under Cook's direction in the description and classification of New Jersey's native plants and fossils. When the studies began in 1880, Cook appealed to the pride and possessiveness of Jerseymen by explaining that for fifty years geologists from outside the state had been visiting New Jersey's rich sources of fossil remains and carrying them away. Articles on the fossils had appeared in a wide variety of publications. Explaining that the New Jersey fossil locations were classic to American geologists and that it was "due to the cause of science that we should contribute to its advancement," Cook proposed to have all the available information compiled, updated, completed, and published in one volume.[44] He engaged Robert P. Whitfield, curator of the geological department of the American Museum of Natural History, to undertake the study of the fossil invertebrates of the Cretaceous formation. Nathaniel L. Britton of the School of Mines of Columbia College promised to complete a catalogue of the flora of the state while John S. Newberry, professor of geology and paleontology of Columbia College and state geologist of Ohio, undertook the descriptions and sketches of the fossil plants and fishes.[45]

In 1878, the survey published *Clay Deposits of Woodbridge, South Amboy and Other Places in New Jersey*. As Cook explained in the introduction, the work was based on his earlier findings in the 1855 and 1868 surveys but John Smock was largely responsible for "the fullness and accuracy of its detailed descriptions and drawings."[46] The report was divided into five parts: Part I on the geography and topography of the Middlesex County clay district, Part II on the geological structure of the district, Part III the composition, properties and origin of the clays, Part IV the commercial uses for the clays, and Part V statistics, directions for exploring, digging, and mining clay, and an account of transportation and market conditions. Accompanying the volume was a topographical map showing the clay district on a scale of three inches to one mile, the first survey map which included contour lines of elevation.

The survey's geological studies in stratigraphy were given particular prominence in the 1882 report with a detailed report on the red sandstone or Triassic district. Henry D. Rogers, William B. Rogers, Edward Hitchcock, W. C. Redfield, and Charles Lyell were among earlier geologists who had concerned themselves with the structure and origin of this formation and it has been the subject of considerable study since Cook worked on it. Situated in the central part of the state roughly seventy miles long from Rockland County, N. Y., southwest to the Delaware River and from fifteen to thirty miles wide where approximately two-thirds of the state's population live, it is a region of great geological complexity. The name "Triassic" derives from Germany where a three-fold (Trias) formation of red sandstone, white chalk, and red sandstone was the subject of early study.[47] New Jersey, like the rest of eastern North America, has only the upper red sandstone layer. The early geologists had difficulty in determining the age of the red sandstone in New Jersey because of the scarcity of fossils. This is evidenced by the fact that in 1882 Cook merely wrote that most geologists put it in the Triassic formation (approximately 200 million years old and a part of the Mesozoic Era).[48] The formation extends from Nova Scotia to North Carolina with many variations. One which Cook pointed out was the fact that in Massachusetts, Connecticut, eastern Virginia, and North Carolina the strata dip towards the south while in New Jersey, Pennsylvania, western Maryland, Virginia and North Carolina, the dip is to the northwest. The formation was figured to be 25,000 feet thick and to include in addition to many varieties of sandstone; shales, limestones, various conglomerates, traprock ridges, and outcrops of earlier rocks. About half of it is north of the terminal moraine and these sections are covered by the miscellaneous sands and gravels deposited by the ice sheet.[49] In many places erosion has worn away the sandstone and shale while leaving the harder traprock. Under the heading of "trap-rock" Cook included all the varieties of igneous rocks found in the belt. George W. Hawes of the National Museum had identified the Bergen Hill rocks as dolerite and Cook accepted this as the prevailing variety. The traprock is now uniformly designated as basalt, dolerite being described as rock formed when the basalt minerals crystallize at a certain rate (diabase and gabbro are formed when they crystallize at other rates).[50] Cook was aware that much remained to be done in determining the exact nature of the traprocks. He wrote, "In the absence of any microscopic examinations, no lithological divisions can be made."[51]

Besides setting forth the composition of the traprocks as far as they were known at that time, Cook also described the sandstones, shales and conglomerates occurring in the formation and grappled with the question of origins. Henry Rogers had attributed the formation to a broad river flowing from a mountainous area in North Carolina, across Virginia, Maryland, Pennsylvania, New Jersey, and New York to the sea. The river had carried down and deposited the components of the sedimentary sandstones, shales, and conglomerates which eventually comprised the Triassic. Cook rejected this explanation because the strata dip toward what would have been the northwest side of the hypothesized river course. After Rogers several explanations were offered for the dip. One supposed that as the mass of sediment turning into rock achieved a depth of five miles it became so heavy that it exercised a tilting effect on that small portion of the earth's crust. Another relied on the effects of the changes in the earth's interior which brought about the massive land flows which erupted from the center of the earth and, in cooling and crystallizing, formed the trap ridges. W. C. Kerr of North Carolina supposed an "up-lift of the intervening tract" between the two divisions which dipped in opposite directions.[52]

Disagreeing with these hypotheses and others which had been offered, Cook suggested that all the detached portions of the formation were once connected (including those in the northeastern Canadian provinces); that the sediments were originally deposited on an uneven underlying rock surface; that this rock was "disturbed by a number of axes of elevation or . . . great faults which . . . crossed the formation obliquely but in a direction much nearer north and south than the general trend of the formation."[53] The Hudson River east to Connecticut would be one of these; the axis crossing the Delaware at Lambertville another; and the area south of the Potomac in Virginia another. The elevation of these axes would give a general dip of WNW on one side, and ESE on the other but not at right angles to the trend of the formation and it would not require as great a thickness for the whole mass as has been generally computed."[54] Geologists continue to refine their knowledge of the origin and structure of the Triassic. In 1964 Widmer evaluated various theories and pointed out that fossil evidence appears to rule out the concept that Triassic sediments in New Jersey and Connecticut were once part of a single great valley. He suggests instead that the depositions had been made in two separate valleys.[55]

The great number of subjects investigated by the survey, added to

Cook's extraordinary competence and care, made the New Jersey survey an outstanding one. This was later recognized by George Otis Smith when he singled out Joseph Peter Lesley's survey of Pennsylvania and Cook's of New Jersey as being especially noteworthy and of a "high order."[56]

Cook's accomplishments as director of the New Jersey survey were his primary achievements in geology and as this work became better known he was more and more drawn into the group of national and international geologists. One of the important steps in this direction was his attendance at the meetings of the International Geological Congress in Paris in 1878. After his trip to see the glaciers and a few detours to agricultural and geological meetings in England, Cook returned to Paris for the Congress meetings.

The primary reason for calling the Congress was the confusion in geological nomenclature. Throughout the nineteenth century as new geological strata were identified they were given local geographical place names. This parochial procedure made it difficult to know how many local names were being used for identical strata found throughout the world. The problem was the old one that Henry Rogers had tried to solve by using Greek terms.[57] In 1876, when the American Academy for the Advancement of Science met in Buffalo, the members of Section E (geology) decided to make an effort to develop one set of names for geological strata that could be recognized and used everywhere. A group of European geologists, in the country to help celebrate the Centennial, attended the meeting and expressed its willingness to cooperate. A committee to consider holding an international congress of geologists was formed and the first meeting of the International Geological Congress in Paris in 1878 was the result.

When the Congress convened in the great hall at the Trocadero for its first meeting there were representatives present from France, Spain, Italy, Switzerland, Austria, Russia, Belgium, The Netherlands, Sweden, and Canada but the Germans and the English had chosen not to come.[58] There were eight Americans in attendance including Cook, Lesley, James Hall, Edward Drinker Cope, Thomas Chamberlin, and T. Sterry Hunt.[59] Professor Hebert of France presided and the proceedings and papers were all read in French except for Hall who insisted on reading his in English and having it translated by a young French geologist.[60] Lesley in a letter to his wife said that for four hours the first day they had sat and listened to papers read so rapidly in French that they could not understand them.[61] Some of the speakers added to the problem by speaking with their backs to the large audience and gesticulating like monkeys. The following day the subject was nomenclature and the coloration of maps and it was easier to understand the papers. Hunt read a paper on the Cambrian, Lesley on the Permian, and Cope on the Cretaceous and Tertiary in the section on the limitations of formations.

Lesley thought that the Congress was a failure but from the first he had been convinced that any unification was impossible and was planning to write a paper expressing his views for the American Philosophical Society. In addition to the language barrier, Lesley felt that there was such a discordance of attitude and experience that cooperation was impossible. Cook, however, who had long experience with the problems of moving forward when forward motion was dependent upon men in organizations, was more sanguine about the Congress. He thought that it had addressed itself to subjects that had to be discussed by geologists from all over Europe and that much benefit could come to the science because of the meeting. He did regret the absence of the English and the Germans because he feared that there would have to be troublesome and tedious discussions on subjects that had come before the Congress and that could have been ironed out and taken care of there.[62] In any event, the delegates decided to reassemble in Italy in two or three years. The Congress was the beginning of a continuing effort to rationalize and consolidate the work of geologists in all countries.

Although Cook had already passed his sixtieth birthday without reaching the ranks of leading American geologists, the fact that he was one of the few geologists from the United States at the Congress plus his renewed work in the areas of theoretical geology marked a turning point in his career and from that time on his prestige increased remarkably.

Besides attending other geological and agricultural meetings and shows, talking with agriculturists and geologists in various places and altogether pursuing any lead that might increase his stock of knowledge of agricultural and geological matters Cook also thoroughly enjoyed the customary pursuits of the tourist and especially took advantage of every opportunity to observe foreign people, their foods and their customs. The year before he had been so seriously ill with some kind of intestinal infection that word of his illness had been published in the newspapers of the state and thoroughly alarmed all his friends.[63] Fortunately, there were no lasting effects and he began his trip with great enthusiasm and his customary powers of endurance unimpaired. (He was, of course, well protected by his sets of winter underwear while traveling on the glaciers.)[64] His routine while abroad was as exhausting as when at home. Almost every morning he arose at 5:30 to write letters to his family or articles he had promised to send to *The Cultivator and Country Gentleman* and the *Newark Daily Advertiser*. Thirty-three of his letters have been handed down in the family and they give us a more complete picture of the kind of man he was than any words that could be written about him. They show his warm and loving devotion to his family, his broad range of interests, the flexibility of his judgments on the strange ways of the natives, and his alertness to anything that would increase his knowledge or understanding.

As on Cook's 1870 European trip where they had met and married, James and Mary Neilson accompanied him. Cook had tried to find enough money to take his daughter Emma along and had even asked Paul if he could contribute something—but in the end he was unable to raise the extra money. He would have liked to have Mrs. Cook with him, especially on his botanizing expeditions, but she was suffering from some sort of physical disability and was having trouble walking.[65] So Cook wrote his letters. He was very careful to write separate letters to each member of the family; some mornings he wrote to all of them, including in each the particular information or comment that he thought would most interest them.

Cook and the Neilsons landed in Glasglow and the next day left for Paris. After getting themselves settled in a "genuine French [boarding] house" Cook went off to the Exposition to take up his duties as commissioner from New Jersey. His primary responsibility was the arrangement of seven boxes of minerals from Franklin, New Jersey.[66] An agricultural show which was part of the Exposition had begun already and the officials asked Cook to be a judge but he declined. He did, however, enjoy the show and saw some of the finest looking cows he had ever seen. One night he attended a meeting and banquet of the French Agricultural Society and listened to a number of talks and a heated discussion on the grape root louse which was attacking the vineyards.[67] Unlike the Neilsons (who were proficient in the language) he had some difficulty in understanding French and seldom attempted to speak it but listened carefully to the speeches and mentioned especially one lady who interrupted a speaker from the floor and was then led to the dais where she talked very eloquently. He was much impressed with the elegance of the banquet, the fine china and silver used, the five wines served and the dozen courses which included soup, salmon, veal, beef, *pâté de foie gras*, capon, turkey, mutton, little pies and mushrooms, strawberries, fresh almonds, figs, apricots, and peaches. Paris pleased him enormously—he pronounced it "pleasanter than any other place in the world."[68] He had visited it in 1852 but since then Napoleon III had built the broad boulevards which added so much to the city's charm. Cook enjoyed the profusion of flowers everywhere, the cleanliness, the trees, a street fair, and the museums of the Jardins de Plantes.

Cook was particularly interested in European drinking habits. He himself sympathized with the temperance movement and welcomed the signs he saw of it in England, but he found conditions in Europe to be different. He reported that there was a great deal of wine and beer drinking but no saloons with screens before the doors, no drinking places that were not as open to women as to men, no drunken brawls and no drunken men staggering about.[69] For himself, he pronounced the *vin ordinaire* to be as refreshing as buttermilk.[70]

After leaving France the first time he had visited an extinct volcano at Clermont and then on to Switzerland and the glaciers. At St. Moritz he made a collection of plants and pressed them to take home to Mary. Leaving Switzerland, Cook and the Neilsons traveled to Milan, Venice, Munich, and Zurich, returning to England in August where, he said, he felt as though his "tongue was loosened again."[71] He went on to Dublin to the meeting of the British Association. Here he met geologists from England and Ireland and made a special friend of Professor Boyd Dawkins of Manchester with whom he went out to a bog at Ballybetagh to see a large number of Irish elk bones.[72]

Cook was beginning to get somewhat homesick and missed his family, worried that he would not find the proper kind of souvenir for each one and hoped never again to take such a long journey without Mary and some of the rest "upon whom I am so much dependent" with him. Toward the last of July a letter from home told him that Sarah had become ill with typhoid fever after drinking water from an impure well while on a visit in the country.[73] On August 23, after Cook returned to Paris for the meeting of the International Geological Congress, he received a letter from Mary saying that Sarah was better but the next day brought letters with the sad news of her death.[74] Cook was badly shaken. The realization that he was not with his family when they most needed him especially grieved him. He wrote in anguish of how at Amiens he had purchased for Sarah some photographs of a statue of a child: "It is marvellously natural though in cold marble. The darling child I thought to please had been in her grave two weeks. Everything reminds me of her."[75] He was helped by the presence of the Neilsons. They mourned together and gave him their warm and genuine sympathy. He found comfort in a sermon at the American Chapel: "If the minister had known us and our circumstances he could not have selected a more appropriate text.''[76] He found most comfort, however, in the thought that

> The dear child has only been a comfort and joy to us from the day of her birth, and it fills me with distress to think what a loss it is to us and to our household. But it must be even greater if possible to her husband. We can only think of her lovely life and conduct to us all, and as you say be thankful that we have enjoyed her life so long. Our loss is a great one and I cannot but weep over it, though everything in the life of our dear child makes me remember that the loss is all on our part, and that she was prepared for the change and that it must be a joyful one to her.[77]

His original return passage was scheduled for September 17. He tried to leave immediately but was only able to have it moved up to September 6.

Upon his return home, Cook plunged anew into his duties with college, farm and survey and undertook new responsibilities in the national agricultural and geological organizations. His family was practically grown by now. Robert graduated from Rutgers in 1879 and began a succession of jobs in various mines and factories. Paul continued to do well at W. and L. E. Gurley and the factory prospered. By 1880 eighty-four men were employed there making sensitive and specialized instruments. The factory supplied the topographic survey with specially constructed instruments including a solar compass.[78]

During the years that Robert was at Rutgers the college attained the largest enrollment in its history. In 1875 there were 188 students enrolled. Of these, seventy were in the Scientific School including four from Japan and one from England.[79] Forty-five of the seventy were full-time students and the rest were part-time or special students.

Fifteen years after the Scientific School had opened, Professor Isaac Hasbrouck worked out a series of statistical compilations on its alumni which appeared to support the criticism that Rutgers in company with other land-grant colleges did not have enough students in agriculture.[80] Before 1880 only four students had written their senior theses on agricultural topics. However, this number was misleading as an indication of the number of students who went into farming. Of the ninety-two graduates and nongraduates that Hasbrouck was able to find for questioning, 11 percent or a total of sixteen were actually engaged in farming.

In 1877 the Rutgers program was criticized by Lewis Sturtevant, editor of the *Scientific Farmer*, who pointed out that few courses in agriculture were taught and inaccurately blamed the college for having only one professor of chemistry, natural history, and agriculture.[81] Two years later he again criticized the college. Cook wrote the following reply:

New Brunswick, N. J. March 6, 1879

Dr. E. Lewis Sturtevant,

Dear Sir,

There is in the March number of the Scientific Farmer, a criticism on the Annual Report of the Rutgers Scientific School, which is intended to be condemnatory, and which I think is unfair. The institution is not as strong as its friends would desire, which is its misfortune and not its fault. It is however doing its duty up to the extent of its means, and is educating a considerable body of students, for industrial pursuits. It has never received any aid whatever from the State, and it honestly pays out for the salaries of teachers more than it receives from the proceeds of the government land grant,—besides providing the necessary buildings, apparatus and farm, from other funds.

The U. S. grant required that a college should be established, in which the "leading object shall be to teach such branches of *learning* as are related to agriculture and the mechanic arts . . . in order to promote the liberal arts in addition to the practical education of the industrial classes in their several pursuits" & etc. . . .

The Trustees of Rutgers College claim that they are faithfully carrying out the prescribed conditions, and the Board of Visitors appointed on the part of the state to see that the laws are properly fulfilled, visit and examine the college regularly, and they report the obligations of the Trustees to the State are most liberally and faithfully carried out. The *name*, Agricultural College, does not fully express the character of the Institution,—but . . . it has been retained. Other industrial arts are as much practiced in New Jersey as agriculture is.

But branches of learning related to agriculture and mechanic arts are taught, and they meet the demands of the students who come to avail themselves of the advantages of the institution.

In Mathematics which the reviewer has not noticed, the students are all taught both the theory and practice of land surveying and leveling, and a large number of them are carried through very full courses of mathematical pure and applied sciences. There are some 40 students who are daily practiced in mathematical and linear drawing.

In Chemistry, which . . . has three professors . . . all the students are instructed by a full course of lectures & experiments and in the analytical laboratory there are 50 students now at work, in various states of advancement,— and in addition to the professors two or three tutors are kept constantly busy.

The departments of Botany and Vegetable Physiology and of zoology and animal physiology are not so fully taught as the others because there is less call for them,—but they are fairly begun and a foundation is laid upon which any one who has been taught how to study can build for himself.

The English studies and modern languages are taught . . . because it is believed that students should in addition to knowing a subject, know how to speak or write upon it. As to the teaching of practical agriculture, it is fairly questionable whether it is at all required in the Congressional Act. The best practical agriculturists in our own as well as in foreign countries are men who have been liberally educated the same as other men, and having a liking for the applications of science to agriculture have successfully turned their attention in that direction. Young men can better learn the practice of farming elsewhere than at a college,—and it is only when they have become familiar with most of the practical details of the art, that they can safely be trusted to undertake any change in established processes—progressive farmers all over the country are receiving their instruction through the press, and this I presume will continue to be the best method of teaching them, and that which will give most productive results. We have a College Farm which if it were supplied with funds could be used for experiments, but it has none,—It was originally poor, wet, and fully half of it in stumps and bush. It has been all cleared and underdrained and sufficiently enriched to produce good crops. It appears to me now that the best use to make of it is to conduct it as a whole on strict business principles, and to publish every year a full account of all expenses and income; to show where there are losses, and where gains are made, and if possible to show that farming, well carried on, will pay. This will make farming respectable in the eyes of many who now turn away from it under its common method with contempt.

We have many farmers' sons who come here to be educated and some unthinking persons expect that after getting an education they will go back and work on their farms in place of laborers who can do as much work as they, and can be hired for $10 or $15 a month. But the fathers themselves do not really mean this. They are willing to have their sons go away for awhile as surveyors, or engineers, or chemists, or in any branch of applied science which will pay better than simple manual labor; for they know that when they have had experience so as to manage men, or conduct business, they will come back to the farm if it offers paying inducements. . . .

This letter is not with a view for publication. . . . Personally I would only like to know if we are wrong in our course, how you think it should be changed. . . ."[82]

In reply Sturtevant protested that he felt Cook misunderstood his position, he was a great supporter of education for the agricultural classes and thought the agricultural colleges to be most desirable: "If I speak harshly it is because I feel friendly towards agricultural education. I would be the last to reflect upon you personally, . . . Please think of me as a strong friend of agricultural education, even though you may criticize my way of showing it: and especially believe that I respect *your* position and and appreciate *your* labors."[83]

The trustees and faculty were pleased with the seriousness of the Scientific School students. They supposed that the fact that what they studied had practical applications as well as being a study of underlying principles had a fortunate effect on conduct. They reported,

Cases of serious discipline in the Scientific School are of the rarest possible occurrence; and while this may be due in part to the earnest and manly character of the young men themselves, who represent largely the real yeomanry of the state, we cannot but think it is in good part attributable to the fact that they are made to see, at every stage of their work, its direct bearing upon the practical business of life upon which they expect soon to enter.[84]

Nevertheless, students continued to fail to respond to the opportunity in the numbers expected. In 1875 only twenty-four of the forty county scholarships were filled.

The emphasis on science continued to grow. The curriculum had gradually been revised to include more science in the classical program as well as in the Scientific School. By 1882 half of the faculty members were teaching science or mathematics. Cook continued to teach geology and organic chemistry, and took the students on the yearly geological expedition. After the high enrollment of 1875, the college faltered in its forward march. Some of the general decline in its liveliness might have been due to the fact that the trio which had done so much to bring it was broken up. Campbell was aging and his always poor eyesight had deteriorated so much that after 1870 he could not read.[85] Murray had left in 1873 to become superintendent of Educational Affairs in Japan, and Cook was kept increasingly occupied with the farm, the survey, and the efforts in Trenton and Washington to secure passage of bills favorable to agriculture, geology, and the land-grant colleges. In addition to his other duties, the day-to-day running of the college fell to him as vice-president during Campbell's illnesses.[86] In 1882, Campbell resigned and was succeeded by Merrill Edwards Gates, then principal of Albany Academy. He thus joined Campbell, Cook, and Murray as the fourth principal of the academy who had come to Rutgers. Cook was becoming increasingly tired and would have liked to give up his teaching duties and the responsibility for the farm. His income from the survey was not large enough to enable him to do this and he looked for other sources of income. He thought that one such possibility might be the East Jersey Proprietors.

The East Jersey Proprietors, or more properly, the Board of Proprietors for the Eastern Division of New Jersey, was established in

1684 to manage the holdings of the twenty-four proprietors William Penn had organized in England for the purchase of the eastern half of New Jersey from the estate of Sir George Carteret. The proprietors were absentee owners and speculators. Penn himself focused his attention on Pennsylvania and, in fact, only one of the original twenty-four proprietors ever visited New Jersey. Their shares were sold or otherwise disposed of and a complicated system of land-purchase developed that caused a considerable amount of dissension over the years.

The land titles in East New Jersey which derive from the proprietary patents originated in the following manner: Ownership of a quarter share of one of the original twenty-four shares made its owner a member of the Board of Proprietors' Council.[87] From time to time the Council issued "dividends," which gave shareholders the right to claim or "locate" a specified amount of land. The first dividend provided 10,000 acres for each full share. The dividends were in the form of warrants of location which allowed the owner to claim a specified number of acres. The owner of a warrant chose his land, applied to the surveyor general of the Board to have a deputy surveyor survey his land and after survey the results were sent to the surveyor general who verified the accuracy of the survey and registered the surveyor's certificate with the register of the Board. The warrant holder was then given title to the lands. By the middle of the nineteenth century almost all land of any value had been located and conveyed to private ownership. There were some oddments still available—beaches or islands along the shore, land which had been located through fraudulent means and could be reclaimed for the proprietors, a few small irregularly shaped pieces in the northern hills, and some lakes. During the 1870s the Council located and sold several lakes.[88]

Cook's interest in the proprietors came about through various friends who were members of the Board as well as through his responsibilities as state geologist. His interest was piqued as well because of his Revolutionary War ancestor who had been commissioned to guard the papers of the proprietors. In 1877 he purchased one quarter of a share and his friend, William Force (who was also a member of the Board of Visitors of the Rutgers Scientific School and of the Board of Managers of the New Jersey Geological Survey) bought a quarter share at about the same time. Force lived in Newark and was a commission merchant with a New York City company dealing in flax seeds, linseed, and their oils. He had been a member of the Executive Committee on Agriculture formed in 1864 to establish the Rutgers Scientific School and farm and was secretary both of the Board of Managers of the State

Geological Survey and the State Board of Agriculture. In their common ventures, Cook and Force had found each other to be conscientious, hardworking, and efficient and they often relied on each other to get things done. When Cook and Force bought their quarter shares, the Board of Proprietors had been a source of annoyance to many of its members for some time. Monroe Howell of Parsippany, who was surveyor general, wrote to Cook about one aspect of the problem, the register, Lawrence Boggs, "It is the same old story, all complain of the manner in which Mr. Boggs treats those having business at the Surveyor General's Office. . . . I am very anxious for a change of some sort, in the location and management of our office, I wish you would talk up the necessity of a change. . . . I would sooner have it anywhere than where it is."[89]

Cook and Force soon began to attempt reforms. In 1879 Force wrote to Cook, "The inefficient organization and neglect to prosecute their claims vigorously has been at the sacrifice of respect for such rights as might have been maintained by them. Large interests have been dribbled away and standing and character have been forfeit."[90]

Cook and Force were both appointed to a committee to investigate and report on the rights of the proprietors to land under water, to the committee on rules and regulations and to committees on tidewater lands, and on books and papers. In the hope that they would eventually be able to realize some profit for themselves they bought up as many warrants as they could. They offered to pay $2.50 per acre and most holders were glad to get rid of them—as recently as 1870 warrants had been selling for about thirty-five cents an acre. Mr. D. A. Ryerson wrote to Cook: "I know that my father had . . . a credit. . . . I do not know that he disposed of it . . . and if you are willing to take the risk you are welcome to them at the price named, $2.50, with thanks."[91]

Some warrant holders wanted more money—one man wrote that he had heard of a warrant for a fraction of an acre selling for $100.[92] He planned to ask around to see what the best offer was and offer his to Cook at that price. From Catherine A. English came the following: "Mother joins me in sincerest thanks to you for the kindness shown in the management of the business, and we trust you will yourself realize satisfactory returns in your own disposal of proprietary rights,"[93] and in another letter, "Your letter . . . was an agreeable surprise to Mother as she scarcely expected to learn of finding any more 'rights of location' to her credit. Her first remark after reading your letter was 'The Lord is good' and 'Professor Cook is a kind and honest man.'"[94]

Force busied himself with the books and records of the proprietors, tracing down owners of the unredeemed warrants and all unclaimed lands. Thomas Kinney and Augustus Cutler, who were also proprietors, supported the reform efforts.[95] Force and Cook originally thought they might turn a profit for themselves on Sandy Hook property. Sandy Hook was owned by the federal government, but Cook and Force and an associate, John Watts Russell, thought that the old maps and records of the proprietors proved that because of an earlier error part of the land still belonged to the proprietors. They invested a considerable amount of money, time, and effort in this endeavor. They had surveys made; John Russell went to Washington to try to persuade the government it did not own as much of the Hook as it thought it did; and William Force spent long hours with the old maps and records of the proprietors.[96] But they were unsuccessful; the government did not allow their claim and all their efforts were for nothing.

Within the Board itself Force and Cook continued to gain power. Force was made a member of the executive committee which eventually took over day to day management of the proprietors, reporting to the Board semiannually.[97] Under Force's influence the committee made a great effort to discover all lands under water that were still owned by the proprietors as well as lands which its original owners obtained by fraud. In 1882 the Board announced its proposal to survey all lands still belonging to it. Force was made trustee for the entire Board and given the responsibility for arranging for the survey and sale of all lands in its possession. He was to be paid a fee for each transaction. Force and Cook and their friends hoped this would prove to be a profitable and well-received undertaking for all the proprietors. They also hoped to make some money themselves.

With the warrants that he had purchased, Cook claimed Oyster Island in New York Harbor (which was wholly under water at high tide). His knowledge of reclamation of tidal lands led him to believe that the island might become a valuable piece of property—an optimistic expectation that proved to be unjustified.

Cook's optimism about the financial condition of the college farm was as unjustified as his expectations of profit from his proprietary interests. In 1876 he summarized his hopes for the farm,

The condition of the farm is such now that it will with reasonable economy, more than meet the current expenses at ordinary good farming. But it is desirable for the interests of New Jersey agriculture, that it should do much more than this. It is ready for experiments on fertilizers, on tillage, on crops, on feeding, or on any part of rural economy, whereby science can lighten labor, or increase its rewards. Such experiments cost money, [require] educated skill and patient work, and these must be provided as rapidly as possible.[98]

Unfortunately, a nationwide agricultural depression which lasted from about 1870 until the end of the century contributed to the chronic financial problems of the farm and the Board of Trustees soon had to borrow money to finance essential repairs and improvements. By 1880 the farm was $4,045 in debt.[99] Later that year the trustees mortgaged it for $6,600 in order to raise money to pay this and other claims.[100]

In spite of financial problems Cook was able to carry on a considerable amount of useful research. His research projects were similar to those carried on by most agriculturists and college farms during the period. Many of these "experiments" on the land-grant college farms should more properly be termed "field trials." For the most part they were not controlled experiments nor did they grapple with fundamental problems of basic reasearch. With a few exceptions like Levi Stockbridge, United States agricultural scientists did not develop basic or original research. Stockbridge began experiments in Massachusetts in 1866 that were designed to test his theory that the soil should not be built up to meet some ideal composition but that the fertilizer needs of each plant should be determined by the chemical composition of the plant. In Illinois Thomas J. Burrill who carried on microscopical observation of the disease of fruit trees was another exception.[101] In all the land-grant colleges, however, investigations and field trials were more structured than when left to amateurs and the results were more systematically communicated and this meant better results for the farmers.

At Rutgers Cook moved into basic research and added specialized scientists to his staff as soon as funds became available. Until that time, within the limits set by financial stringency, he carried on useful studies in field crops, dairy science, horticulture, agricultural economics, agricultural chemistry, and, with the help of the New Jersey Geological Survey, in the study of soils.

Among Cook's trials of various new field crops, he was particularly pleased with a new bean he found in Munich during his 1878 trip. He wrote to Mary, "In the Agricultural Experiment Station at Munich I found them experimenting in growing a new pea or bean for a fodder plant. It comes from Japan and it is named *soja hirsuta* [soy bean]. It is very promising and I got some seeds. I will put 3 or 4 in this letter and shall be glad to have them planted singly in some rich ground. They will not ripen, of course, but we can see how they grow, and I have some more seeds for next spring."[102] James Neilson was able to get more soybean seeds in Vienna and the first crops were gathered at Rutgers in 1879, one of the earliest recorded plantings of soy beans in the United States. Cook reported on the crop at the next annual meeting of the New Jersey State Board of Agriculture and in the annual report of the State Board he included a translation of a paper on soy beans published by the Bavarian Experiment Station.[103] A table compared the composition of soy beans with twelve other fodder plants such as timothy, corn, oats, and cured corn and showed that the soy bean had a higher nutritional value than any other fodder analyzed. It was highly recommended as a rich and healthful food for cattle. Cook's trial plantings of five varieties of soy beans showed that one did not grow well at all and two needed a warmer climate, but two others did very well. Farmers were too conservative to adopt the plant at the time, however, and the soy bean was not accepted for another fifty years or more.

Seven years after he had begun trials of fertilizers on Indian corn in 1872, Cook reported on them in the annual report.[104] The trials showed that in the soil around New Brunswick muriate of potash and barnyard manure were beneficial, sulphate of ammonia had a deleterious effect on the corn, and phosphates had no effect.[105] Indian corn was thus established as a potash crop. Similar fertilizer tests were made on wheat, cabbage, and potatoes and helped to establish the fact that in different soils crops needed different fertilizers.

The dairy herd continued to be an important part of the farm and was improved when possible. Production records showed that in 1877 the herd averaged 2,660 quarts annually per milking cow.[106] The Rutgers herd participated in a comparative study made by Edward Lewis Sturtevant, editor of the *Scientific Farmer*. Results published in 1877 showed that of the eight herds studied, the greatest amount of milk (measured over a period of three years) was produced by a selected herd of five to seven Ayrshires at Rutgers which produced 3,013 quarts per year.[107] The lowest was 2,482 quarts from Sturtevant's herd.

In a sense Cook's investigation of the marl beds during the Kitchell geological survey began the classification and analysis of soils in New Jersey. The efforts to restore and improve soils dated from the first fertilizer experiments in 1867. Results became increasingly significant as these studies were extended. The long-term studies of Indian corn were especially important but the fertilizer tests with wheat, corn, cabbages, and potatoes were also useful. Some study of the physical handling of the soil was done in investigations of deep and shallow ploughing experiments. Fertilizer analysis was stepped up after the establishment of the State Board of Agriculture.

Cook had begun keeping records on temperature, rainfall, and barometric pressure when he moved to New Brunswick and during his absences his wife or one of his children recorded the information. In the 1868 *Geology of New Jersey* he had included meteorological tables compiled from the records of the Smithsonian Institution and the Department of Agriculture with some additional information from William A. Whitehead, a New Jersey resident interested in weather. The data given included mean temperatures at selected locations in the state, a chart of wind directions in five locations, and monthly rainfall figures for 1854-67.[108] Climatology tables were included in annual reports of the survey in 1876, 1879, 1880, 1881 and Volume I of the final report published in 1888. In 1876 Cook published the first of a series of annual reports on rainfall in New Brunswick.[109] The *Annual Report of the Rutgers Scientific School for 1880* included weather tables showing rainfall and temperature readings at the college farm.[110]

In 1880, cooperating with the Division of Telegrams and Reports for the Benefit of Commerce and Agriculture of the Chief Signal Office of the War Department, Cook organized a squad of people throughout New Jersey to make weather observations.[111] Rain gauges, snow gauges, thermometers, and graduated cylinders were sent out as well as blank forms to be filled out by the observers.

New Jersey farmers appreciated Cook's efforts on the farm and welcomed the annual reports of the Scientific School. He continued to deliver agricultural lectures even though he was no longer obligated to speak annually in every county. In 1880 he lectured at the State Normal School in Trenton and in Warwick, Manasquan, Kirkwood, Moorestown, Burlington, Somerville, Stockton, Locktown, and Jamesburg.[112] His subject for most of these lectures was "How to Make Farming Pay," something which, as one farm correspondent wrote, "is just what we are anxious to know." By the time the Rutgers College Farm was established, the disastrous practices of early New Jersey settlers who cropped their farms until the land was worn out and then moved on was pretty much a thing of the past. Farmers were anxious to maintain their farms and repair damages caused by earlier neglect. Though farmers who stubbornly scorned "book farming" still spoke loudly in parts of the Midwest, in New Jersey most such men had already lost their farms and moved west or disappeared into the limbo of the laboring men in industry or business. Farmers asked the largest number of questions about fertilizers, rotation of crops, new or improved varieties of seeds and crops, comparative value of different breeds of domestic animals, and the best kind of feed.[113]

During his 1878 European visit as in 1870 Cook took every opportunity to visit farms, agricultural schools, experiment stations, exhibitions, and shows. He wrote reports for the *Cultivator and Country Gentleman* of his investigations of agricultural sites in England, Italy, Belgium, France, The Netherlands, and Bavaria.[114] As in the past, these observations of European experiment stations made him even more anxious to have one in New Jersey. His goal for the farm became a kind of holding action—to make it self-supporting and lay a stable foundation for more extensive experimentation in the future. "The farm should be made an experiment station," he wrote, "with a competent chemist and assistants permanently employed in the analysis of fertilizers and the investigation of matters of agricultural interest . . . [carrying out] experiments which require accurate records of weight, measure and time. . . ."[115]

Of the twelve experimental land-grant farms in existence before 1875, New Jersey's was the only one which had been bought and was maintained by a private college.[116] Not that support in other states was very often generous. Pennsylvania was an exception. There part of the land-grant fund had been used to buy three farms in different sections of the state and $2,000 was appropriated annually for *each one*. Although New Jersey was largely agricultural in the nineteenth century, the controlling interests on the political scene were the railroads (especially the Camden & Amboy) and the business and industrial concerns. But agricultural interests were persistent. In 1877 a committee of the Board of Visitors was appointed to talk to the New Jersey Senate Committee on Agriculture and the Agricultural College but decided a request for help would be inappropriate in view of the financial condition of the state. Both the Board of Visitors of the Scientific School and the State Board of Agriculture repeatedly urged the state to appropriate money for the support of the Scientific School and the farm. Governor Newell, William H. Hendrickson of Middletown, William Parry of Burlington County, and James Neilson especially criticized the legislature—not only for failing to provide for more rapid development of the farm, but even worse, for forcing the college to meet all expenses.

When help did not seem to be forthcoming from the state, Cook turned to the federal government. Although the second Morrill bill had failed in 1875, its supporters thought they could smell victory in 1876. Cook was more involved than ever in the lobbying efforts in 1876. He visited Washington himself to testify before the Education Committee and was in regular correspondence with such men as General J. B.

Bowman, president of the College of Kentucky, and Colonel W. S. Clark, president of Massachusetts Agricultural College. George Atherton from Rutgers also testified before the Committee. Cook's primary source of information was Representative Augustus W. Cutler of Morris County. A fervent supporter of Morrill's bill, Cutler was anxious for Cook's help and conscientious about reporting what was going on, and he acted as a liaison between Cook and Morrill. However, he expressed reservations on the possible success of the bill because of opposition from the Texas Pacific Railroad. Two members of the Education Committee were friends of the railroad.[117] Cutler wrote that he thought the bill would have a chance only if they could

manufacture public opinion in favour of the *Public Lands for Free Schools* and gather strength under that *watch word*. . . . A portion of the fund can be diverted for National Colleges . . . Texas Pacific cannot stand *against it,* and we cannot get up public sympathy so quick and readily as upon the cry of *Free Schools.* . . . I think policy demands that we adopt this course at present. But I did not want to adopt it without advising you of the present situation and the views that actuate me in advising this line of action. . . . If you were here and saw the situation I know you would agree with me.[118]

By April Clark was writing Cook that he was not hopeful of getting "any good thing out of the present Congress," and Cutler wrote, "the Educational *sticks,* I do not know what the matter is."[119] He wrote that he had never changed his mind about the hostility, hoped he was mistaken, but feared he was not. The hopes and the flurry of activity proved to be in vain. The bill did not pass. But Morrill reintroduced his bill year after year and it finally was passed the year after Cook's death.

Meanwhile, Cook and his associates continued to press for state aid to the Scientific School and the college farm and the establishment of a state-supported agricultural experiment station. In 1877 the Board of Visitors succeeded in persuading Governor Joseph D. Bedle to come to some of its meetings and his message to the legislature the following year included a mild statement that the Board of Visitors was "deeply impressed with the importance of enlarging the scope of experiments on the farm. In view of the benefit to the farms generally, I think a moderate appropriation wise."[120] The same year William A. Newell, William Parry, Patrick T. Quinn, and Cook were constituted a committee to visit the legislature and when that did not produce results the offensive was stepped up and the entire board in a body visited Trenton.[121] In 1879 Senator George C. Ludlow of Middlesex County introduced a bill to establish an agricultural experiment station; the Board of Visitors testified before both Assembly and Senate committees where the bill received unanimous approval—but the Senate turned it down.[122]

Thomas Kinney (whose newspaper the *Newark Daily Advertiser* in 1864 had published the editorial bemoaning Princeton's loss of the land grant) was president of the State Board of Agriculture and an impassioned supporter of the Rutgers Scientific School and its farm. In a dramatic plea for support he excoriated the legislative bodies for failing to recognize their obligation to agriculture and for wasting their time instead on "political intrigues, sectional jealousies, social problems, and financial experiments."[123] At the same time he berated them for their shameful treatment of the State Board which had, he said, "the cheap privilege of doing its work at its own expense, with the exception of allowing a small stipend to the efficient secretary who performs the work."[124] The president of the Board of Visitors, Thomas Dudley, formerly American consul in Liverpool, was similarly though less colorfully a staunch supporter of state aid for an experiment station.

The opposition came from these who opposed any extension of government responsibility at all as well as from those who objected specifically to Rutgers as the land-grant college. Cook saved a clipping from an unidentified newspaper which expressed one such point of view: "The connection of a state farm with a particular sectarian college is anomalous at best, and can only be excused by certain considerations of economy coupled with Mr. Cook's special fitness. Should further expense be meditated at the expense of the State then the whole affair should be detached from Rutgers and made thoroughly independent."[125]

In 1880 the State Board of Agriculture presented a petition to the legislature calling for an experiment station with a director, a chemical laboratory, and a full time agricultural chemist to analyze fertilizers. It recommended that more studies be made of the feeding and fattening of farm animals and that a botanist or entomologist be engaged to study diseases and insect menaces to sweet potatoes, clover, and cranberries.[126] In response to this Senator Isaac L. Martin, who had succeeded Ludlow as senator from Middlesex County, introduced a bill to establish an experiment station and in March 1880 all the efforts of Cook and the other supporters of the experiment station were rewarded. The Senate voted 17 to 3 in favor of the bill on the third of the month.[127] It reached the Assembly the next day and was scheduled for a second reading four days later, but a petition from the Burlington County Agricultural Society was presented asking that the bill be passed. Thereupon, under a suspension of rules it was immediately given its third reading, passed by a vote of 37 to 3 and on March 10 was signed into law by Governor George B. McClellan.

The bill provided for an annual appropriation of $5,000 and gave control of the station to a Board of Directors, consisting of the governor of the state, the Board of Visitors of the Scientific School (who were appointed by the governor) and the president and professor of agriculture of Rutgers College.[128] The Board was empowered to select a location for the station and branches, to appoint a director and to employ chemists and other assistants. Before the month was out the Board had decided to locate the station at Rutgers and had chosen Dr. Cook as the first director.

New Jersey thus became the third state to establish an agricultural experiment station by legislative act.[129]

1880-1889
The Climax of
Two Careers

The last years of Cook's life were a culmination of his efforts in both agriculture and geology and brought him national recognition. The creation of the New Jersey Agricultural Experiment Station was a step in this direction but the funds provided (first $5,000 a year, later $8,000, and eventually $11,000) allowed for only a small increase in true agricultural experimentation. Most of the money went to support the fertilizer analysis and control program.

When the station began operations in 1880 with Cook as its director it included a chemist, two assistant chemists, a mail clerk, and a young woman clerk who took care of a branch office in Camden. Fertilizer analyses were carried on in a two-room laboratory in Van Nest Hall on College Avenue under the supervision of Arthur Taylor Neal, the chief chemist. Neal, a graduate of Wesleyan College in Connecticut, had studied in Germany at the University of Griefswald and at the Experiment Station in Halle. He had assisted Wilbur Olin Atwater, pioneer in the analysis of fertilizers, who was to become the first director of the Office of Experimentations of the United States Department of Agriculture.[1] Neal, a "frank, earnest, and capable fellow," later was made director of the Delaware Experiment Station.[2] At Rutgers he was responsible for fertilizer analysis and, with the other chemists, supervised field experiments with fertilizers, trials of new crops and varieties, and studies in feeding livestock.

Because the establishment of the experiment station did not provide any state support for the college farm it continued to have financial problems. So precarious was the monetary situation that it became a regular practice to borrow from Benjamin West, manager of the farm, to buy brewer's grains to feed the cows. These transactions were not entirely without profit to Mr. West; the trustees always paid him 6 percent interest. However, by June 1885, the trustees' funds had reached such a calamitous state that they owed Mr. West over $4,000. In desperation they planned to take out another mortgage on the farm but were saved from this embarrassment by a generous gift of $5,000 from one of their number, the wealthy Newark brewer Robert F. Ballantine.[3] Mr. West was not the only employee who lent money for farm expenses; the trustees' minutes also record that they owed Professor Cook $286.21 for funds advanced.[4] The agricultural committee of the trustees, Henry Rutgers Baldwin, a physician from New Brunswick, and George C. Ludlow, ex-ambassador, ex-governor and President of the New Jersey State Board of Agriculture, reported that they were repeatedly mortified when they had to go to the bank every three months to ask that a loan of $1,634, incurred for farm expenses, be renewed.[5] The income from the farm provided enough for the interest on the loan and for payment of a salary to the farmer but there was never enough to pay the principal.

Realizing that extensive experimentation on the farm was out of the question, Cook turned to several farmers around the state for their help in experiments with fertilizers on field crops. This system, already used in some other states, provided a means of testing fertilizers on different kinds of soil. For example, the farm of Stephen C. Dayton of Basking Ridge was located on traprock soil; Dr. C. W. Larrison's farm in Ringoes was on red sandstone soil while in New Brunswick Adrian Vermule's farm provided an example of red shale soil and in Burlington William S. Taylor performed his trials on clay marl soil.[6] Each year the list of participating farmers grew. By 1889 the station had sponsored more than one hundred fertilizer field experiments.[7] The cooperating farmers were sent careful instructions from Cook telling them how to mark out their plots, how to plow, what fertilizers to apply to each plot, how and what to plant, and how to keep records.[8] They agreed to carry the experiments through a full four-year rotation and over the years they conducted experiments on sweet potatoes, oats, hay, corn, wheat, and peach trees. Results were reported in the annual reports of the Experiment Station.

The experiments provided valuable information for all New Jersey farmers. At this stage in the development of agriculture many fundamental questions remained. Not for another ten years would the role of nitrogen in fertilizing be determined. Cook emphasized another basic fact in the annual report on the Experiment Station for 1882: "That it is unsafe for farmers in one section to follow the methods of those of another is again forceably illustrated. Phosphoric acid and potash gave on one farm a heavy profit, on the other a decided loss. Each farmer must make similar experiments for himself, or where soils are known to be similar, club together and divide the labor and expense of the trial."[9] Ever aware of agricultural education in the broadest sense, Cook pointed out that for a small investment of time and money the local experiemental plots gave farmers and their sons and neighbors a chance to gain basic knowledge of agricultural chemistry.

The raising of dairy cattle and studies in breeding and feeding, begun in the first few years in the effort to earn farm income and limited to average milk production in various breeds in the 1870s, blossomed in the 1880s into a variety of investigations which focused on a search for the least expensive feed that would produce the best yields of high-quality milk. Most significant among these experiments were those on silage. A major problem in the management of stock had always been the difficulty of feeding cattle over the winter when they could not graze in open fields. An important factor in the agricultural revolution in England in the eighteenth century had been the introduction of turnips as a winter feed. In the latter part of the nineteenth century, agriculturists became excited about the storage of green fodder as a supplement to the common practice of drying hay before storage. Several state and college experiment stations including those in Vermont, New Hampshire, North Carolina, Tennessee, Wisconsin, Michigan, and New Jersey conducted studies relating to silage. Alfred C. True, in his *History of Agricultural Experimentation and Research in the United States*, singles out the work of Manly Miles in Illinois, Charles Goessman in Massachusetts, and George Cook in New Jersey as the earliest significant experiments.[10]

Several important questions had to be answered before the use of stored green fodder could be adopted by practical and conservative farmers: Could it be stored without rotting? Would cows eat it? Would it affect the taste of milk and butter? What chemical changes took place in the stored fodder? Would these changes affect the health of the cows or the quantity or nutritional quality of the milk? In Illinois Miles initiated the experimentation by feeding cattle cornstalks and broom-corn seed which had been stored in open pits covered with straw and earth.[11] Stimulated by Miles's work Cook began silage feeding experiments. At first the fodder was put into tight bins in the cellar of the barn, but the following year a silo was built and in 1883, with an appropriation of $2,000 from the legislature for "proper and sufficient receptacles for the preservation of green fodder," a better silo constructed.[12] During the first year of experimentation Cook found, as had Miles, that the cows would eat the silage (which has a taste similar to that of sauerkraut), that there was no loss of weight, and that the milk flow remained the same.[13] In the years following Cook carried on a variety of studies of changes in composition in ensiled corn compared with cured fodder corn; comparative values of clover, sorghum, green rye, and rye silage; and a comparison of dried corn fodder, green fodder corn, and corn silage. These experiments were reported in the annual reports or in bulletins issued by the station.[14] Cook also lectured on silage to farmers' clubs throughout the state. Notes written in his hand giving specific measurements for the building of silos, space allotments for each cow, and the comparative costs of silage are found in his collected papers. He pointed out that among the benefits of using silage were an increase in the number of stock that could be economically managed on any given farm, a consequent increase in the amount of manure, independence from the vagaries of the weather and the possibility of better utilization of high-priced farm land. The New Jersey Board of Agriculture did its part to spread information on silage. During the annual meetings in Trenton farmers came in large numbers to hear papers read by the experts. In 1883 they filled to overflowing the courthouse where the meetings were held. Silage was one of the main topics of the day and Cook was there to talk of his experiences. When some farmers remained skeptical he told them that he had heard rumors that a large milk condensing establishment in New York had ordered its suppliers to discontinue the use of silage and that one gentleman had told him that butter made from the milk of cows eating silage carried an unmistakable taste. "But," said Cook, "those who are engaged in the sale of milk believe that it is the best food that can be used; that the milk is as rich and that the flavor is not influenced by it. I believe farmers generally will adopt its use."[15] George Farlee of Trenton, himself a dairy farmer, came to Cook's support saying that the cows liked it and seemed to thrive upon it and (more convincingly perhaps) added that his dairy women of thirty years experience said that it made the best butter.

The 1881-82 report of the United States Commissioner of Agriculture referred to the work on silage in New Jersey: "The question has attracted so much attention that we have collected and tabulated two analyses made at the department and one at the New Jersey Experiment Station giving averages of compositions of nine specimens as given in bulletin #11 of the New Jersey Station."[16] Eventually results at the various stations persuaded farmers that silage did indeed provide a better feed for cattle during the winter than did dry fodder and the silhouette of the silo became a common feature of the countryside. Experiments on silage were carried on at the station after Cook's death, and in 1904 two of

Cook's enthusiasms were brought together in an experiment which proved that milk could be produced at a lower cost by substituting soybean silage for commercial concentrated feeds.[17]

Along with questions about silage Cook encouraged investigations of other aspects of dairy farming. Several members of the Board of Managers of the Experiment Station, including James Neilson, Thomas Dudley, and William S. Taylor, owned dairy farms and contributed in special ways to the work of the station. Neilson made several European trips and wrote Cook lengthy letters about his visits to experimental farms and stations. Dudley visited England and at Cook's insistence made a special trip to the famous experiment station at Rothamsted. The three worked together on a committee of the Board to plan milk experiments.[18] In one of the experiments that resulted, six Jersey cows from Taylor's herd of thirty-three cows, along with six Ayrshires and six native cows from the college farm, were used in an attempt to discover the best breed of cow for dairy purposes.[19] At this primitive stage in the development of dairy science the station furnished brewer's grains and cottonseed meal as a part of the total feed mixture but each farm supplied its own hay, straw, and turnips. Afterward Cook realized it would have been better if these, too, had come from the same source. The cows were milked twice a day with a ten-hour interval during the day and a fourteen-hour interval at night. The milk of each cow was weighed, strained, and mixed with the rest of the milk from that herd. Then a pint from the morning yield was mixed with a pint from the evening yield and sent to the laboratory. There the milk was analyzed for total solids, caseine, albumin, sugar, butterfat, protein, and ash. Mr. Taylor's cows were given numbers but the college farm cows rejoiced in the names of Dominie, Kicker, Strawberry, Susie, Camel, Lophorn, and Sutphen.[20] The chart accompanying the first annual report of the station showed that the native cows yielded the largest amount of milk, but more butter could be made from the milk of the Jerseys.[21] Cook made it plain in his summation that these experiments were introductory and unsatisfactory. He expected to arrange for further experiments in which average herds of all breeds common to the state would be represented.

Another experiment carried on at the farm in an effort to improve the methods of dairy farming was concerned with the search for a well-balanced diet for cows. Based on studies of animal nutrition carried on in Europe and on a book on animal nutrition written by Henry P. Armsby, Cook's friend and former associate at Rutgers, six cows of various breeds were chosen for the experiment.[22] For thirty days the cows were fed the "ideal ration" advocated by these experts—a mixture of clover, hay, wheat straw, brewer's grains, turnips, and cottonseed meal. The milk production and weight of the cows were measured carefully and results published in the first report of the station and in *Bulletin 10* which was reprinted in many of the state's newspapers.[23] Working farmers found the reports valuable because they showed that the ration used cost 30 percent less than feeding cows on clover hay alone. The savings were even greater when compared to a ration of clover and Indian cornmeal. Along with this immediately practical information, Cook included an explanation of the principles of animal nutrition and the cow's need for certain proportions of protein and carbohydrates. Discussing a fact which some farmers still find hard to apply, he referred to the experiments of the German agricultural chemists who found that feeding a cow more than the basic requirements of protein, fat, and digestible starchy material would not increase the milk flow. The search for the best feeds and fodders for New Jersey cattle was complicated by the fact that the only available tables analyzing feeds and fodders had been made in Germany, where the soil, climate, and maturation of crops was quite different from that found in New Jersey. Further tedious and lengthy studies at the station dealt systematically with the analysis of foods and fodders grown on the various Jersey soils and with such complex factors and the fact that crops like Indian corn and timothy hay were more digestible at one period of their growth than at another. In addition, the excreta of the animals was analyzed to discover the proportion of food remaining undigested.

By 1888 Cook could report that analyses of 461 samples of fodders and feeds had been made and the results put in tabular form for comparison with the analyses of the German expert, Professor Kuhn, and Dr. E. H. Jenkins, who had collected and arranged American averages.[24] The feeds and fodders were analyzed for their content of water, crude protein, crude fat, crude fiber, carbohydrates and ash (minerals). The relative amount of each nutrient present in each sample was presented quantitatively and the relative monetary value of each kind of feed and fodder was given. Tables showing the pounds per day of each nutrient needed by animals under varying conditions, such as a horse at light work, growing cattle, milk cows, swine being fattened, and others, were included.[25] Six pages of this sort of information enabled the farmer to work out the feed necessary for any animal for any period desired.

The extensive work of analyzing and supervising the experiments on cattle absorbed only a small part of the time of Cook, Neale, and their small staff. The primary focus of the chemists was on fertilizer analysis.

Begun under Cook's direction as a responsibility of the State Board of Agriculture in 1874, it was continued by the experiment station. Working with Arthur Neale who had primary responsibility for the enterprise was a succession of assistants among whom three later achieved notable success in agricultural chemistry. Louis A. Voorhees served as chief chemist of the New Jersey Station from 1896 until 1905; Joseph L. Hills became director of the Vermont Agricultural Station; and Edward B. Voorhees served as director of the New Jersey Station from 1896 until 1911. Beginning with ninety-two samples of fertilizers analyzed in 1880, the number rose to 303 in 1886 and 314 in 1889.[26] Of all the work done by the experiment station in New Jersey and elsewhere, it was the information on fertilizers that was best understood and appreciated by farmers. At first fertilizer samples were selected by chemists at the New Jersey Station or sent in by farmers who suspected the efficacy of certain fertilizers, but after 1884, although the station chemist made surprise visits to virtually every fertilizer manufacturer in the state to collect samples, most of the samples were sent in by volunteer farmers in all counties except Hudson.[27] The volunteers, who received expenses but no further compensation, included William B. Ward of Newark who was also a member of the Board of Managers and Woodnut Pettit, son of David Pettit, one of Cook's first friends and supporters from Salem County. Careful instructions and a special sampling tube were sent to each farmer by the experiment station. Each procured samples of every fertilizer sold in his county. In the laboratory, the chemists put the samples through chemical tests to determine the amount of nitrogen, potash, and phosphoric acid each contained. As methods of analysis were not yet sophisticated enough to allow testing for the element potassium, tests were made for compounds.[28] Most important was the publication of the analyses. All work done at the station's laboratory was available for publication, even that done for manufacturers for a set fee. The results, which took about eighty pages in each annual report, were the subject also of thirty-eight of the first sixty bulletins issued by the experiment station. One of the features of the fertilizer reports which farmers found helpful but which roused opposition from dealers was the practice of publishing the relative economic value of each type of fertilizer. Comparative amounts of nitrogen, phosphoric acid, and potash were given as well as the cost per pound. At one time the opposition of dealers became so intense that the Board of Managers voted to discontinue publishing these facts. Three months later the members of the Board stiffened their spines and resumed publication of the information. A few years later the fertilizer manufacturers made a futile attempt to push a bill through Congress which would have cut off federal aid to stations publishing commercial valuations.[29] By 1888 requests for New Jersey bulletins had reached 11,000 a year.[30] Besides allowing the farmer to choose better fertilizers for his money, the reports and bulletins taught him to select brands with the largest amount of the specific plant food he needed for a particular crop, stabilized the fertilizer trade, and protected reputable manufacturers.[31]

In addition to fertilizer and fodder analyses, Neale and his assistants also analyzed soils, water, milk, and whatever else was sent to the laboratory. The annual reports announced that they were prepared to identify grasses, wheats, and insects as well but there seems to have been little demand for this service.

In 1881 the growing of sorghum for the manufacture of sugar and syrup, tried on a small scale by individual farmers for some thirty years, was spurred on by a tariff on Cuban sugar and the promise of a state bounty of a dollar for every ton of cane grown and a penny for every pound of sugar produced.[32] A request to the experiment station from the New Jersey Senate for help in the project led to trial crops of fourteen varieties on the college farm. In addition, for a number of years Neale spent several months in Cape May County at the Rio Grande Sugar Company in an effort to boost the yield of sugar. He achieved positive results, increasing the crop of cane by doubling the number of hills per acre and fertilizing with potash and nitrate of soda but when the tariff on Cuban sugar was removed and the sugar beet turned out to be a better source of sugar than sorghum, the Rio Grande Company folded. Cook and Neale continued to experiment together with Henry A. Hughes of the original company but after Cook died, Neale resigned, and the weather caused a poor crop in 1889, the struggle was abandoned. Before this happened, Neale, working with Harvey W. Wiley of the U. S. Department of Agriculture, had perfected a diffusion process of milling sorghum by first using hot water on the shredded cane and then clarifying the product by steaming with slaked lime. This proved to be a significant innovation in the manufacture of sugar from sorghum.

Among the various other problems of New Jersey farmers taken up at the station at one time or another, the culture and diseases of cranberries were among the most important as was the culture of peach trees, a study of the diseases of sweet potatoes, and the results of trial plantings of alfalfa, cotton, tobacco, black grass, and cow peas.[33]

In the evolution of agricultural science there was an intrinsic conflict between the desire for research for the sake of knowing and the need to make studies which would produce immediate increases in farmers' incomes. The analyses of fertilizers carried on by almost all the first state experiment stations were supported by legislatures because they clearly responded to economic urgencies. The continual growth of support for the experiment station in New Jersey was not inevitable but was a result of Cook's recognition of the importance of responding to the needs of the farmers. If he had not he might well have lost their support as did the director of the Connecticut Experiment Station in Storrs, W. O. Atwater. Atwater insisted on pursuing studies on human diet, nutrition, and metabolism when the farmers were only willing to support research that would aid their pocketbooks. Eventually he was forced to resign because of the unpopularity of his program. His successor in 1912, Edward Hopkins Jenkins, like Cook, built close ties with the working farmers and found that he could then also pursue lines of original research because the farmers trusted him.[34] By 1880 Cook was a master of this kind of strategy. His own service on the New Jersey Board of Agriculture and as state geologist and his close personal friendship with many of the state's farmers were of vital importance. The bond was cemented as farmers began to rely on the station, not only for inspection and control duties but also as a disseminator of agricultural information. Cook and the station easily weathered the few attacks that were made.

New Jersey's experiment station was one of the most respected of the early stations but its work inevitably exhibited to some degree the same weaknesses that True found common to all early station work.[35] Too many experiments were superficial, sporadic, and diffuse. In New Jersey this was partly due to Cook's quick response to requests for information or aid. He was willing to try to grow anything—soybeans, cotton, tobacco, cow peas, alfalfa, or sorghum—and in this willingness to attack so many problems he spread the resources of the station very thin. His enthusiasm fortunately did not lead to the carelessness found in many stations. Experiments were carefully planned, executed in accordance with then current practices, and meticulous records were kept. A letter from Edwin H. Bogardus, who had taken a job with the New Haven Experiment Station after his responsibilities with the New Jersey Geological Survey ended, while perhaps not a fair evaluation of that station, gives some indication of the standards set by Cook:

I am told that the Jersey Station did more work last year than was accomplished here. I am not surprised to hear this. . . . It would be proper to call this place the great Connecticut smoking and whistling station. . . . I am busy but many of the other men are not. . . . A project for a plant house was abandoned after much trouble and expense and as a consequence also the scheme for soil analysis. . . . It looks as if the lab is to be conducted on the old plan, and fertilizers to constitute the main work for the future.[36]

Fully as important in the development of agricultural science as research and experimentation was the communication of the results to farmers and other agricultural scientists. The annual reports and bulletins of the New Jersey Experiment Station (which numbered sixty-four regular and ten special bulletins by the end of 1889) were augmented by Cook's lectures to the State Board of Agriculture and such groups as the Newark Board of Trade and various farmers' clubs. In 1884 he lectured on "How to Make Farming Pay." As J. G. Hitall of the Woodbury Grange Road wrote, "That is just what we are anxious to know," while George M. Rogers from Kirkwood urged that he talk to the "more rural or newer settlers who are doing nothing right."[37] During the winter months Cook frequently gave two or three lectures a week.[38] One of the most satisfying of his many contacts with agriculturists, this time outside of the United States, was that with J. H. Gilbert and others at the British Experiment Station at Rothamsted. The highlight of this relationship was an 1884 visit of Dr. Gilbert to the campus for a special lecture.[39]

The connections Cook had established with other professors of agriculture and experiment stations in the United States exemplified a more generalized development of the 1880s. As the various groups with agricultural interests pushed for tighter organization and greater federal support for agricultural colleges and experiment stations, they coalesced, gathered strength, and reinforced each other. Cook played an ever more significant role. An important milestone was the Convention of Agriculturists called in 1882 by George Baily Loring who had just been appointed Commissioner of Agriculture by President Cleveland. Loring had presided at the convention of 1872 and hoped that he could use the agriculturists as the lever to pry greater support from the government for his department.[40] His expectations miscarried as the agriculturists were more interested in promoting their own interests than in helping him. The program at the convention included papers on agricultural education by Cook and by George Chapman Caldwell of the Cornell Experiment Station. Cook's paper (read first) stirred up an interest in the establishment of experiment stations in the states which Caldwell's paper reinforced.

Cook began by talking of his long-held conviction that agriculturists needed the same "broad liberal education as the foundation for superior attainments" as did any other specialized professional.[41] He expressed his dismay that many people thought of agricultural colleges as havens for those who did not have the mental capacity or the basic education to succeed in other colleges. This gave a false picture of the nature of scientific agricultural education. A more valid (though equally distressing) deterrent to the growth of agricultural colleges was the sad fact that young men found when they had graduated from college that they could frequently only get farm jobs as common laborers. At the same time the practicing farmer failed to make as good a profit as he might because he did not have adequate scientific knowledge of farming matters. The logical resolution of this contradiction, said Cook, was to educate the farmers themselves. The chief end of agriculturists should be to give "more attention . . . to the investigation of those subjects which have their application in the cultivation of the soil and the increase of its learning" so that farmers may appreciate "the real interests and importance of their . . . calling and . . . treat it with becoming earnestness and dignity."[42] To illustrate, he cited specific examples of work being carried on at the New Jersey station on sorghum, fertilizer analysis, silage, and the balanced ration for cattle. Not only did the results of these studies when applied increase profits for the farmer but they brought scientific students in the college into direct contact with the working farmers. This stimulation of inquiry and care in farm operation, said Cook, provided the best kind of agricultural education. "The agricultural colleges," he concluded, "are at their best and legitimate work when they are training men for the work of investigation, for determining the best methods of applying known principles, for settling those which heretofore were unknown, and generally for doing work . . . for the common benefit of all classes of the community."[43] He advocated that such colleges be increased and liberally supported. "The experiment station," he said, "takes up the work where the agricultural college leaves it, and carries it forward till its benefits are . . . enjoyed in every household and upon every farm."[44] He emphasized the way in which the two institutions could work together to achieve desired ends.

Caldwell's paper supported Cook's ideas and a considerable amount of enthusiasm began building for the establishment of more college-attached experiment stations. Such a development would not further Loring's intention to use the influence of the organization to obtain greater government support for his department. He therefore advocated instead a series of conjoint experiments in the colleges and stations to be administered by his office.[45] His suggestion stymied the push for state-run experiment stations temporarily, but shortly after the convention Eugene Woldeman Hilgard, director of the California Agricultural Station at Berkeley, published an article in the *Atlantic Monthly* attacking both the Department of Agriculture and the land-grant colleges that had not set up experiment stations.[46] He suggested that Congress provide subsidies to set up college-attached stations.

For several years thereafter the spokesmen for the experiment stations patiently worked to develop a plan for the most workable relationship between the federal government and state experiment stations and its embodiment in a bill that could pass the Congress. Most influential in the formulation of the concept was Seaman A. Knapp, professor of agriculture and later president of the Iowa State Agricultural College and the foremost promoter of the agricultural extension program.[47]

Loring called another agricultural convention the following year at which he tried to keep advocates of experiment stations from speaking but New Jersey's Thomas Dudley managed to gain the floor long enough to advocate the establishment of an experiment station and farm in every state.[48] This opened up the debate and the delegates began discussing the exact form that an expanded experiment station program should take. President Theophilus Abbot of the Michigan Agricultural College argued in support of a system that would provide for a professor of agricultural science to work part time on special experiments controlled by the college. Under such a system experiment stations would have been set up as departments of the colleges.[49] The alternative was to have the stations established as independent autonomous units.

In 1885 a new Commissioner of Agriculture, Norman J. Coleman, called a special convention of delegates from the agricultural colleges and put experiment stations on the agenda as a major topic for discussion. In New Jersey Cook and Dudley had succeeded in having the state legislature send petitions to Congress advocating federal aid for state experiment stations. Between February 1883 and March 1885 similar petitions had come in from ten other states and in the winter of 1884-85 a group of college presidents traveled to Washington to argue for passage of the bill, but they were unsuccessful.[50]

Twenty-eight states and three territories were represented at the agricultural convention held in 1885.[51] Cook reported to the delegates on the lobbying efforts of the previous year and told the convention that he found when he had appeared to testify before the House Committee on Agriculture that the bill was first received with indifference. George Atherton, by then president of Pennsylvania State College, was also lobbying for the bill and after two months during which, Cook said, "the subject grew upon them" the committee voted unanimously to support the bill when it came before the House. There were enough votes in the House to pass it but the pressure of business at the end of the session prevented it from ever being brought out of committee.[52] Cook's letters during these years show that on several occasions he acted as a goad to spur his colleagues into action. Since 1864 when he had been involved in the struggle to have Rutgers made the land-grant college of New Jersey, Cook had known that it was votes that counted. In addition to working closely with Atherton he corresponded with President Andrew D. White of Cornell, M. C. Fernold at the Maine State College in Orono, William R. Lazenby of the Ohio State Experiment Station, W. S. McMurtrie of the Illinois Industrial University, and William R. Brewer of the Sheffield Scientific School, urging them to send representatives to Washington to appear before the committee. The response was not encouraging. White said that it would be difficult for Cornell to be represented although he would do what he could and he would certainly write letters if Cook would tell him where to write. Fernold replied that it would be impossible to send anyone but that a Maine senator and representative he had talked to thought the bill would pass. Lazenby indicated that while the Ohio people had been actively writing letters he didn't think that anyone from their experiment station could go to Washington. McMurtrie said that they could do nothing as their regent did not favor the bill.

Fortunately, B. F. Howey, congressman from New Jersey, conscientiously sent copies of the various versions of the bill to Cook and arranged with Senator Hatch for Cook and other representatives of the experiment stations and colleges to appear before the committee. When Cook testified before the committee he reminded the senators that the reason for the new bill was the inadequacy of the land-grant arrangements made in the 1862 Morrill Act.[53] That act had failed to provide sufficient support for agricultural education in all states. Farmers, said Cook, did not need help in the simple operations which they carried on but in areas where they lacked the skill or means to carry on investigations. For the most part they could not cope with the trouble and expense of weighing and measuring necessary for scientific experimentation. He called the attention of the committee to the seventy-five or more experiment stations in Europe and the state experiment stations in existence in the United States and gave examples of the work closest to him—that done in New Jersey to control commercial fertilizers and feeding stuffs and the experiments to find the best fodders and to ferret out deficiencies in various soils. He spoke also of the need for further investigation of such matters as diseases in peach trees, sweet potatoes, and cranberries.

During the next year Cook and Atherton were joined by T. C. Chamberlin, the geologist who had worked on the terminal moraine and was soon to become president of Wisconsin University but was at the time in the Department of Interior working on the geological survey. Henry Armsby, now associate director of the Wisconsin Experiment Station, and Merrill Gates, president of Rutgers, were also active. During 1887 Cook and Atherton carried on an extensive correspondence on the various bills and amendments to bills, made trips to Washington to talk with congressional agricultural committees and speculated as to which congressmen were best able and willing to aid their cause.

Thanks to the efforts of Congressman William H. Hatch, after whom the bill was named, it passed the House in 1886 and Senator James George tried to get it to the floor of the Senate.[54] Finally in January 1887 the bill was brought to the Senate but it became apparent that while there was sufficient support for federal subsidy of agricultural experimentation there were some concerns as to whether or not the bill would protect the autonomy of the state experiment stations. Amendments were added which incorporated some of the provisions of an alternative bill which had been offered by Senator Joseph E. Hally of Connecticut.[55] These included the requirement of assent of the state legislatures for the creation of a college station. A requirement that each station operate an experimental farm was dropped and the stations were not to be required to aid the Department of Agriculture. The Commissioner of Agriculture was given no powers beyond those of aiding and assisting the state stations. The bill was finally passed after much discussion, amendment, and shuttling from Senate to committee to House to committee and back. President Grover Cleveland signed the bill on March 2, 1887.

Unfortunately, in the confusion a provision for money to implement the bill was omitted—"one of the Senate's 'improvements,'" Atherton wrote.[56] Cook and Atherton again began lobbying efforts. In a special act in February 1888 the omission was remedied and the agricultural colleges were able to establish federally supported experimental stations.

Immediately after the passage of the Hatch Act in 1887 Cook proceeded to carry out his dream of establishing a well-staffed experiment station. He was able to hire a number of competent specialists. One of the most outstanding was Byron D. Halsted who held a Ph.D. from Harvard. Thirty-six years old when he came to New Jersey, Halsted soon became one of the nation's leading experts in plant pathology and mycology. Another new man was Julius Nelson, whose son and granddaughter later followed him in service to the station. He was best known for his studies of the oyster. These two, along with John B. Smith, the indefatigable entomologist, and Edward Voorhees, constituted what has been called "a group of agricultural scientists unexcelled in any American agricultural experiment station."[57]

In the last annual report Cook wrote, he announced that the New Jersey Agricultural Experiment Station would continue to work on analyses of fertilizers, feeds, and fodders, questions connected with the production and quality of milk, and various field experiments, while the Agricultural College Experiment Station (as the federally supported station was called) would extend the work in the direction of "investigation of the principles of science which underlie the various branches of agricultural and horticultural practice."[58] To this end Cook started Nelson on the study of the oyster and directed George E. Hulst, the first entomologist at the station, to include in his report detailed drawings and descriptions of the life cycles of several of the more destructive insects.[59] Cook held out great hopes for the efforts of Horace Bushnell Patton, a Ph.D. from Heidelberg, who was hired as a chemical geologist. Patton proposed to continue the preliminary soil analysis made for the New Jersey Geological Survey in 1878 and to "study the whole process of soil formation including the effects of tillage."[60] Patton left the station the year after Cook died but soil research continued under the direction of Edward Voorhees and eventually led to the preeminence of Rutgers in soil research with the work of Jacob G. Lipman and Selman A. Waksman, discoverer of streptomycin.

At the same time that the struggle to pass the Hatch Act was going on, agriculturists were trying to establish a permanent national organization of agricultural colleges for the purpose of sharing knowledge and working together on research and experimentation. The effort had begun in 1871 when the Friends of Agricultural Education convened in Chicago following the meetings of the AAAS.[61] As a result of that meeting Cook was made the representative from New Jersey.[62] Although a desire for a permanent organization had been expressed by a majority of those present and informal meetings were held yearly after 1881 by professors of agriculture in eight midwestern colleges, no one assumed leadership in gathering the agriculturists together.[63] The establishment of a permanent organization was not considered seriously again until Commissioner Loring called the agriculturists together in

1885. When the delegates had met in national convention in 1882 and 1883, George Atherton had been the leading advocate for the formation of a permanent organization. At the Convention of Agriculturists in 1885 Atherton was made chairman of an executive committee (of which Cook was a member) to plan for a permanent organization and to convene the group again.[64] Atherton did not move very rapidly and in reply to a letter from Cook early in 1887 said that he expected that a meeting might be held that fall. The group finally met in Washington in October 1888 after the Hatch Act had passed. Of the thirty-five men in attendance about half were college presidents and the rest professors of agriculture or directors of state experiment stations. The new organization was called the Association of American Agricultural College and Experiment Stations and both colleges and stations were entitled to membership.

One of the great problems that became apparent at the meeting was the difficulty of establishing the experiment stations authorized by the Hatch Act. Most of them were to be attached to the land-grant colleges but few people knew how to go about organizing an experiment station. As John A. Myers from the Agricultural College in Mississippi wrote to Cook, "We shall have to make some provisions for the newcomer and exactly what it shall be is the problem that racks the brains of our officials. . . ."[65] Colleges needed advice on the best organizational structure for an experiment station, what equipment they should buy for the station, how they could decide on what research to try, and how they could find out about previously accumulated data in the research area they decided to follow.[66] They wondered how much teaching their professors should do while trying to carry on research and whether this added responsibility should add to their salaries.

At the 1887 meeting Cook spoke on the organization of work under the Hatch Act while W. O. Atwater discussed the coordination of work in experimentation and S. W. Johnson of Connecticut talked on the proper interpretation and applications of the Hatch Act. The three were asked to serve on a committee to arrange for publication of a paper incorporating the material in their papers. Atherton was elected president of the organization and Cook was elected one of the five vice-presidents.[67]

The Atwater-Johnson-Cook "Report on Station Work" did not set forth a rigid set of standards or procedures but approached the problem by printing replies to questionnaires previously sent to existing experiment stations.[68] The questions were concerned particularly with the kind of experimental work they expected to be doing. The report recommended the writing of monographs explaining results of experiments and including descriptions of apparatus and research methods.[69] The committee recommended as well that new stations embark upon short-term experimentation or research on immediate problems facing farmers in their states. This would provide a prompt response and direct, practical advice and thus provide to the farmers justification for their existence. At the same time, they should begin long-range projects on more abstract research which might lead to results of profound permanent value to scientific agriculture.

The three authors warned that directors of experiment stations should not forget that their mission was to teach as well as to experiment and that they must seek ways to bring their discoveries "not 'down to the farmer,' but home to him!"[70] If they honestly and earnestly pursued the effort to help the farmer, they were told, both farmers and the general public would respond with support and understanding for their basic research projects.

The report recognized that the individual states would have varying personnel and factional problems and attitudes to deal with as well as varying agricultural problems. The committee offered no specific directions as to how a variety of men, some without scientific training or any experience in practical farming problems, could establish experiment stations. The committee aimed only to "inquire and to suggest."[71] When the next meeting of the association was held in Knoxville, Tennessee, in January 1889, Cook chaired the section dealing with the problems of cooperation among stations. After three days of discussion and debate the group decided to leave interstation cooperation on a voluntary basis.[72]

Thus Cook's long struggle to encourage the establishment of agricultural experiment stations and his experiences on the Rutgers College Farm had prepared him not only effectively to implement agricultural experimentation in New Jersey but also to provide needed advice and leadership on the national scene.

Cook's reputation and role among geologists took much the same course as they did among agriculturists and there also his abilities were not fully appreciated or called upon until he was in his sixties. His reputation rested primarily on his demonstrated scientific achievements and administrative and political skills as director of the New Jersey Geological Survey. In particular he was recognized for making New Jersey the first state in the Union to have a complete topographical survey and mapping. The topographical mapping program in New

Jersey was given a boost in 1884 when John Wesley Powell, director of the United States Geological Survey, began the preparation of a topographical and geological map of the United States. The New Jersey survey had by that time completed about half of the field work and mapping of the state. In return for copies of the completed maps, the USGS undertook to fund the remainder of the work. While technically the project thus came under the direction of the USGS, in fact the arrangement made no difference in the personnel or control of the mapping operation. Cook's staff was paid by the USGS and the project remained under his direction. This was especially good news for Cook and Smock as it meant that they no longer had to sacrifice part of their salaries to finance the topographical work. From July 15, 1884, the date on which the USGS took over, the funds of the New Jersey Survey were freed for use on geological studies. Smock resigned his position as assistant geologist in 1885, accepting a post at the Museum of Natural History of New York State in Albany. Bowser and Vermeule stayed on until the topographic survey and mapping were completed in 1887.

The New Jersey maps covered the entire state with seventeen overlapping maps on a scale of one inch to the mile. Manuscript maps were prepared on a scale of three inches per mile and tolerances were held to one-fiftieth of an inch (approximately thirty feet). The map series was drawn on a polyconic projection and each map was published as it was completed, beginning in 1882. The entire series cost $6.93 per square mile for both field work and manuscript preparation. As the nineteenth century topographic maps of Great Britain have been estimated to have cost $200 per square mile, it is clear that Cook's survey was carried out very economically.

Topographic mapping was essential for accurate geological mapping but it had other uses as well. For example, a water commission appointed by the state legislature in 1883 found that the survey's topographic maps and hydrologic data greatly expedited their work on a plan for the state water supply. As Cook reported in 1888, maps drew attention to New Jersey's advantage of location, varied terrain, healthful seaside and mountain resorts, water supply, and then unequaled means of travel and communication. Cook added, "The maps are studied by engineers for projected improvements, by citizens seeking homes in the country, by land owners who desire to improve or open their properties, as well as by intelligent and inquiring citizens of all kinds who are interested in the development and prosperity of the state."[73] The first edition of the topographic map was completely sold out (at cost) and a second edition printed by 1888. Citizens were directed to send twenty-five cents per sheet to the Office of the Geological Survey in New Brunswick.

According to State Geologist Kemble Widmer, the maps have successfully withstood the test of time.[74] Seventy-five years after the last map of the first series was completed, considerable demand for copies still existed and well over 100,000 maps have been distributed since 1900. Since the original series was published only two major changes in format have been made. In 1903 the overlapping system was changed to an edge-match system and in 1956 two additional colors were added to improve readability and contrast.

After the maps were published praise came from all over. W. P. Garrison, publisher of the *Nation* wrote, "And so the great map . . . is finished! And what a beautiful piece of work it is! It will make many envious to possess it who have perhaps small claim on the bounty of the state."[75] Probably most important to Cook was the praise from other geologists. Henry F. Osborne from Princeton's Museum of Geology and Archaeology wrote, "Allow me to express my heartiest congratulations upon the termination in so successful a manner of this portion of your work. The series are models of topographic work and richly deserve the flattering notice they have received from the press."[76] T. C. Chamberlin wrote, "I have the greatest pleasure in acknowledging your magnificent atlas. It is superb and is a grand example for other states to follow."[77]

From foreign lands as well came flattering words: James Geikie at the University of Edinburgh commented on the beautiful execution of the maps and added, "I hope they will be duly patronized by the folk for whom in the first place they are intended. By foreigners like myself I am sure they will be highly appreciated."[78] Charles Barrois of the faculty of Sciences in Lille, France, wrote, "I have received . . . the fine geological and topographical maps you were so kind as to send me. I thank you very much indeed and beg to congratulate you most heartily for the completion of those grand pieces of work."[79]

In *The Mapping of New Jersey*, John P. Snyder, paying tribute to the maps, writes, "At long last, accurate maps of the state could be prepared with confidence. Subsequent refinements consisted chiefly of updating and procedural details. Two hundred years of reshaping New Jersey maps had come to an end."[80]

Credit for the actual work on the topographical survey belongs largely to C. C. Vermeule. The following passage from a letter he wrote to Cook after the completion of the maps indicates the relationship between them.

I take the opportunity which I have not had before to express to you my regret that circumstances make it necessary to sever those relations which have existed between us for ten years past and to assure you of my sincere and heartfelt appreciation of all your kindness to me in that period. I assure you that I never expect to find a kinder friend or pleasanter associate. Whatever success has been achieved in the New Jersey work I know to be due to your active interest and sympathy and cordial support, to your leaving me untrammeled to work out my plans yet interposing sound and well-timed advice when your greater experience showed you that it was needed. I need not tell you how much I have had that work at heart, nor do you need my assurance that I feel that I have done my very best and have nothing to reproach myself with excepting that I have now and then attempted too much more than I could well accomplish. . . ."[81]

For Cook a most important result of the progress of the topographical mapping was that geological and stratigraphical studies of the state could be perfected and refined. In 1882 the annual report included a lengthy account of the characteristic features of the Triassic red sandstone and traprock and some information on the igneous rocks in Sussex County's Kittatinny Valley. The 1883 report included material on the Tertiary and Cretaceous formations of southern New Jersey, more on red sandstone and traprock strata, and a lengthy description of the Archaean rocks (now characterized as early Precambrian). In 1884 sketches of sections showed the stratification of various deposits beneath the surface and the manner in which they extended out under the ocean. Cook judged that the rocks of the Green Pond Mountain Range, first examined by Rogers, were Silurian with possibly some Devonian. In commenting on the Archaean rocks which he had re-examined, Cook noted that in much of the area covered by the rocks in the mountain ridges the formations were massive and unstratified. The 1885 report was accompanied by several geological sections illustrating the Archaean and the Quaternary geology. Work had begun on the study of the Highlands Archaean rocks and iron ores with the aid of the topographic maps as well as a detailed study of the Quaternary formations along the seashore.

In the winter of 1885 the State House in Trenton burned, destroying some of the properties of the survey. The most important loss was the collection of minerals, fossils, building stones, rocks, woods, and other natural products of the state which had been placed in a museum in the State House. Fortunately, the best of the specimens were away on loan to the 1884 New Orleans Exposition. Plans for starting a geological museum in a new State House were immediately begun. Meanwhile, what had been saved was stored in the State Arsenal in Trenton. The new museum was scheduled to be ready in 1888 and Cook expected to include implements and other relics of Indians as well as fossils and collections of plants and animals and rocks, minerals and ores. He urged all interested citizens to send their contributions to him.

In 1886 Cook continued the study of Archaean rocks with special attention to geological age, the succession of members, the geological structure and the lithology. Paleozoic rocks, the Triassic formation, and the surface geology were also briefly considered. In 1887, the year in which the topographic survey and maps were completed, some field work was done in the exploration and study of the Archaean rocks in Sussex County and of the glacial and terrace deposits in the valley of the Delaware above the Water Gap.

A detailed critical analysis of Cook's stratigraphical work is beyond the scope of this book. The enlargement of stratigraphic knowledge depends upon careful examination and description and the general status of the science but it is also dependent upon the state of the technology. While the nature of strata can be deduced from natural outcrops, more exact data are available when the passage of rail or automobile roads necessitates tunnels and cuts or when the development of mines opens up new areas underground. Thus the complex mineral deposits at Franklin, New Jersey, and the nature of that occurrence were not discovered until deeper shafts were opened in the zinc mines and many new minerals discovered. It was not until 1959 when sixty years of records of the New Jersey Zinc Company were made available to researchers that old questions on the formation of the limestone could be reconsidered with new evidence.

Rogers had not considered Precambrian rocks (which he termed "Primary") except to divide them into gneisses and granites. The significance of his "Primary" category was that he found no fossils in them.[82] As Frank L. Nason pointed out in 1889, Rogers was a careful observer and recorded the facts he observed meticulously so that the limitations of his work are primarily due to the limitations of the science at that time.[83] Kitchell made little advance in this area except to record some new facts. Cook's 1868 *Geology of New Jersey* includes theories consistent with ideas prevalent at that time. He used the term "Azoic" (in later years he used "Archaean") instead of "Primary" and the accompanying map achieved a higher degree of accuracy. In its 1873 map, the New Jersey Survey made the first attempt to group together the allied rocks of the Precambrian (Azoic, Archaean) and in 1884 the desirability of graphically representing the various characters of the Precambrian (Archaean) on a geological map was recognized, although it was also pointed out that because the rocks were often concealed and had been subjected to considerable faulting and displacement this might be an impossible task.[84] The completion of the topographical maps enabled the survey to refine the mapping of the various rock groups and in 1885 N. C. Britton and J. H. Merrill began systematically studying the formation. By 1888 the accumulated data indicated that the Precambrian (Archaean) rocks were not homogeneous and that the various belts needed to be traced. Cook's conclusions on the stratigraphy of the marl formations which have been treated in earlier chapters were particularly important for both the advance of basic stratigraphic knowledge and for the practical exploitation of the clay and marl beds and the water-bearing strata.

In 1885 Cook introduced the subject of forestry and forest fires in the annual report of the survey. The topographical survey had provided new information about the state's forest area. The state had 2,300,000 acres of forest land, 1,485,290 of which was in the southern pine forests. The most common tree in northern New Jersey was the chestnut—used for railroad ties and telegraph poles. The southern forests were primarily made up of pine and cedar trees. The pine sometimes was cut for lumber but much of it was used for firewood and charcoal while the cedar trees were made into shingles, strips, or siding. Cook was convinced that more profit could be realized from the lumbering industry in the state than was generally thought and he recommended that most of the forest land should be used for raising timber because it was largely unsuitable for cultivation. He explained that the Paleozoic and Archaean rocks yielded rocky soil that was not tillable. Most of the woodlands on the Triassic formation were on farms and could therefore expect to decrease somewhat as the wood was used. Cook expected that in the years to come there would be pressure to bring much of the pine forest area under cultivation but suggested that it would be conducive to the best interests of the state to leave at least one and a half million acres permanently in forest land.

The annual reports through the 1880s continued to update information on water supply, marl, zinc and iron mines, and water supply. In addition, both Cook and Smock were interested in meteorology. Cook had kept records of rainfall and weather in New Brunswick from the time he arrived in 1854, and in 1876 began publishing a series of annual reports on rainfall in New Brunswick in the reports of the Rutgers Scientific School. In the Geological Survey Report of 1880 he included a few pages on the climate of New Jersey.[85] Tables gave temperature and atmospheric precipitation at twenty locations throughout the state. In 1886 the State Weather Service was organized in cooperation with the U. S. Weather Bureau. Cook was made director. Volume I of the "final report" of the geological survey issued in 1888 included a lengthy discussion of climate by John Smock.

In 1886 and 1887 Cook reported on drainage projects in the state. Of the large tracts of wetlands for which the geological survey had been petitioned to provide drainage plans only one had been completed—the tract in the Great Meadows on the Pequest River in Warren County. The valley was some seven and a half miles long and one and a half miles wide. Approximately ten thousand years before a lake had been formed by a dam of glacial drift deposited across the valley. The lake had disappeared but in its place remained a meadow on the accumulation of sediment, vegetable matter and peat. The Pequest River wound its way through this meadow in a small, crooked channel which overflowed and flooded the entire valley after every heavy rain. The water ran off very slowly, leaving the land in such a swampy condition that it could not be safely crossed. In the past ineffectual attempts had been made to drain the meadows but the efforts had always focused on the meadow itself rather than the outlet of the river. The geological survey plan provided for widening and deepening the channel so that the stream could carry off all the water. Begun in 1872 the project was successfully completed in 1878. The water stayed within the banks of the stream; the swamps became dry enough for cultivation; and corn, hay, and grass were being raised. This made the fields worth three or four times as much as the fields in the surrounding uplands. A further benefit was the reduction of various kinds of fevers and malarial diseases which had been very common in the area.

After Dr. Britton finished his preliminary catalogue of the flora of New Jersey in 1881, six hundred copies were distributed to botanists throughout the state for their comments, corrections, and additions. The botanists returned the catalogues after two or three years and their notes were used in completing the final catalogue.

Membership on the Board of Managers of the survey had, of course, changed since its formation in 1864 but the calibre of the men who served on it remained much the same. The original membership of ten was raised to seventeen when congressional districts were reallocated in 1875. Remarkably, in 1888 William Parry, Henry Aitkin, and William M. Force, three of the original members, remained on the Board. Seldon T. Scranton, appointed in 1866, Thomas T. Kinney in 1870, and Augustus W. Cutler in 1872 were other long-time members who were particularly interested and active. The support of the Board for the survey continued to be enthusiastic and helped to insure renewal of the enabling legislation and appropriation when it periodically expired. Because the expenses of the survey were kept to a minimum, the work carried out in the most economically possible way, and the results easily understood, approval by the legislators was always virtually unanimous.[86] In 1872 the survey was extended for four years with an appropriation of $5,000 a year; in 1876 the legislature increased the appropriation to $8,000 a year and extended it for five more years and the legislatures of 1880 and 1885 voted to continue this appropriation.[87]

As the magnitude of the survey increased, Cook inevitably became more and more involved in administration and was less able to get into the field. His ability to decide what should be done and procure the money and men to do it was as important to the successful completion of the survey as was his expert knowledge of the geology of New Jersey. However, his geology notebooks show that during vacations he continued to travel throughout the state to inspect various geological sites.

In addition to the extraordinarily loyal and competent staff led by John Smock and C. C. Vermeule, he also enlisted the services of Nathanial C. Griffin of the Columbia College School of Mines to work on the Archaean rocks and a catalogue of the flora of the state, and Fred J. H. Merrill to help with the cross sections of the Highlands and coastal area. R. P. Whitfield prepared the lists of Cretaceous invertebrate fossils and Gastropods. J. S. Newberry continued to do the paleontological description of the fossil flora of the Triassic and Cretaceous systems and the fishes of the Triassic.

In 1888 the first volume of Cook's second "final" survey (the first having been the 1868 *Geology of New Jersey*) was completed. It included reports on the geodetic, topographic, and magnetic surveys, the climate of the state, and two maps, one showing civil divisions and the other elevations, mountains, ridges, valleys, plains, rivers, and drainage areas. The second volume, almost ready for publication, included catalogues of the state's minerals, wild plants, and vertebrate and invertebrate animals.

Cook noted that so much attention had been given to the study and description of the geological structure of the rocks in the state in reports prior to 1888 that the work remaining consisted largely of analyzing and synthesizing data collected in the past. The marl and clay formations in the middle of the state and the limestones, slates, and sandstones in the north and northwestern portions had been especially carefully studied. He pointed out that there were still some obscure and difficult points of structure in the red sandstone and the gneissic rocks but he thought that important progress had been made in clearing up the difficulties. He expected to publish a volume on structural geology next and a final volume on economic geology would complete the series.

Among geologists as in agricultural circles, Cook was increasingly honored as an elder statesman and called upon to assume important positions in the national organization. After his attendance at the meetings of the International Geological Congress in Paris in 1878 he had been appointed to the American Committee which served as a liaison with the Congress. He was unable to go to subsequent meetings in Bologna and Berlin because delegates had to pay their own way and he could not afford it but he was active in the preparatory work for the meetings and in 1883 compiled a table of then current names, equivalents, and subdivisions of the strata for the Mesozoic and Cenozoic of the eastern United States.[88] The next meeting was scheduled for London and Cook became even more deeply involved in the preparations. James Hall was chairman of the committee but he was very much concerned with personal problems connected with his work on the New York State Survey and was relatively inactive. Cook frequently was called upon to preside at the meetings of the committee. Persifor Frazer, who had worked on the Pennsylvania survey, was the secretary of the committee and managed its work. The committee was divided into subcommittees, each charged with the responsibility of preparing a report on a specific geological period. Cook was appointed reporter for the Mesozoic and was a member of the Quaternary and Recent of which Major John Wesley Powell, director of the United States Geological Survey, was reporter.

By 1887 the International Congress had established as its primary goals the uniform classification of major divisions of historic and stratigraphic geology and the establishment of a uniform system for the coloring of geological maps. Some agreement had been reached on common usage of major chronological and stratigraphical terms, rules for paleontological nomenclature had been adopted, and a geologic map of Europe was almost finished. Great difficulties stood in the way of the adoption of universal chronological and stratigraphical terms. This had become apparent at the Paris meeting and the problems had not diminished in subsequent years. In the European countries where the strata had been first studied the names given to the successive strata were generally known and accepted. American geologists had tried to fit American geological strata into these classifications but the system was not comprehensive enough to meet conditions throughout the world.[89] Natural forces had been at work in different ways in America and the labels were not always appropriate. European geologists found it very difficult to abandon terms which they had grown accustomed to and, in fact, developed a national pride in their own system of nomenclature. Because attendance at the congresses was voluntary and members paid their own way, the largest representation was always from the host country and they could always outvote the visitors. At the Paris meeting there were 194 French representatives and 110 foreigners, at Bologna 148 Italians and seventy-five foreigners and at Berlin 163 Germans and ninety-three foreigners. For the next meeting of the congress the American committee was planning to present a consensus report on recommendations for terms conforming to the American strata. Then an effort to reconcile the terms used by Europeans with the American terms would be made.

Unfortunately, the problem was complicated by the inability of the Americans to agree among themselves. They even disagreed about the feasibility of having a uniform classification of strata. Most of the opposition came from Powell. His assistant and supporter, Grove Carl Gilbert, happened to be serving as vice-president of Section E of the American Association for the Advancement of Science (the parent organization of the American committee) in 1887 and in his presidential address Gilbert said that the concept of a worldwide unity of geological systems was a fallacy. He declared, "Uniformity is not worth purchasing at the price of falsification."[90] He argued that geologists in meetings were attempting to establish geological facts by vote instead of by observation. "The entire science of geology," he proclaimed, "is constituted by the aggregation and arrangement of facts, and none of its results can be rendered more true, or be more firmly established, or be prevented from yielding to contradictory facts, by conventional agreement."[91]

Gilbert's address conflicted strongly with Frazer's conviction that because the American geologists had been among the strongest advocates for the convening of the congresses, all American geologists should support its work. Otherwise, he thought, the development of the classification system would be controlled by "the divided energies of a handful of leaders, each using the resources of his government to enable him to show that all the rest are hopelessly wrong and himself phenomenally and wholly right."[92]

Frazer's zeal at times wearied the rest of the committee as he tended to "drag the committee about when there was nothing to do."[93] James Dwight Dana, who at Cook's suggestion had been made a member of the committee in 1887, wrote to Cook that there was considerable dissatisfaction with Frazer because he was not openminded enough.[94] Dana thought that Frazer was developing a clique and he strongly disapproved of cliques of any sort, whether USGS or any other. He wrote, "I have confidence only in Hall, Newberry and yourself of the Committee."[95]

Throughout 1887 Cook proceeded with the gathering of opinions for his report on the Mesozoic. He found two hundred papers written by almost one hundred people on the Triassic alone. His final report consisted of a short narrative and several tables and focused particularly on the Triassic. He identified the principal problems on the Triassic as being a scarcity of marine invertebrate fossils, a tendency of the rock to disintegrate easily, which meant it was covered with earth almost everywhere, and the unusual uniformity of color and composition which made it difficult to trace faults or other disturbances.[96]

His report identified the Triassic on the Atlantic slope as represented by the red sandstone and as the lowest strata of the Mesozoic, above the Paleozoic group and below the Cretaceous stage, as is the Keuper of Europe. (Cook used the term "Cretacic," probably in an attempt to make it correspond to the suffixes of Jurassic, Triassic, and Mesozoic—however, the idea was not generally adopted.) He characterized the rock material of the system as largely granitic and even-bedded, the materials being derived from the older rocks bordering it on the other side. He pointed out also the remarkable incidence of eruptive rocks. Because of faults in the rocks, which dipped mainly in one direction and were little curved or folded, measurements were unsatisfactory but estimates as to its thickness varied widely—from 1,500 feet to 15,000 feet or more. Cook described the Cretaceous as well represented in the eastern United States beginning with a lower strata of sands of estuary origin, a middle strata of the Raritan clays, and then the series of greensand marls and limestones. Also widespread west of the Mississippi, the Cretaceous in that area included material which varied from that of the East but fossil remains indicated a positive correlation.

When the time came to give reports to the committee, Powell refused to present a written one. He proposed that all geologists who had opinions about the work of the subcommittee should come to a meeting of the International Committee and express their views orally.[97] Frazer grumbled that Powell's concept of his position as director of the USGS was like that of a commander of an army of geologists.[98] In fact, the determination and iron will which had served Powell well in making his trip down the Colorado was not helpful in establishing workable relationships with his fellow geologists. Frazer had hoped that at the final meetings of the International Committee with Cook in the chair and himself on the floor, they could keep Powell from being too disruptive. But no one could restrain Powell and the meeting "got into a snarl" (to use Hall's words) when Powell tried to persuade the committee that the written reports of the other subcommittees should not be accepted.[99] He was unsuccessful in this effort and the committee presented its preliminary report to Section E the following week.[100] From the chair Gilbert tried to discredit the subcommittee reports by ruling that a vote was not in order as the reports were merely the individual opinions of the reporters; but he could not prevent the section from unanimously approving the work of the committee.[101] The final reports of the subcommittees were accepted by the international committee in December 1887 at a meeting at which Cook again presided. Powell's dissatisfaction with the committee came to a head in April 1888, when he withdrew his report on the Quaternary and resigned.[102]

On the whole Cook agreed with Frazer rather than with Powell and Gilbert although he had some doubts as to the practical results of the international congresses.[103] He sympathized with Powell's assertion that no final and universal geological classification could be achieved at that time but thought it useful for geologists to get together and present their cases to each other, thus demonstrating the complexity of the task and providing communication if not agreement.

Cook's work on the international committee greatly enhanced his reputation for sagacity and administrative abilities among the geologists and at the conclusion of the Section E meeting in 1887 he was elected vice-president. His vice-presidential address, delivered the following year at the annual meeting in Cleveland, was on the role of American geologists at the International Geological Congress.[104] After tracing the history of the congresses and explaining its problems with representation and language, he described what he saw to be the most important tasks for geology and geography at that time. First he stressed the need for good topographic maps—here the United States was far behind the European countries. He also explained that the difficulties in universalizing classification of strata rose because, although geological strata occur throughout the earth, the fact that Europeans had begun the systemization meant that the system was not comprehensive enough for universal application and that because of this American geologists had great difficulty in trying to transfer the classifications of the German, English, and French systems to their country. He suggested that because the host country representatives outnumbered outsiders to such a great extent decisions could only be tentative. He thought a more equitable representation was necessary before final decisions could be made. In any case, he argued that because the geological time column was still in the process of being developed all naming should be considered tentative. "Names must be given in describing new kinds of occurrences of rocks, but they should be provisional and dropped whenever some more characteristic or generally appropriate name can be found."[105] He was unable to suggest a solution to the problems of representation and expenses but urged that the goals of the congress were worthy and useful and would help geologists in developing a fuller understanding of the whole field of geological science as well as allow for more careful and precise study of special fields.[106]

The same year in which he was elected vice-president for Section E brought Cook the greatest honor of his career. As early as 1881 James Hall had proposed him for election to the National Academy of Science and in 1885 he received the largest number of nominations, but it was not until 1887 that he was elected. J. P. Lesley, director of the Pennsylvania Geological Survey, wrote to ask him for a summary of his most important scientific works. Cook answered that he hardly knew what to reply because his work had always been related to the New Jersey Geological Survey and while he always tried to include something of scientific interest he had concentrated on economic matters. He finally decided to list four scientific studies which had involved much labor in their preparation:

(1) The description of the stratigraphy and mineral composition of the several beds which constitute the greensand marl formation of New Jersey, (1854) often republished, much extended but not changed; (2) The paper "On a Subsidence of the Land, On the Sea Coast of New Jersey and Long Island" (1857); (3) The Southern Limit of the Last Glacial Drift across New Jersey and the Adjacent parts of New York and Pennsylvania (1877); and (4) A description of the Fire Clay deposits of Woodbridge, Amboy and other places in New Jersey (1878).[107]

During the 1880s Cook began to feel that he was trying to do too much. He was anxious to complete the geological survey and to fulfill his growing responsibilities in national agricultural and geological circles but he kept hoping that he would be able to retire from teaching. When he was named director of the Agricultural College Experiment Station established under the terms of the Hatch Act and given a salary of $2,000, he tried again to give up his teaching. But the trustees decided that his duties at the college should continue though they would no longer pay him the $1,500 salary he had been getting from the college.[108]

The income from his farm and the investments in mortgages that he had managed to make over the years did not provide enough money for him to retire.

When Merrill Gates began his presidency of Rutgers College in 1882 the fortunes of the college were declining. When Campbell retired there were only 113 students and roughly half of these were scholarship students. But Gates was young and vigorous and had decided ideas about improving the college. A firm believer in discipline—both moral and academic—for students, he did not look with great favor upon the development of the elective system which allowed them to choose some of their own courses. Nor did he have any patience with the tendency to high jinks or experimentation with new life styles that college men often desired. He treated the members of the Board of Trustees much as he did the students and lectured them upon occasion. He was similarly impatient with the shortcomings of faculty members and managed to persuade a few of the weaker ones to resign. His relations with Cook remained very cordial, however, as the following letter testifies:

New Hampshire, 1887

Dear Dr. Cook,

. . .If anything occurs to you which I can do this summer for the college, I shall be glad to have you suggest it. I am at work easily on next year's lectures now.

To Dr. Doolittle, Dr. Meyer, Prof. Van Dyck, Dr. Austin, Dr. Scott, and Prof. Wilbur, please give my cordial regards when they drop in (as we are all so fond of doing) at your office to exchange greetings with you.

Cordially,

Merrill Gates[109]

The fortunes of the Rutgers Scientific School (or the Agricultural College as it continued to be popularly and erroneously known) remained uninspiring. Although students enrolled in the engineering and chemistry curricula, few were interested in the agricultural program. Rutgers continued to share this misfortune with all other land-grant colleges. In 1885 fewer than one farmer's son out of each 15,000 of the right age was receiving instruction in agriculture at all the colleges established by the Morrill Act.[110] The student enrollment at the Scientific School increased dramatically after Cook hired new professors and began new programs with the Hatch Act money, but he did not live to see it.

The philosophy of education remained that which had been held from the first years of the Scientific School. In 1887 a leaflet issued by the Board of Visitors reiterated these concepts:

The college, then is to teach branches of *learning*, not branches of the arts—but such sciences as explain the *principles* which underlie the arts,—such sciences as require apparatus, experiments and observation to make them fully understood—and such other branches of learning as may best fit young men as citizens to speak or write upon the subjects they have studied, as well as to put them in practice. The subject of study and experiment are such as can not be profitably studied in the common school, or by boys,—but such as need the arrangements and instruments for surveying, draughting,—and the farm and stock for field and farming practice. These are provided and the college is doing its work well. Appointments have been made to all the forty scholarships this year, and there are now 36 students in college who occupy state scholarships, the others having been left vacant by some change of purpose in the student appointed, or by failure in preparation.[111]

By 1887, the Board of Visitors could report that 155 students had been graduated from the Scientific School and over 150 others had taken partial courses of study. These students were employed as farmers, surveyors, engineers, mechanics, manufacturers, chemists, geologists, and some were in trade. The Board also pointed out in the 1887 leaflet that many states had made appropriations to pay for a farm or for buildings. In New Jersey, however, such improvements had been paid for by the trustees of Rutgers College at their own expense and no assistance had ever been received from state funds.

After the passage of the Hatch Act, the state did finance the building of New Jersey Hall to house the activities of the State Experiment Station and the College Experiment Station.

The Act of 1880 which established the experiment station had placed it under the control of the Board of Managers rather than the Trustees of the College, perhaps to avoid the antagonism throughout the state against having the still largely Dutch Reformed Board of Trustees running the State Experiment Station. The Act of 1888 accepting the Hatch Act reaffirmed that Rutgers Scientific School was the State Agricultural College and recognized the trustees of Rutgers College as the authority maintaining the Agricultural College.

Although the state financing of New Jersey Hall was a great triumph for Cook, it meant more work for him. He tried to cut back on some activities, resigning from the New Brunswick Water Commission in 1888 after fifteen years of service, but this was apparently all he was able to eliminate. He had become more and more deeply involved with the East Jersey Proprietors and finally was named surveyor general. He continued to hope that he would make some money from his investments in land purchased from the proprietors but he never did. In the end, Mary Cook's prophesy turned out to be correct. She had warned him that if he became involved in the proprietors he would have his work for his pains and William Force would make the money. In 1887 he decided she was right and began to sell his shares. (After Force's death, the proprietors brought suit against his estate claiming that Force had allowed himself too generous fees for his services. The judge ruled that his estate should return a few thousand dollars to the Board and faulted Cook for allowing Force to dominate him even to the extent of carrying on some negotiations which Cook was not aware of.) Another money-making scheme of Cook's that did not work out was an investment in a silver mine in Colorado managed by John Halsey, a cousin of Mary's.

Increasingly, during these years Cook wrote to Paul of his fatigue and the effort required to accomplish all that he had to do.[112] The end came quite suddenly on September 22, 1889. He had complained of pains in his chest a few days before and had called the doctor, who told him to rest at home. However, the next day he felt better and went back to his office where he was stricken again. He was taken home and, surrounded by his family, soon died. A service was held in Kirkpatrick Chapel and in the Second Reformed Church and he was buried in Elmwood Cemetery.

After his death, the *American Journal of Science, The American Geologist* and *The National Academy of Science Biographic Memoirs* published laudatory memorial essays and in June 1890, a memorial service was held in New Brunswick. A memorial booklet included essays by James Neilson, Abram S. Hewitt, John Wesley Powell, and Dr. T. S. Doolittle. In the years that followed Cook was not forgotten. In 1894 the state legislature appropriated money for an oil portrait to be hung in the State House; the honorary agricultural society at Rutgers College was called the George H. Cook Society and finally, in 1972, an undergraduate liberal arts college established at Rutgers University to succeed the College of Agriculture and Environmental Science was named Cook College.

Of the thousands of laudatory words which have been written about George Cook, perhaps the ones which best characterize him were those of George Merrill in *The First One Hundred Years of American Geology*, when he praised him as a man who stood out among American geologists as "a devotee of science free from the narrowness of the specialists of the personal idiosyncrasies that so frequently mar the character of men of this class. . . . [He] loved science for science's sake, yet did not close [his] eyes to its economic bearing, nor call upon an overtaxed public to support [him] in the work [he] loved, regardless of its outcome. . . . Never had anyone the interests of the public more at heart than [this man]. . . . For [himself he] asked simply the privilege of doing the work and doing it to the best of [his] ability."[113]

But perhaps Cook himself would have been more pleased at an assurance that he had indeed lived up to the motto found among his papers after his death. Dated 1860, it read, "Whatsoever ye do, do heartily, as to the Lord and not unto men."

Notes

NOTES FOR CHAPTER 1

1. *A History of Morris County*, Vol. I (New York, 1914), p. 3.

2. Ibid., p. 2, and John Whitehead, *The Passaic Valley: New Jersey in Three Centuries* (New York, 1901), p. 174.

3. State of New Jersey, Department of State, Census Bureau, *Compendium of Censuses, 1726-1905 together with tabulated returns of 1905* (Trenton, 1906).

4. Henry Cook to G. H. C., March 8, 1852.

5. Matthias and Mary Cook to G. H. C., May 29, 1843.

6. William Parkhurst Tuttle, *Bottle Hill and Madison: Glimpses and Reminiscenses from its Earliest Settlement to the Civil War* (Madison, New Jersey, 1916), p. 46.

7. J. A. Ferguson, *A Historical Sketch of the Presbyterian Church of Hanover, New Jersey* (Newark, 1877), p. 7.

8. Whitehead, *Passaic Valley*, p. 167.

9. Gilbert Seldes, *The Stammering Century* (New York: John Day, 1928), p. 6.

10. Whitehead, *Passaic Valley*, p. 174.

11. George H. Cook, *Notes for a Genealogy of the Cook Family* (privately printed), p. 4.

12. MS genealogy of the Cook family, Cook papers.

13. *History of Morris County*, p. 46.

14. MS genealogy of the Cook family.

15. *History of Morris County*, p. 47, 512.

16. G. H. C. to Isaac Cook, January 17, 1841.

17. *History of Morris County*, p. 101; Charles A. Philhower, *Brief History of Chatham* (New York, 1914), p. 42; MS copy of Jephtha Munn's speech to

Lafayette in Cook papers.

18. Conversation with Margaret Cook Thomson.

19. Isaac Cook to G. H. C., February 27, 1841, and G. H. C. to I. C., June 17, 1841.

20. Mary and Matthias Cook to G. H. C., May 29, 1843.

21. MS talk given by G. H. C. to the Teacher's Institute, New Brunswick, n.d.

22. Mary Cook to G. H. C., May 15, 1845.

23. Henry Cook to G. H. C., June 10, 1852.

24. David Cook to G. H. C., July 1, 1838, and May 24, 1840.

25. Matthias Cook to G. H. C., February 22, 1849.

26. Mary Cook to G. H. C., November 14, 1838.

27. Mary Cook to G. H. C., January 19, 1841.

28. *History of Morris County*, p. 11.

29. John Bodine Thompson, "The Middle of the Century," in David Murray, *History of Education in New Jersey*, U. S. Bureau of Education Circular of Information No. 1, 1899 Whole Number 252; *Contributions to American Educational History*, edited by Herbert B. Adams, No. 23 (Washington, D. C., 1899), p. 138.

30. Murray, *Education in New Jersey*, p. 37.

31. Ibid., p. 128f.

32. Eliza Joanna Cook to G. H. C., January 19, 1841.

33. Murray, *Education in New Jersey*, p. 37, and Eliza J. Cook to G. H. C., February 3, 1839.

34. Murray, *Education in New Jersey*, p. 141.

35. Eliza J. Cook to G. H. C., January 19, 1841.

36. Matthias and Mary Cook to G. H. C., May 29, 1843, quoting Eliza.

37. Ibid.

38. Bill from Thomas Dooley to John Cook, March 16, 1836; and Philhower, *History of Chatham*, p. 31.

39. John Ball to G. H. C., July 26, 1843; Theodore R. Sizer, *The Age of the Academies* (New York, 1964), passim.

40. David Cook to G. H. C., November 15, 1840; David, Mary and Eliza Cook to G. H. C., February 3, 1839.

41. David Cook to G. H. C., November 15, 1840.

42. David, Mary, and Eliza Cook to G. H. C., February 3, 1839; Joanna Munn to G. H. C., February 2, 1839.

43. Mary Cook to G. H. C., August 1840.

44. G. H. C. account book for 1836; *History of Morris County*, p. 110f.

45. Cook correspondence for 1836-40, passim.

46. *History of Morris County*, p. 11.

47. Isaac Cook to G. H. C., January 28, 1839.

48. Balthasar Henry Meyer, *History of Transportation in the United States before 1860* (Washington, 1917), p. 360; William F. Helmer, *Rip Van Winkle Railroads* (Berkeley, 1971), p. 19.

49. Ephraim Beach to G. H. C., June, 1838; Cook diary, July 9, 1838.

50. Memorandum to Assistants and Field men of the Engineering Department of the Canajoharie & Catskill Railroad, June 28, 1838, from Lewis J. Germain, First Assistant, Cook papers.

51. Cook diary, July 11, 1838, and August 3, 1838.

52. Lewis Germain to G. H. C., February 2, 1839, and January 13, 1839.

53. Lucius Barrows to G. H. C., January 6, 1837, and February 25, 1837.

54. Cook diary, July 1838.

55. Isaac Cook to G. H. C., December 20, 1836.

56. William Gurley to G. H. C., March 7, 1860.

57. Cook diary, September 2, 1838, and December 10, 1838.

58. Temperance pledge, Easton, Pa., February 11, 1838.

59. Cook diary, October 19, 1838.

60. Memorandum from "John Fingus," Newark, March 2, 1837.

61. Cook diary, August 26, 1838.

62. Cook diary, September 5, 1838.

63. Isaac Cook to G. H. C., November 25, 1838; Cook diary, October 9, 1838.

64. Cook diary, July 9, 1838.

65. The Catskill & Canajoharie Railroad was never finished. Eleven miles had been built by 1840 when floods tore away bridges and sections of track and the company went into bankruptcy.

NOTES FOR CHAPTER 2

1. Isaac Cook to G. H. C., January, 1839.

2. Stephen Van Rensselaer to the Reverend Samuel Blatchford, quoted in Ethel M. McAllister, *Amos Eaton, Scientist and Educator, 1776-1842* (Philadelphia, 1941), p. 368.

3. Ibid.

4. McAllister, *Amos Eaton.*

5. Amos Eaton to John Torrey, February 29, 1819, quoted in McAllister, *Amos Eaton,* p. 192.

6. James Bryant Conant, *Two Modes of Thought: My Encounters with Science and Education* (New York, 1965), p. 43.

7. Cook papers, passim.

8. George P. Merrill, *The First One Hundred Years of American Geology* (New Haven, 1924), p. 75.

9. Ibid., p. 132.

10. Palmer C. Ricketts, *History of Rensselaer Polytechnic Institute: 1824-1934* (New York, 1934), 3rd ed., p. 230.

11. Handwritten certificate signed by Amos Eaton, Troy, September 24,

1839, Cook papers.

12. G. H. C. to Major Ephraim Beach, June 24, 1839 (draft).

13. Cook diary, July 1, 1839.

14. G. H. C. to Isaac Cook, May 28, 1840.

15. Articles of Agreement between Amos Eaton and George Cook, March 27, 1840.

16. Ibid. and Cook diary for March 24, 1840.

17. G. H. C. to Isaac Cook, March 19, 1841.

18. Cook diary, March 24, 1840.

19. G. H. C. to Isaac Cook, May 28, 1840.

20. Cook diary, March 24, 1840.

21. Cook diary, May 12, 1840, and May 29, 1840.

22. G. H. C. to Isaac Cook, May 28, 1840.

23. Cook diary, April 20, 1840.

24. Cook diary, April 30, 1840.

25. G. H. C. to Isaac Cook, May 28, 1840.

26. Cook diary, April 30, 1840.

27. G. H. C. to Isaac Cook, July 17, 1840.

28. G. H. C. to Isaac Cook, October 1840.

29. G. H. C. to Isaac Cook, July 17, 1840.

30. G. H. C. to Isaac Cook, October 2, 1840.

31. McAllister, *Amos Eaton*, p. 472.

32. Robert Cook to G. H. C., June 29, 1879.

33. Cook diary, February 21, 1841.

34. G. H. C. to Isaac Cook, March 19, 1841.

35. Receipted bills, Cook papers, 1844, 1845.

36. McAllister, *Amos Eaton*, p. 474.

37. Ibid., p. 475.

38. Ibid., p. 469.

39. W. G. Vought to G. H. C., February 21, 1842.

40. Mary H. Thomas to Nathan Thomas, January 21, 1842, Thomas papers.

41. Mary Cook to G. H. C., June 1841.

42. David Cook to G. H. C., July 1841, and April 2, 1842.

43. G. H. C. to Isaac Cook, n.d., 1841.

44. Amos Eaton to G. H. C., November 27, 1841.

45. Amos Eaton to G. H. C., November 18, 1841.

46. Memorandum, Cook papers, November 13, 1841.

47. McAllister, *Amos Eaton*, p. 414.

48. *Troy Whig*, January 18, 1842, as quoted in McAllister, *Amos Eaton*, p. 357.

49. Cook diary, January 24, 1842.

50. E. W. Cotes to G. H. C., July 24, 1842.

51. *Troy Whig*, May 17, 1842, as quoted in McAllister, *Amos Eaton*, p. 508.

52. G. H. C. to Isaac Cook, March 19, 1841.

53. Merrill, *First Hundred Years*, p. 233.

54. James Hall to G. H. C., September 17, 1842.

55. John M. Clarke, *Life of James Hall* (Albany, 1921), p. 46f.

56. Ricketts, *Rensselaer Polytechnic*, p. 91.

57. Calvin Park to G. H. C., July 31, 1842.

58. George Daniels, "The Process of Professionalization in American Science: The Emergent Period, 1820-1860," *Isis*, Vol. 58, 1967, pp. 151-166.

59. J. R. Bradway to G. H. C., September 16, 1842.

60. Cook diary, December 23, 1843.

61. Cook diary, December 26, 1843.

62. Cook diary, December 31, 1843.

63. Cook diary, December 26, 1843.

64. Ibid.

65. Cook diary, December 31, 1843; Samuel Rezneck, *Education for a Technological Society: A Sesquicentennial History of Rensselaer Polytechnic Institute* (Troy, N. Y., 1968), p. 71.

66. Daniel Cady Eaton to G. H. C., February 24, 1843.

67. Rezneck, *Education*, p. 71.

68. Subscription list for a course of lectures on chemistry, 1844, Cook papers.

69. Rezneck, *Education*, p. 73.

70. Report of Board of Examiners for September 30, 1844; list of men for examination, Cook papers.

71. Mary Thomas to Patty S. Thomas, July 10, 1846, Thomas papers.

72. S. Mandeville to G. H. C., March 23, 1846.

73. Samuel Joseph May to G. H. C., September 17, 1846.

74. David Collin, Jr., To G. H. C., February 17, 1844.

75. J. Barber to G. H. C., September 17, 1846.

76. C. Van Schaick to G. H. C., April 17, 1841; diploma naming William P. Van Rensselaer honorary member of Troy Lyceum of Natural History, February 15, 1845; R. Bridges to G. H. C., June 28, 1844.

77. Jephtha Munn to G. H. C., August 1844.

78. Conversation with M. Halsey Thomas, grand-nephew of Mary Thomas Cook.

79. Mary T. Cook to Nathan Thomas, n.d., Thomas papers; Mrs. Russell Sage, *Emma Willard and Her Pupils, or Fifty Years of Troy Female Seminary, 1822-1872* (New York, 1898), pp. 212, 244.

80. Mary Thomas to a brother, February 13, 1846, Thomas papers.

81. Elihu W. Cotes to G. H. C., June 17, 1841.

82. Calvin Park to G. H. C., September 19, 1841.

83. Joanna Munn to G. H. C., November 21, 1844.

84. Joanna Munn to G. H. C., January 5, 1846.

85. Jephtha Munn to G. H. C., April 23, 1846.

86. Mary Thomas Cook to Nathan Thomas, May 14, 1846, Thomas papers.

87. W. L. Adams to G. H. C., July 17, 1846.
88. Mary Thomas Cook to Patty S. Thomas, July 10, 1846, Thomas papers.
89. Ibid.
90. Mary Thomas Cook to James W. Thomas, n.d., 1845, Thomas papers.
91. Mary Thomas Cook to Nathan H. Thomas, June 4, 1846, Thomas papers.
92. Agreement signed April 15, 1846, Cook papers.
93. Jephtha Munn to G. H. C., December 26, 1845; Patty S. Thomas to Nathan Thomas, March 23, 1846, Thomas papers; Benjamin Mott to George Cook, November 21, 1845; Albert Fox to G. H. C., November 27, 1845.
94. Patty S. Thomas to Nathan Thomas, March 23, 1846, Thomas papers.
95. Agreement of April 15, 1846, signed by Amos Dean, Cook papers.
96. Receipt, November 30, 1846, signed by Amos Dean, Cook papers.
97. *Hoffman's Albany Directory and City Register,* 1847-48 (Albany, 1848), pp. 150-245.
98. Draft of letter to person unknown, probably 1846.
99. Cook notebook, August 1841 through 1842 with some entries for 1846.
100. Benjamin Nott to G. H. C., August 5, 1846; Jonas Tower to G. H. C., December, 1845; Benjamin Nott to G. H. C., August 31, 1846; Benjamin Nott to G. H. C., August 5, 1846.
101. Lewis Germain to G. H. C., April 14, 1847.
102. Reuben Isaac Germain to G. H. C., October 27, 1846.
103. Lewis Germain to G. H. C., April 14, 1847.
104. Benjamin Franklin Greene to G. H. C., January 18, 1843.
105. Charles Riborg Mann, quoted in Ray Palmer Baker, *A Chapter in American Education: Rensselaer, 1824-1924* (New York, 1925), p. 150.
106. Rezneck, *Education,* p. 121, 123-125.

NOTES FOR CHAPTER 3

1. Warren C. Scoville, *Revolution in Glassmaking: Entrepreneurship and Technological Change in the American Industry: 1880-1920* (Cambridge, Mass., 1948), p. 53ff.
2. Cook Account Book and diary, March 29, 1844 to November 14, 1846, entry for November 14, 1846.
3. Receipt, G. H. C. from R. Boyd, November 1, 1847.
4. William Arthus to G. H. C., December 27, 1847.
5. Lewis Germain to G. H. C., February 22, 1848.
6. Draft of a letter, G. H. C. to Charles Valentine, June 17, 1848.
7. Nathan H. Thomas to James W. Thomas, February 28, 1847, Thomas papers. Mary Cook to Henry Cook, April 29, 1848.

8. Mary Halsey Thomas Cook to Tibby Thomas, May 2, 1848, Thomas papers.

9. Ibid.

10. Lansing & Pruyn to G. H. C., April 6, 1849, and Judgment, Supreme Court, County of Albany, Andrew White *vs* George H. Cook and Theodore Olcott, September 25, 1848.

11. G. H. C. to Charles Valentine, June 17, 1848 (draft).

12. Bill of sale, July 14, 1848, July 22, 1848.

13. Judgment, Supreme Court, County of Albany, Andrew White *vs* George H. Cook and Theodore Olcott, September 25, 1848.

14. B. F. Greene to G. H. C., February 1848; Alex Holland to G. H. C., March 21, 1848.

15. Elias Gates to G. H. C., June 14, 1848.

16. *Albany Academy Centennial Celebration* (Albany, 1917), p. 18.

17. *Albany Academy Semi-Centennial* (Albany, 1864), p. 13.

18. Joel Munsell, *The Annals of Albany* (Albany, 1850), p. 76.

19. *Albany Academy Semi-Centennial*, p. 168.

20. Ibid., p. 23.

21. Ibid., p. 18.

22. G. H. C. account book, 1846-1855.

23. Ibid., entry for June 17, 1851.

24. Bill to G. H. C. for pew rent. Teacher's letter to G. H. C., July 3, 1850.

25. Account book, 1846-1855, entry for December 1850.

26. Lewis Caleb Beck to G. H. C., January 11, 1853.

27. Testimonial from medical students, n.d., 1853.

28. John M. Clarke, *James Hall of Albany, Geologist and Paleontologist* (Albany, 1921), p. 191.

29. Circular for Albany University, March 4, 1853.

30. Copy of letter, Christopher Morgan to R. Gere, April 16, 1850.

31. George H. Cook, *Experiments and Observations Made Upon the Onondaga Brines*, Annual report of the Superintendent of the Onondaga Salt Springs of New York for 1851 (Albany, 1852) Assembly #43, p. 27.

32. *Annual Report of the Superintendent of the Onondaga Salt Springs: 1854* (Albany, 1855), passim.

33. *Annual Report of the Superintendent of the Onondaga Salt Springs for 1853* (Albany, 1854), passim.

34. James B. Lobb to G. H. C., August 1, 1852, and Letter of Introduction from Administration Generale des Anciennes Salines Nationales de L'est Rue Miromenil 30, n.d., 1852.

35. Henry Cook to G. H. C., April 21, 1853.

NOTES FOR CHAPTER 4

1. William Campbell to G. H. C., July 20, 1853.

2. Mary Thomas Cook to G. H. C., January 20, 1854.

3. Mary Thomas Cook to G. H. C., January 25, 1854.

4. William A. Miller and others to G. H. C., n.d., 1853.

5. Oscar M. Young and others to G. H. C., n.d., 1853.

6. Draft of letter, G. H. C. to C. Y. Lansing, February 19, 1859.

7. For a recent history of Rutgers, see Richard P. McCormick, *Rutgers: A Bicentennial History* (New Brunswick, N. J., 1966).

8. *History of Rutgers College by a Trustee*, n.p., 1833.

9. William Campbell to G. H. C., October 7, 1853.

10. Theodore Frelinghuysen to G. H. C., September 28, 1853.

11. Mary Thomas Cook to G. H. C., January 27, 1854.

12. Ibid.

13. Mary Thomas Cook to G. H. C., February 27, 1854.

14. Austin F. Park to G. H. C., February, n.d., 1853.

15. William A. Miller to G. H. C., February 25, 1854.

16. Mary Thomas Cook to G. H. C., February 2, 1854, and February 22, 1854.

17. Mortgage, March 24, 1855, between George H. Cook and Mary H. Cook and James and David Bishop (Cook papers).

18. J. P. Wall, *Chronicles of New Brunswick* (New Brunswick, N. J., privately printed, 1931), p. 431.

19. *New Brunswick Weekly Fredonian*, May 30, 1854.

20. Ibid., January 11, 1854.

21. Ibid., June 6, 1854.

22. Wall, *Chronicles*, p. 315.

23. Ibid., p. 348.

24. Draft of letter, G. H. C. to C. Y. Lansing, February 19, 1859.

25. McCormick, *Rutgers Bicentennial*, p. 74.

26. Minutes of the Faculty of Rutgers College, December 19, 1855.

27. Abraham Polhemus to G. H. C., n.d., 1857.

28. Trustees minutes, April 13, 1858.

29. Draft of letter, G. H. C. to C. Y. Lansing, April 13, 1859.

30. Benjamin C. Taylor to G. H. C., March 6, 1860, March 14, 1860, and March 23, 1860.

31. Draft of letter, G. H. C. to C. Y. Lansing, February 19, 1859.

32. Thomas C. Strong to G. H. C., May 6, 1859.

33. Thomas C. Strong to G. H. C., May 6, 1859, Draft of letter, G. H. C. to Thomas C. Strong, May 13, 1859.

34. Joseph Henry, *Syllabus of a Course of Lectures on Physics* (Smithsonian Report, 1856).

35. Draft of letter, G. H. C. to Thomas E. Vermilye, August 22, 1859.

36. Minutes of the Board of Trustees for April 12, 1859.

37. Trustees minutes, June 21, 1859.

38. Faculty minutes, June 18, 1857.

39. Rutgers College Catalogue, 1856-57.

40. Faculty minutes, March 9, 1855, March 11, 1855, March 14, 1855, April 12, 1858, April 13, 1858.

41. Faculty minutes, March 9, 1855, March 11, 1855, March 8, 1855, June 14, 1855, April 3, 1856.

42. Faculty minutes, June 21, 1855, July 14, 1855, December 19, 1855.

43. Faculty minutes, March 8, 1855, March 11, 1855.

44. McCormick, *Rutgers Bicentennial*, p. 75.

45. Faculty minutes, June 18, 1862, Draft letter, G. H. C. to Isaac Taylor, June 21, 1862, Isaac Taylor to G. H. C., June 19, 1862.

46. Isaac Taylor to G. H. C., June 19, 1862.

47. G. H. C. to Isaac Taylor, June 21, 1862.

48. Trevainon Haight to G. H. C., June 28, 1860.

49. Ibid.

50. Draft letter, G. H. C. to Trevainon Haight, June, n.d., 1860.

51. J. B. Dodd to G. H. C., June 30, 1863.

52. *Rutgers College Quarterly* Vol. I (New Brunswick, 1859).

53. John S. Chapman to G. H. C., December 27, 1861; The Reverend Mr. Ostrom to G. H. C., November 8, 1859.

54. *Rutgers College Quarterly*, Vol. III, No. 1, 1860.

55. Thomas Brinsmade to G. H. C., July 21, 1859.

56. Draft letter to Thomas Brinsmade, July 27, 1859.

NOTES FOR CHAPTER 5

1. Jephtha Munn to Rodman Price, Price papers, April 28, 1854.

2. For a discussion of the development of professionalization see George G. Daniels, "The Process of Professionalization in American Science: The Emergent Period, 1820-1860," *Isis*, Vol. 58 (1967), pp. 151-166.

3. Frank Dawson Adams, *The Birth and Development of the Geological Sciences* (New York, 1938), p. 70.

4. George W. White, "Early American Geology," *The Scientific Monthly* Vol. 76 (March 1953), p. 138f.

5. Charles Schuchert, "A Century of Geology: The Progress of Historical Geology in North America," in Edward Salisbury Dana, ed. *A Century of Science in America* (New Haven, 1928), p. 69. Also see Bradford Willard, "Pioneer Geological Investigation in Pennsylvania," *Pennsylvania History*, Vol. 32 (July, 1965), p. 246.

6. George P. Merrill, *The First One Hundred Years of American Geology* (New York, 1904), p. 4, 17.

7. George P. Merrill, *Contributions to a History of American State*

Geological and Natural History Surveys, National Museum Bulletin 109 (Washington, D. C., 1920), pp. 537-538.

8. Edward Hitchcock, *Final Report on the Geology of Massachusetts* (Northampton, Mass., 1841).

9. *New York State Geological Survey* (New York, 1843).

10. For a discussion of this problem, see Gerald D. Nash, "The Conflict Between Pure and Applied Science in Nineteenth Century Public Policy: The California State Geological Survey, 1860-1874," *Isis,* Vol. 54, 1963, pp. 217-228.

11. Peter D. Vroom, "Governor's Message," *Votes and Proceedings of the 56th General Assembly,* Trenton, N. J., October 24, 1832.

12. For a discussion of Rogers's mountain-building theories see Patsy A. Gerstner, "A Dynamic Theory of Mountain Building: Henry Darwin Rogers, 1842," *Isis,* Vol. 66, March 1975, pp. 26-37.

13. Henry Darwin Rogers, *The Geology of Pennsylvania,* 2 vols. (Philadelphia, 1858).

14. Henry Darwin Rogers, *Description of the Geology of the State of New Jersey* (Philadelphia, 1840).

15. George H. Cook, *Annual Report of the State Geologist for the Year 1885* (Trenton, 1885), p. 158.

16. Cook, *Annual Report of State Geologist,* 1885, p. 155.

17. Rogers's division of the state into four distinct geological periods was only partly original—James Pierce writing in the *American Journal of Science and the Arts* had used three divisions although recognizing that the Highlands— and both Evans's map and Maclure's map had shown four very imprecise divisions. Pierce included the northwestern parts of Sussex and Warren counties with the Highlands to the south.

18. George H. Cook, *Geology of New Jersey* (Newark, 1868), p. 468.

19. Eric Kerridge, *The Agricultural Revolution* (New York, 1968), p. 250.

20. W. H. R. Curtler, *A Short History of English Agriculture* (Oxford, 1909), p. 113.

21. Mark Reeves, "On the New Jersey Marls," *Memoirs of the Philadelphia Society for Promoting Agriculture* (Philadelphia, 1826), p. 1.

22. Rogers, *Geology of New Jersey* (1840), pp. 230-255.

23. Kemble Widmer, *The Geology and Geography of New Jersey* (Princeton, N. J., 1964), p. 92f.

24. Rogers, *Geology of New Jersey* (1840), p. 205.

25. Ibid., p. 206.

26. Ibid., p. 227.

27. Ibid., p. 228.

28. Ibid., p. 206.

29. Ibid., p. 208ff.

30. Ibid., p. 213.

31. George H. Cook, *Geology of New Jersey* (1868), p. 680; Herbert P. Woodward, "Copper Mines and Mining in New Jersey," Bulletin 55, Department of Conservation and Development (Trenton, 1944), pp. 124-129.

32. Jennie Barnes Pope, "The Old Iron Industry," Chapter IV in William Myers, *Story of New Jersey* (New York, 1945), p. 66.

33. Rogers, *Geology of New Jersey*, 1858, p. 159f. Dr. William M. Jordan informs me that although there are no major copper deposits in New Jersey those that do exist are now characterized as vein deposits because they are of hydrothermal origin.

34. Widmer, *Geology and Geography*, p. 26.

35. Charles Palache, *The Minerals of Franklin and Sterling Hill, Sussex County, New Jersey*, Geological Survey Professional paper 180 (Washington, D. C., G.P.O., 1935), p. 14, quoting A. C. Farrington, "Historical Sketch of the Zinc Mines of New Jersey," in *Report of the New Jersey Zinc Company* (1952).

36. Widmer, *Geology and Geography*, p. 34; Palache, *Minerals*, p. 14.

37. Palache, *Minerals*, p. 14.

38. Widmer, *Geology and Geography*, p. 30.

39. Bruce's *Mineralogical Journal*, published in 1814, was a tour de force. He was unable to continue publishing, but the *Journal* is invaluable as a source for early American mineralogy history.

40. Palache, *Minerals*, p. 15.

41. M. P. Berthier, "Analysis of two Zinc Ores. . . ." *Journal of American Science*, Vol. II, No. 2, 1820. Footnote, p. 319.

42. Ibid., p. 323.

43. Palache, *Minerals*, p. 15. Eventually the area, like the Langban deposits in Sweden, became world renowned for the variety of minerals found there. But most of the more than two hundred varieties, of which thirty or so are found nowhere else in the world, were so deep in the earth that they did not come to light until the shafts and tunnels of the zinc mining companies were sunk to a depth of 6,000 ft.

44. James Pierce, "Geology, Mineralogy . . . of the Highlands of New York and New Jersey," *American Journal of Science*, Vol. II, 1822, p. 26.

45. Rogers, *Geology of New Jersey*, 1840, p. 70.

46. George White, "Histories of Geology in America," *Isis*, Vol. 64, June, 1973, p. 208.

47. See Walter F. Cannon, "The Uniformitarian-Catastrophyist Debate," *Isis*, Vol. 51, Part I, No. 163, March 1960, pp. 38-55, for an indication of the complexities of the debate.

48. Henry D. Rogers, *Geology of Pennsylvania* (1858), p. vii.

49. George P. Merrill, *First Hundred Years*, p. 168; Joseph Borrell, "A Century of Geology—The Growth of Knowledge of Earth Structures," in Edward Salisbury Dana, *A Century of Science: 1818-1918* (New Haven, Conn., 1918), p. 171.

50. Cook, *Annual Report of the State Geologist*, 1885, 159f.

51. Walter B. Hendrickson, "Nineteenth Century State Geological Surveys: Early Government Support of Science," *Isis*, LII (September 1961), p. 364.

52. Carl Raymond Woodward and Ingrid Nelson Waller, *New Jersey's*

Agricultural Experiment Station: 1880-1930 (New Brunswick, N. J., 1932), p. 16, n 1; Minutes of the New Jersey Assembly, 1852, p. 824; "Governor Price's Inaugural Address," *New Jersey Journal*, January 24, 1854.

53. *Acts of the 78th New Jersey Legislature*, Chapter LXXVII, p. 176, Mar. 2, 1954.

54. George P. Merrill, *Contributions to a History of American Geology* (Washington, 1906), p. 703.

55. George Vail to Governor Rodman M. Price, Feb. 20, 1854, Price papers.

56. Francis Moran to Rodman M. Price, Feb. 1854; Zachariah H. Price to Rodman M. Price, Mar. 20, 1854, Price papers.

57. Egbert L. Viele (1825-1902) was born in New York City, and graduated from the United States Military Academy in 1847. He joined the Infantry but resigned in 1853 while a first lieutenant. He became a brigadier general in the U. S. Volunteers in 1861 and resigned in 1863. He served as park commissioner of New York City in 1863-64 and was member of the U. S. House of Representatives from New York, 1885-1887.

58. Joseph Leidy to G. H. C., June 16, 1858, Dec. 14, 1858, Dec. 22, 1858.

59. Cook, *Annual Report of the State Geologist, 1885*, p. 186.

60. William Kitchell, *Report of the State Geologist* (Trenton, 1854), pp. 162-163.

61. Ibid., p. 165.

62. Cook, *Report of the State Geologist, 1885*, p. 163.

63. G. H. C. to William Kitchell, Jan. 13, 1855, Kitchell papers.

64. Kitchell, *Report of the State Geologist of New Jersey for 1855*, p. 202.

65. Ibid., p. 204.

66. Ibid., p. 205.

67. James Hall to G. H. C., April 3, 1855.

68. Kitchell, *Report of the State Geologist for 1854*, p. 197.

69. George H. Cook, "The Marls of New Jersey," *Mining Magazine*, Vol. 5 (1855), p. 142f. (This essay is identical to that in the Kitchell report for 1854, pp. 194-215.

70. Ibid., p. 144.

71. Cook, *Report of the State Geologist for 1855*, pp. 82-83.

72. George H. Cook, "Subsidence of Land on the Seacoast of New Jersey and Long Island," *American Journal of Science and Arts*, XXIV (Nov. 1857), p. 345.

73. Kitchell, *Report of the State Geologist for 1855*, 79f; George Cook, *Geology of the County of Cape May* (Trenton, 1857), p. 37f.

74. Cook, *Report of the State Geologist for 1856*, p. 85.

75. George H. Cook, "On a Subsidence of the Land on the Sea-Coast of New Jersey and Long Island," read at the Montreal meeting of the American Association for the Advancement of Science, 1857, *Proceedings of the AAAS*, 1857, p. 159.

76. Cook, *Mining Magazine*, 1855, pp. 132-146.

77. George H. Cook, *Geology of Cape May*, p. 86f.

78. Ibid., p. 91ff.

79. Ibid., p. 133ff.

80. Ibid., p. 29.

81. Ibid., p. 30.

82. Kitchell, *Report of the State Geologist for 1855*, pp, 899-900, 905.

83. George Merrill wrote: "The magnetic ores were regarded as deposited contemporaneously with the sedimentary rocks in which they were enclosed, and the white crystalline limestone of the highlands was classed as Azoic." (George Merrill, *Contributions to the History of American Geology*, Report of the U. S. National Museum for 1904, Washington, 1906, p. 460.) Kitchell, in his report for 1854, had written that two great dynamic forces, igneous and aqueous, alternately exerted themselves in forming and modifying the surface. The water of the ocean covered it at one time and deposited materials which now constitute sedimentary rocks. At another time igneous agencies upheaved them from their ocean beds, forming the mountains and valleys, filling sedimentary deposits with rich ores and minerals and thus here bringing together the three principal classes of rocks, aqueous, metamorphic and igneous." (Kitchell, *Report for 1854*, p. 180ff.) John S. Albanese writes: "Some theories suggested for the origin of the unusual ore deposits at Franklin and Sterling are: 1. igneous injection, 2. sedimentary deposition, 3. contact metamorphism, 4. replacement from magmatic solutions, and 5. metasomatic emplacement. In his 1855 Report Kitchell proposed the theory of sedimentary deposition and in 1959, the geologists of the New Jersey Zinc Company released scientific data which showed no igneous origin. The minerals were all formed from re-crystallized sediment and all the primary materials (franklinite, willemite, etc.) had their origin in sediments enclosed in the limestone—Precambrian muds were deposited in a sea floor at the time the limestone was formed in the shallow sea." (Albanese, John S., Notes on the Minerals of Franklin and Sterling Hill, Vol. I (Union, N. J., Oct., 1959), p. 2.) Widmer says that the origin of the complex ore bodies probably will remain one of the great unsolved geologic mysteries. Iron and zinc minerals might have been introduced into the limestone by pneumatolytic (hot gases) and/or hydrothermal (hot water) action resulting from nearby igneous intrusions. Great disagreement also exists in the interpretation of the significance of the mineral relationships where ore body and pegmatites intersect. There is evidence that the pegmatites came after the ore or that the pegmatite intrusion came into the limestone before the ore was formed. (Widmer, *Geology of New Jersey*, p. 35.)

84. Egbert Viele to G. H. C., Dec. 20, 1854, Jan. 4, 1855, Nov. 18, 1856.

85. Rodman Price to G. H. C., Dec. 28, 1856.

86. William Newell to G. H. C., Dec. 10, 1857.

87. Jephtha Munn to G. H. C., Jan. 2, 1858.

88. G. H. C. to L. D. Chandler, Feb. 1, 1858 (draft).

89. William A. Newell, *Governor's Message*, Jan. 18, 1859.

90. G. H. C. to William A. Newell, Feb. 25, 1858 (draft).

91. G. H. C. to William Phelps, July 19, 1858 (draft).

92. William A. Newell, Message to the Legislature, Jan. 18, 1859.

93. William A. Newell to G. H. C., Dec. 6, 1858, William A. Newell, Message to the Legislature, Jan. 11, 1860.

94. G. H. C. to William Kitchell, Feb. 20, 1860 (draft).

95. Senate Bill 120, March 1860, Charles Morgan Herbert to G. H. C., Mar. 23, 1860.

96. William Kitchell to G. H. C., May 11, 1860.

97. James Dwight Dana, *Manual of Geology*, 4th Edition (New York, 1894), pp. 348-350; Dana, *Manual of Geology*, Revised Edition (Phila., 1864); pp. 586-588; *American Journal of Science and Arts*, LXXIV (Nov., 1857), p. 433.

NOTES FOR CHAPTER 6

1. William H. Campbell to G. H. C., 10/13/64.

2. William H. S. Demarest, *A History of Rutgers College: 1766-1924* (New Brunswick, N. J., 1924), p. 381.

3. Faculty minutes, September 19, 1863 and Cook letterbook G. H. C. to Campbell 6/12/64.

4. David Murray to G. H. C., 7/n.d./1863.

5. David Murray to G. H. C., July 6, 1863.

6. Sandford Doolittle to G. H. C., October 6, 1863.

7. Sandford Doolittle to G. H. C., July 20, 1864.

8. Peter Stryker to G. H. C., October 13, 1863.

9. Abraham Ackerman to G. H. C., summer 1864; shipping receipt from L. Burkette, master of the ship *St. Paul*, Amoy, December 1, 1862.

10. *Addresses Commemorative of George H. Cook* (New Brunswick, 1891), p. 39.

11. F. B. Meek to G. H. C., June 5, 1863. Fielding Bradford Meek assisted David Dale Owen in the surveys of Wisconsin and Minnesota in 1848-49 and James Hall from 1852-58. He was associated with F. V. Hayden on the Western Surveys and in 1858 moved to Washington where he worked as paleontologist in the Smithsonian Institution. In the latter part of his life he was completely deaf and therefore took special pleasure in his scientific correspondence.

12. F. V. Hayden to G. H. C., October 16, 1862.

13. Joseph Henry to G. H. C., June 13, 1863, printed acknowledgement form to G. H. C. from Smithsonian Institution February 19, 1862.

14. Joseph Leidy to G. H. C., February 2, 1862.

15. Joseph Leidy to G. H. C., June 27, 1862.

16. Joseph Leidy to G. H. C., December 19, 1862.

17. Nathan Reingold, *Science in Nineteenth Century America* (New York, 1964), p. 236ff.

18. *New Brunswick Fredonian,* June 19, 1862.

19. *Fredonian,* June 19, 1862.

20. McCormick, *Rutgers Bicentennial,* p. 85; notes of meeting February 18, 1863, in Dr. Campbell's study, Cook papers.

21. Demarest, *Rutgers College,* p. 400.

22. The section on the selection of New Jersey's land-grant college first appeared in somewhat different form in an article by the author, "George Hammell Cook and the Rutgers Land Grant," *Proceedings of the New Jersey Historical Society,* Vol. 82 (October, 1964), pp. 223-240.

23. Carl Becker, Cornell University, *Founders and the Founding* (Ithaca, New York, 1943), p. 34f.

24. Public Laws of the United States, 1862, Ch. 130, *An Act donating public land to the several states and territories which may provide Colleges for the Benefit of Agriculture and the Mechanic Arts,* Section 4, as quoted in George A. Works and Barton Morgan, *The Land Grant Colleges,* Staff Study, No. 10, prepared for the Advisory Committee on Education (Washington, D. C. Government Printing Office, 1939), p. 110. Hereafter cited as the Morrill Act.

25. Faculty minutes, December 8, 1863.

26. Faculty minutes, December 8, 1863.

27. Trustees' minutes, January 13, 1864.

28. Minutes of Votes and Proceedings of the Eighty-Eighth General Assembly of the State of New Jersey (Hackensack, N. J., 1864), p. 10.

29. *Daily Fredonian* (New Brunswick), February 5, 1864; *Minutes of the Eighty-Eighth General Assembly,* p. 4f.

30. Carl R. Woodward, *The Development of Agriculture in New Jersey, 1640-1880* (New Brunswick, N. J., 1927), p. 159.

31. *The Congressional Land-Grant for Agricultural and Other Purposes as related to the College of New Jersey* (n.p., n.d.). Hereafter cited as the Princeton pamphlet.

32. *Fredonian,* February 11, 1864; Demarest, p. 399f.

33. *New Brunswick Times,* February 2, 1864.

34. *Fredonian,* February 18, 1864. No copy of the original pamphlet has been found.

35. Garrett D. W. Vroom to G. H. C., February 11, 1864.

36. Princeton pamphlet, p. 2.

37. Princeton pamphlet, p. 3f.

38. James Bodine Thompson to G. H. C., February 1864.

39. Abraham Messler to G. H. C., February 1, 1864.

40. Samuel Lockwood to G. H. C., March 28, 1864.

41. James Bodine Thompson to G. H. C., March 28, 1864.

42. J. H. Frazee to G. H. C., March 24, 1881.

43. Draft of letter, G. H. C. to Joseph P. Bradley, January 29, 1864.

44. J. R. Wortendyke to G. H. C., January 28, 1864.

45. J. R. Wortendyke to G. H. C., January 29, 1864.

46. C. D. Deshler to David Bishop, February 3, 1864, Cook papers.

47. *Fredonian*, February 26, 1864.

48. *Fredonian*, April 7, 1864.

49. Garret D. W. Vroom to G. H. C., April 6, 1864.

50. *Newark Daily Advertiser*, June 30, 1864.

51. Earl D. Ross, *Democracy's College, the Land Grant Movement in the Formative Stage* (Ames, Iowa, 1942), p. 173.

52. C. M. Harrison to G. H. C., January 27, 1862.

53. G. H. C. to David Cole, October, 1863; draft; C. M. Harrison to G. H. C., May 22, 1862.

54. C. M. Harrison to G. H. C., May 22, 1862.

55. John J. Brower to G. H. C., November 19, 1864.

56. Hugh N. Wilson to G. H. C., June 20, 1862, David Bishop to G. H. C., March 8, 1862.

57. Henry E. Dixon to G. H. C., October 15, 1862, William Rankin Duryee to G. H. C., September 25, 1862, S. M. Woodbridge to G. H. C., August 14, 1862.

58. Sarah Cook to G. H. C., June 11, 1862.

59. William B. Merritt to G. H. C., May 23, 1864.

60. McCormick, *Rutgers Bicentennial*, p. 95.

61. Receipt from Patent Office for Petition for Improvement in Composition for Lining Tobacco Pipes, November 16, 1861.

62. T. R. Porter to G. H. C., February 7, 1863; U. S. Patent Office to G. H. C. and T. R. Porter, April 11, 1863; T. R. Porter to G. H. C., March 12, 1863, and April 1, 1863.

63. John T. McKnight to G. H. C., April 20, 1862.

64. David Murray to G. H. C., May 6, 1862.

65. R. V. DeWitt, Jr. to G. H. C., October 24, 1862.

66. *Laws of New Jersey*, 1864, Chapter CCCXXXII.

67. G. H. C. to Mary T. Cook, April 9, 1864.

68. G. H. C. to Mary T. Cook, April 6, 1864.

69. G. H. C. to Mary T. Cook, April 9, 1864.

70. William Gurley to G. H. C., September 18, 1863.

71. McCormick, *Rutgers Bicentennial*, p. 76.

72. Ibid., p. 77.

73. Henry Cook to G. H. C., June 17, 1861.

74. W. Aitken to G. H. C., August 29, 1863.

75. Mary Thomas Cook to G. H. C., July 22, 1863.

76. M. T. C. to G. H. C., July 15, 1863.

77. M. T. C. to G. H. C., July 22, 1863.

78. M. T. C. to G. H. C., July 15, 1863.

79. G. H. C. to Rodman Price, June 9, 1863, Price papers.

80. William F. Force to G. H. C., May 12, 1863, May 20, 1863.

81. William F. Force to G. H. C., May 6, 1863.

82. *Report of the Geological Survey*, 1885, p. 166.

83. G. H. C. to Mary T. Cook, August 13, 1863.

84. G. H. C. notebook #20, pp. 49-50.

85. G. H. C. letterbook 1863-64, draft of letter to Captain Morrison, March 5, 1864.

86. G. H. C. letterbook 1863-64, draft of letter to James Jenkins, January 16, 1864.

87. *Legislative Documents* for 1864, Document C.

88. *Laws of New Jersey*, 1864, Chapter CCCXXXVII.

NOTES FOR CHAPTER 7

1. Most of material in this chapter on the land-grant colleges appeared originally in an article written by the author. See footnote 22, Chapter 6 above.

2. G. H. C. to William Gurley, July 16, 1867, draft.

3. Trustees' minutes, Dec. 21, 1864.

4. Minutes of committee meeting, June 2, 1864, Cook papers.

5. Abraham Messler to G. H. C., July 21, 1864.

6. Woodward and Waller, *New Jersey's Experiment Station*, p. 25, n. 16.

7. Jonathan Ingham to G. H. C., May 12, 1866.

8. *Report of the Board of Visitors, Agricultural School of New Jersey*, to the Legislature, January 19, 1865. These reports were called "Annual Reports of the Rutgers Scientific School," after 1869 and hereafter will be so designated.

9. Luther H. Tucker to G. H. C., February 5, 1864.

10. *Plan and Course of Instruction of the Rutgers Scientific School*, 1865, pp. 10-11.

11. L. H. Tucker to G. H. C., April 27, 1865.

12. Paul W. Gates, *Agriculture and the Civil War* (New York: Alfred A. Knopf, 1965), p. 269.

13. Gould P. Colman, *Education and Agriculture: A History of the New York State College of Agriculture at Cornell* (Ithaca, N. Y., 1963), p. 52; Alfred Charles True, *A History of Agricultural Education in the United States: 1785-1925* (Washington, D. C., 1929), U.S.D.A. Misc. Pub. No. 26, p. 155. This practice did enable students to earn money to pay their way through college.

14. William Campbell in Annual Report of the New Jersey Agricultural College for 1869, p. 19.

15. Samuel Dumont Halliday, *History of the Agricultural Land Grant Act of July 2, 1862* (Ithaca, N. Y., 1905), p. 20.

16. G. H. C. to John T. Blair, Cook letterbook, May 1864-March 1865.

17. Circular letter of the Board of Visitors, January 13, 1873.

18. Report of the Commissioners of the Agricultural College Fund. *Legislative Documents of New Jersey*, 1866, pp. 742-43.

19. Woodward and Waller, *New Jersey's Experiment Station*, p. 25; McCormick, Rutgers Bicentennial, p. 89.

20. True, *Agricultural Education*, p. 118.

21. Trustees' minutes, June 10, 1865.

22. *Catalogue of Officers and Alumni of Rutgers College* (Trenton, 1916), passim.

23. Ezra Cornell to M. E. Viele, April 29, 1865; J. D. Dana to G. H. C., May 8, 1865; Col. B. P. Johnson to G. H. C., May 13, 1865.

24. Faculty minutes, September 27, 1864.

25. Ibid., September 18, 1864.

26. L. H. Tucker to G. H. C., February 13, 1866, June 14, 1866.

27. *The Country Gentleman*, Vol. XXVI, No. 5 (August 3, 1865), p. 80.

28. Manuscript lecture, Cook papers, 1865.

29. Ibid.

30. G. H. C. to W. Campbell, February 26, 1876.

31. G. H. C. to W. Gurley, July 16, 1867.

32. Colman, *Education and Agriculture*, pp. 47, 48.

33. *Report of the Board of Visitors for 1866*, p. 10.

34. Ibid., pp. 6-8.

35. *Report of the Rutgers Scientific School for 1868*, p. 6.

36. Trustees' minutes, June 20, 1865.

37. *Report of the New Jersey Agricultural College for 1867*, p. 8.

38. Wilson Smith, "'Cow College' Mythology and Social History: A View of Some Centennial Literature," *Agricultural History*, Fall, 1971, p. 301.

39. Edward Danforth Eddy, *Colleges for Our Land and Time: The Land-Grant Idea in American Education* (Conn., 1973), p. 67.

40. Colman, *Education and Agriculture*, p. 69.

41. *Practical Farmer*, Vol. VIII, No. 8 (August, 1871), p. 184.

42. G. H. C. to W. Campbell, April 14, 1869.

43. Manuscript agreement in Cook papers, signed January 13, 1865 by John H. Knight and by G. H. C. as chairman of the subcommittee.

44. N. Norris Halsted to G. H. C., April 17, 1865, May 31, 1865; Isaac R. Cornell to G. H. C., April 3, 1865.

45. Benjamin Haines to G. H. C., 1865.

46. N. N. Halsted to G. H. C., 1865.

47. Woodward and Waller, *New Jersey's Experiment Station*, p. 27, quoting *Rutgers Scientific School Report, 1870*, p. 44.

48. Woodward and Waller, *New Jersey's Experiment Station*, p. 26, quoting *New Jersey State Board of Agriculture Annual Report, 1874*, p. 25.

49. Ibid.

50. *Report of the Rutgers Scientific School for 1865*, p. 11.

51. *Report of the Rutgers Scientific School for 1866*, p. 6.

52. *Report of the Rutgers Scientific School for 1865* (Trenton, 1866), p. 12.

53. Cook papers, draft of letter to W. Campbell, April 1, 1868.

54. *Report of the Rutgers Scientific School for 1868*, Appendix C, p. 23.

55. Woodward, *Agriculture in New Jersey*, p. 285.

56. Charles A. Browne, "Justus Von Liebig—Man and Teacher," in

Forest Ray Moulton, ed. *Liebig and After Liebig: A Century of Progress in Agricultural Chemistry*, Publication of the American Association for the Advancement of Science, no. 16 (Washington, D. C., 1942), p. 6.

57. *Report of Rutgers Scientific School for 1867*, p. 12f.

58. *Report of Rutgers Scientific School for 1869*, p. 5; Minutes of the Board of Visitors, June 17, 1869.

59. G. H. C. to W. Kitchell, January 13, 1855, February 16, 1855, November 30, 1854, Kitchell papers; David Pettit to G. H. C., December 25, 1854, Cook papers.

60. F. X. Adams to G. H. C., November 10, 1868; J. Smock to G. H. C., May 17, 1867; S. W. Ingham to G. H. C., February 11, 1867.

61. Bill, November, 1868, Woodbury, New Jersey, Cook papers.

62. *Report of the Rutgers Scientific School for 1867*, p. 11f.

63. Ibid., pp. 17-34.

64. Ibid., pp. 20-23.

65. Ibid., pp. 20-23.

66. Ibid., p. 35.

67. Woodward and Waller, *New Jersey's Experiment Station*, p. 18.

68. Minutes, Board of Visitors, December 20, 1871.

69. Charles Sears to G. H. C., n.d., 1855.

70. *Targum*, March 16, 1920.

71. Henry Steele Commager, *The Search for a Usable Past and Other Essays in Historiography* (New York, 1967), p. 211.

72. George H. Cook, *Geology of New Jersey* (Newark, 1868), Preface, p. xiv.

73. Notebook #24, entry for August 24, 1865.

74. Notebook #24, entry for August 17, 1865.

75. Notebook #22, entry for September 22, 1864.

76. Cook, *Geology of New Jersey*, 1868, Preface, p. xiv.

77. Ibid., pp. 453-458.

78. Ibid., p. 288.

79. Ibid., pp. 459-461.

80. Ibid., pp. 462-464.

81. Ibid., p. 250.

82. Ibid., p. 685.

83. William Coleman, "Limits of the Recapitulation Theory," *Isis*, Vol. 64 (September, 1973), p. 341.

84. James Dwight Dana, *Manual of Geology* (Philadelphia, 1864), p. 587; and Fourth Edition (New York, 1894), p. 350.

85. John Smock, "George H. Cook, Late State Geologist of New Jersey," *The American Geologist* (December, 1889), Vol. IV, p. 324.

86. Frank Nason, "Geological Studies of the Archaean Rocks," *Annual Report of the State Geologist for 1889*, p. 15.

87. Cook, *Geology of New Jersey*, p. 61.

88. Kemble Widmer, *The Geology and Geography of New Jersey* (New

York, 1964), p. 32.

89. Ibid., p. 31.

90. Cook, *Geology of New Jersey*, 1868, p. 337.

91. Ibid., p. 200.

92. Ibid., p. 340.

93. Merrill, *First Hundred Years*, p. 640.

94. Cook, *Geology of New Jersey*, 1868, p. 342.

95. Ibid.

96. Merrill, *First Hundred Years*, p. 392, 401.

97. Gerald D. Nash, "The Conflict Between Pure and Applied Science in Nineteenth Century Public Policy," *Isis*, LIV (June, 1963), pp. 223-25.

98. Walter B. Hendrickson, "Nineteenth-Century State Geological Surveys: Early Government Support of Science," *Isis*, LII (September, 1961), p. 368.

99. Cook, *Geology of New Jersey*, 1868, Preface, pp. xi, xii.

100. *Report of the State Geologist for 1885*, p. 171.

101. James Jenkins to G. H. C., March 14, 1869.

102. Isaac R. Cornell to G. H. C., March 30, 1869; Karl Biedel to G. H. C., April 22, 1869; C. H. Hitchcock to G. H. C., April 15, 1869; F. B. Meek to G. H. C., May 12, 1869.

103. S. F. Baird to G. H. C., March 25, 1869.

104. S. W. Johnson to G. H. C., March 29, 1869.

105. F. Sterry Hunt to G. H. C., April 6, 1869.

106. J. M. Safford to G. H. C., June 29, 1869.

107. Othniel C. Marsh, *American Journal of Science*.

108. Joseph B. Lyman to G. H. C., March 25, 1869.

109. E. L. Viele to G. H. C., March 24, 1869.

110. Merrill, *First Hundred Years*, p. 392.

111. Mary Cook to G. H. C., September 18, 1866.

112. Mary Cook to G. H. C., April 29, 1866.

113. Mary Cook to G. H. C., May 3, 1866.

114. Mary Cook to E. M. Thomas, December 13, 1868 and March 14, 1870, Thomas papers.

115. David D. Demarest to G. H. C., April 13, 1870; Gardner A. Sage to G. H. C., April 13, 1870.

116. Mary Cook to E. M. Thomas, February 7, 1879, Thomas papers.

117. William Gurley to G. H. C., December 30, 1870.

118. Edward Thomas to G. H. C., January 13, 1872.

119. N. J. Bishop to G. H. C., n.d., 1868.

120. Sage, *Emma Willard* (New York, 1898), p. 812.

121. Mary Cook to Mrs. Uriah Lewis Davis, n.d., 1869, Thomas papers.

122. Sarah Cook, diary, Cook papers.

123. Sage, *Emma Willard*, p. 1671.

124. Sarah Cook, diary.

125. A. Hewitt to G. H. C., September 29, 1865.

126. J. H. Willard to G. H. C., n.d.
127. W. Gurley to G. H. C., December 15, 1869.
128. John Willard to G. H. C., November 23, 1867.
129. Mrs. Emma Scudder to G. H. C., n.d.
130. Rutgers catalogue, 1867-68.
131. W. Gurley to G. H. C., September 5, 1866.
132. W. Gurley to G. H. C., May 5, 1866.
133. James Hall to G. H. C., July 25, 1868; David Murray to G. H. C.

NOTES FOR CHAPTER 8

1. Gerald D. Nash, "The Conflict Between Pure and Applied Science in Nineteenth Century Public Policy," *Isis*, June, 1963, Vol. 54, pp. 220, 223, 225.

2. John M. Clarke, *James Hall of Albany* (Albany, 1921), p. 503.

3. *Report of the State Geologist for 1872*, p. 9.

4. *Report of State Geologist for 1869*, p. 13f.

5. *Report of State Geologist for 1885*, p. 175.

6. *Report of State Geologist for 1870*, p. 18.

7. William Gurley to Paul Cook, November 25, 1870; J. D. Buckelew to G. H. C., November 11, 1870, and November 10, 1870; James Neilson to G. H. C., September 25, 1870.

8. Trustees' minutes, June 21, 1870.

9. William Gurley to G. H. C., August 2, 1870.

10. William Gurley to G. H. C., August 2, 1870.

11. George H. Cook, "European Agriculture IV: Observations in Norway," *The Cultivator and Country Gentleman*, Vol. 36 (March 30, 1871), p. 195.

12. *Report of the Rutgers Scientific School for 1872*, p. 25.

13. *Report of Rutgers Scientific School for 1871*, p. 31.

14. *Report of State Geologist for 1870*, pp. 58-61.

15. Rosamund Sawyer Moxon, William Parker Hudson and Marjorie Isabelle Merritt, *Woodlawn: The Story of the Neilson Home* (New Brunswick, N. J., 1941), p. 6.

16. *The Cultivator and Country Gentleman*, Vol. 36 (February 16, 1871), p. 99.

17. *Report of State Geologist for 1870*, p. 19.

18. *Laws of New Jersey*, 1871, Chapter 132, p. 25 as noted in *Report of State Geologist for 1871*, p. 10.

19. Ibid., p. 11.

20. *Report of State Geologist for 1872*, p. 11.

21. *New Jersey Journal*, February 13, 1872, p. 14.

22. *Report of the State Geologist for 1875*, p. 20.

23. *Report of the State Geologist for 1874*, p. 8-10. John P. Snyder, *The Story of New Jersey's Civil Boundaries*, Bureau of Geology and Topography, Bulletin 67 (Trenton, 1969), p. 14.

24. George H. Cook, *Report on a Survey of the Boundary Line Between New Jersey and New York* (New Brunswick, 1874), p. 48.

25. Snyder, *Civil Boundaries*, p. 14.

26. *Report of the State Geologist for 1875*, p. 25.

27. Ibid., p. 29.

28. Ibid., pp. 9, 12.

29. John C. Smock to G. H. C., August 10, 1875.

30. John C. Smock to G. H. C., August 24, 1875.

31. John C. Smock to G. H. C., August 27, 1875.

32. John C. Smock to G. H. C., September 15, 1875.

33. John C. Smock to G. H. C., September 25, 1875.

34. John C. Smock to G. H. C., October 6, 1875.

35. *Report of the New Jersey Commissioners on the Centennial Exhibition* (Trenton, N. J., 1877), p. 47.

36. *Report of the State Geologist for 1876*, p. 9.

37. *Report of the New Jersey Commissioners on the Centennial Exhibit*, p. 47.

38. *Report of the State Geologist for 1874*, p. 8.

39. *Scarlet Letter* (1889), p. 130.

40. Woodward and Waller, *New Jersey's Experiment Station*, p. 27.

41. *Report of the Rutgers Scientific School for 1876*, p. 9.

42. *Proceedings of the New Jersey Horticultural Society at its Second Annual Meeting*, New Brunswick, February 1 & 2, 1877 (Newark, 1877).

43. Woodward and Waller, *New Jersey's Experiment Station*, p. 27.

44. *Report of the Rutgers Scientific School for 1876*, p. 31, subscription list, Cook papers, 1876.

45. Edwin Bogardus to G. H. C., August 14, 1874.

46. O. H. Gallup to G. H. C., September 29, 1876.

47. E. Burrough to G. H. C., May 12, 1876; David Pettit to G. H. C., January 14, 1876; W. W. Pierce to G. H. C., March 12, 1876; William Tory to G. H. C., September 23, 1876; George T. Ingham to G. H. C., September 28, 1876; Woodward and Waller, *New Jersey's Experiment Station*, p. 31.

48. *Report of the Rutgers Scientific School for 1872*, p. 26.

49. Harry B. Weiss, *History of the New Jersey State Board of Agriculture, 1872-1916* (Trenton, 1949), p. 20f.

50. Elizabeth A. Osborne, *From the Letter Files of S. W. Johnson* (New Haven, Conn., 1913), p. 107.

51. Agreement, February 1, 1872, between Alexander S. Conover and G. H. C. and between Patrick Healy and G. H. C., n.d., 1871.

52. *Report of the Rutgers Scientific School for 1871*, p. 51.

53. Gould P. Colman, *Education and Agriculture: A History of the New York State College of Agriculture at Cornell University* (Ithaca, N. Y., 1963), p. 54.

54. *Proceedings of the National Agricultural Convention Held at Washington, February 15, 16, & 17, 1872*, U. S. Congress, 2d Session, Senate Misc. Doc. 164), p. 17.

55. Ibid., p. 35.

56. Ibid., p. 17.

57. John H. Klippart to G. H. C., July 19, 1872.

58. G. H. C. to Governor Joel Parker, March 1872 (draft).

59. Ibid.

60. P. S. Gold to G. H. C., July 19, 1872.

61. J. H. Klippart to G. H. C., July 19, 1872.

62. Carl Raymond Woodward, *Agriculture in New Jersey: 1640-1880* (New Brunswick, N.J., 1927), p. 229.

63. Alfred Charles True, *A History of Agricultural Experimentation and Research in the United States: 1607-1925*, Misc. Publication No. 251, U. S. Dept. of Agriculture (Washington, D. C., G.P.O., 1937), p. 82.

64. Woodward, *Agriculture in New Jersey*, p. 231.

65. Weiss, *State Board of Agriculture*, p. 14.

66. Woodward, *Agriculture in New Jersey*, p. 231.

67. True, *Agricultural Education*, p. 196.

68. Earle D. Ross, *Democracy's College: The Land Grant Movement in the Formative State* (Ames, Iowa, 1942), p. 173.

69. Ibid., p. 174.

70. Ibid.

71. James McCosh to G. H. C., September 2, 1872, October 1, 1872, October 30, 1872.

72. Minutes of the Board of Visitors of the Rutgers Scientific School, June 13, 1873.

73. Ross, *Democracy's College*, p. 175.

74. Ibid.

75. Demarest, *Rutgers College*, p. 433; McCormick, *Rutgers Bicentennial*, p. 103.

76. G. W. Tryon to G. H. C., November 15, 1876; H. A. Ward to G. H. C., July 3, 1875; J. R. Hackett to G. H. C., January 31, 1876; Kemble Widmer, *Geology in New Jersey*, typescript, 1965, p. 10f.

77. Isaac Hasbrouck to G. H. C., December 27, 1872.

78. Isaac Hasbrouck to G. H. C., April 14, 1873.

79. Francis Cuyler Van Dyck to G. H. C., January 24, 1871.

80. David Murray to G. H. C., October 21, 1870.

81. *Report of the Rutgers Scientific School for 1873*, p. 39.

82. Woodward, *Development of Agriculture*, p. 258f.

83. *Report of the Rutgers Scientific School for 1870*, p. 8.

84. Woodward, *Development of Agriculture*, p. 263.

85. McCormick, *Rutgers Bicentennial*, p. 101.

86. Trustees' minutes, March 7, 1876.

87. S. W. Johnson to G. H. C., September 13, 1876.

88. G. H. C. to Henry P. Armsby, September 18, 1876.
89. J. T. Ellis to G. H. C., May 3, 1872.
90. August Cutler to G. H. C., September 9, 1874.
91. W. W. Pierce to G. H. C., March 28, 1875, December 13, 1875; Edward Baker to G. H. C., July 31, 1876; D. C. Paul to G. H. C., November 8, 1876.
92. Conversations with Margaret Cook Thomson and Van Wie Ingham.
93. W. R. Janeway to G. H. C., October 29, 1872.
94. Mary T. Cook to G. H. C., May 2, 1875; Elijah Thomas to G. H. C., May 1, 1875, Thomas papers.
95. Mary T. Cook to G. H. C., May 2, 1875 (in possession of Margaret Cook Thomson.
96. William Gurley to G. H. C., May 26, 1874.
97. Asher Anderson to G. H. C., September 15, 1871.
98. Clara Gurley to G. H. C., November 15, 1871, and January 2, 1871.

NOTES FOR CHAPTER 9

1. G. H. C. to Anne Cook, July 14, 1878.
2. Augustus W. Cutler to G. H. C., October 31, 1877; Thomas Dudley to G. H. C., April 10, 1877.
3. C ok notebook #44, entry for August 8, 1875; notebook #45, entry for May 4, 1876, May 5, 1876; John C. Smock, "On the Surface Limit or Thickness of the Continental Glacier in New Jersey and Adjacent States," *The American Journal of Science and Arts*, CXXV (1883), p. 339.
4. Richard Foster Flint, "Glacial Geology," *Geology: 1888-1938*, Fiftieth Anniversary Volume, Geological Society of America (1944), p. 27f; Warren Upham, "Obituary Memorial of Professor Henry Carvill Lewis and his Work in Glacial Geology," *American Geologist* (December, 1888), p. 374.
5. Herbert E. Gregory, "A Century of Geology," in Edward Salisbury Dana, ed., *A Century of Science* (New Haven, Conn., 1918), p. 139.
6. John C. Smock to G. H. C., April 13, 1877.
7. John C. Smock to G. H. C., August 20, 1877.
8. George H. Cook, "On the Southern Limits of the Last Glacial Drift Across New Jersey and the Adjacent Parts of New York and Pennsylvania," *Transactions of the American Institute of Mining Engineers*, Vol. VI (1879), pp. 467-470.
9. *Report of the State Geologist for 1877*, p. 11.
10. Ibid., p. 19.
11. Ibid., p. 21.
12. G. H. C. to Mary Cook, July 7, 1878.
13. G. H. C. to Emma Cook, July 14, 1878.
14. G. H. C. to Mary Cook, July 14, 1878.

15. *Report of the State Geologist for 1878*, p. 13ff.

16. John C. Smock, "On the Surface Limit of the Continental Glacier." See note 3 above.

17. *Report of the State Geologist for 1880*, p. 1, 57.

18. John C. Smock, "George Cook, Late State Geologist of New Jersey," *The American Geologist*, Vol. LV (December, 1889), p. 325.

19. *Report of the State Geologist for 1873*, p. 13.

20. *Report of the State Geologist for 1888*, p. 4.

21. *Report of the State Geologist for 1885*, p. 185-203.

22. John P. Snyder, *The Mapping of New Jersey: The Men and the Art* (New Brunswick, N. J., 1973), p. 116.

23. C. C. Vermeule to G. H. C., May 13, 1882.

24. *Report of the State Geologist for 1885*, p. 190.

25. Ibid., p. 180.

26. Ibid., p. 179.

27. *Report of the State Geologist for 1880*, p. 187.

28. *Report of the State Geologist for 1881*, pp. 84, 86.

29. *Report of the State Geologist for 1885*, p. 176.

30. *Report of the State Geologist for 1880*, p. 161.

31. James M. Chapman to G. H. C., August 13, 1877; J. C. Bates to G. H. C., January 8, 1879; A. Q. Keasdey to G. H. C., January 25, 1879; Samuel Allinson to G. H. C., February 15, 1879; Thos. Kinney to G. H. C., March 6, 1879; A. C. McLean to G. H. C., March 14, 1879; J. M. Bancroft to G. H. C., April 14, 1879; David Ripley to G. H. C., May 22, 1879.

32. *Report of the State Geologist for 1880*, p. 162.

33. Ibid., p. 171.

34. *Report of the State Geologist for 1884*, p. 121ff.

35. *Report of the State Geologist for 1885*, p. 179.

36. John C. Smock in the preface to Cornelius Clarkson Vermeule, *Report on Water Supply*, Vol. III, Final Report of the State Geologist (Trenton, N. J., 1894), p. vi.

37. Conversations with Van Wie Ingham and with Margaret Cook Thomson.

38. George H. Cook, "The Change of Relative Level of the Ocean and the Uplands on the Eastern Coast of North America," *Proceedings of the American Association for the Advancement of Science*, Vol. XXXI (1882), p. 404.

39. William Stoke, *Essentials of Earth History* (Englewood Cliffs, N. J., 1960), p. 41f.

40. *The Sunday Times* (New Brunswick), June 16, 1929.

41. Henry Kummel, "New Jersey Coast—The Two Feet per Century Myth," *American Association for the Advancement of Science, Bulletin*, Vol. 44 (1933), p. 178.

42. Widmer, *Geology and Geography*, p. 139.

43. "Unstable America," *Newsweek*, October 16, 1973, p. 77.

44. *Report of the State Geologist for 1880*, pp. 54, 56.

45. *Report of the State Geologist for 1881*, p. 85.

46. "Clay Deposits of Woodbridge, South Amboy and Other Places in New Jersey," *Report of the State Geologist for 1878*, p. 4.

47. Widmer, *Geology and Geography*, p. 61.

48. *Report of the State Geologist for 1882*, p. 14.

49. *Report of the State Geologist for 1880*, p. 18.

50. *Report of the State Geologist for 1882*, p. 22; Widmer, *Geology and Geography*, p. 66, 73.

51. *Report of the State Geologist for 1882*, p. 47.

52. Ibid., p. 13.

53. Ibid., p. 14.

54. Ibid.

55. Widmer, *Geology and Geography*, p. 62.

56. George Otis Smith, "Government Geological Surveys," in Edward Salisbury Dana et al., *A Century of Science in America: With Special Reference to the American Journal of Science: 1818-1918* (New Haven, Conn., 1918), p. 201.

57. See Chapter 5.

58. G. H. C. to Mary T. Cook, September 1, 1878, Thomson papers.

59. Persifor Frazer, "The International Congress of Geologists," *The American Geologist*, Vol. I (1888), p. 4.

60. G. H. C. to Mary T. Cook, September 1, 1878, Thomson papers.

61. Mary Lesley, *Life and Letters of Peter and Susan Lesley*, Vol. II (New York, 1909), p. 199.

62. G. H. C. to Mary T. Cook, September 1, 1878, Thomson papers.

63. E. Burrough to G. H. C., April 12, 1877; Joseph P. Bradley to G. H. C., March 27, 1877; Arnold Guyot to G. H. C., April 12, 1877.

64. G. H. C. to Anne Cook, July 21, 1878, Thomson papers.

65. Paul Cook to G. H. C., November 22, 1878; G. H. C. to Mary T. Cook, July 23, 1878, Thomson papers.

66. G. H. C. to Mary T. Cook, July 16, 1878; G. H. C. to Mary T. Cook, June 26, 1878, Thomson papers.

67. G. H. C. to Mary T. Cook, June 23, 1878, Thomson papers.

68. G. H. C. to Mary T. Cook, July 30, 1878, Thomson papers.

69. G. H. C. to Anne Cook, June 30, 1878, Thomson papers.

70. G. H. C. to Anne Cook, July 21, 1878, Thomson papers.

71. G. H. C. to Mary T. Cook, August 11, 1878, Thomson papers.

72. G. H. C. to Emma Cook, August 25, 1878, Thomson papers.

73. Conversations with Margaret Cook Thomson and Van Wie Ingham; G. H. C. to Mary T. Cook, August 14, 1878, Thomson papers.

74. Mary T. Cook to G. H. C., August 13, 1878 and August 16, 1878, Thomson papers.

75. G. H. C. to Mary T. Cook, September 1, 1878, Thomson papers.

76. G. H. C. to Mary T. Cook, August 28, 1878, Thomson papers.

77. Ibid.

78. *Report of the State Geologist for 1888*, p. 298.

79. *Rutgers Scientific School Report for 1875*, p. 7.

80. *Rutgers Scientific School Report for 1880*, p. 12.

81. *The Scientific Farmer*, Vol. 2 (1877), p. 83.

82. G. H. C. to Lewis Sturtevant, March 6, 1879.

83. Lewis Sturtevant to G. H. C., March 13, 1879.

84. *Rutgers Scientific School Report for 1875*, p. 9.

85. McCormick, *Bicentennial History*, p. 110.

86. William Campbell to G. H. C., February 24, 1876.

87. Richard P. McCormick, *New Jersey from Colony to State: 1609-1789*, The New Jersey History Series (New Brunswick, N.J., 1964), p. 32.

88. *Board of General Proprietors of the Eastern Division of New Jersey* vs *Force*, New Jersey Court of Errors and Appeals (1894), p. 890.

89. Monroe Howell to G. H. C., September 13, 1877.

90. William Force to G. H. C., February 10, 1879.

91. D. A. Ryerson to G. H. C., November 10, 1879.

92. Edward J. C. Atterbury to G. H. C., November 17, 1879.

93. Catherine A. English to G. H. C., September 17, 1880.

94. Catherine A. English to G. H. C., July 14, 1880.

95. Thomas Kinney to G. H. C., May 6, 1879.

96. William Force to G. H. C., May 16, 1879, November 29, 1879.

97. *General Proprietors* vs *Force*, p. 895.

98. *Rutgers Scientific School Report for 1876*, p. 32.

99. Trustees' minutes, March 2, 1880.

100. Ibid., June 16, 1880.

101. True, *History of Agricultural Experimentation*, p. 81.

102. G. H. C. to Mary T. Cook, August 4, 1878.

103. *Report of New Jersey State Board of Agriculture for 1879*, Legislative Documents, Doc. 49, p. 26.

104. *Rutgers Scientific School Report for 1879*, p. 53.

105. Ibid.

106. Woodward, *Agriculture in New Jersey*, p. 249.

107. *The Scientific Farmer*, Vol. I (August, 1877), p. 103.

108. Cook, *Geology of New Jersey*, pp. 56-70.

109. *Report of the Rutgers Scientific School for 1876*, pp. 17-19.

110. Ibid., p. 35.

111. James Fenwick to G. H. C., March 15, 1880; A. C. Noble to G. H. C., January 1, 1880; C. F. Van Invegen to G. H. C., January 13, 1880; Robert Craig to G. H. C., February 12, 1880.

112. J. C. Whitehall to G. H. C., January 23, 1880; C. M. Rogers to G. H. C., February 5, 1880; Thos. J. Beans to G. H. C., February 17, 1880; William S. Taylor to G. H. C., June 2, 1880; W. S. Potter to G. H. C., January 20, 1880; E. P. Tomlinson to G. H. C., August 25, 1880; John D. Buckelew to G. H. C., November 15, 1880.

113. *Report of the Rutgers Scientific School for 1874*, p. 21.

114. *The Cultivator and Country Gentleman*, Vol. XLIII (1878), pp. 419, 451, 457, 499, 570, 755.

115. *Report of the Rutgers Scientific School for 1874*, p. 21.

116. True, *Experimentation Research*, pp. 67-82.

117. Augustus W. Cutler to G. H. C., January 15, 1876.

118. Augustus W. Cutler to G. H. C., January 12, 1876.

119. Augustus W. Cutler to G. H. C., April 3, 1876.

120. Joseph Bedle, "Governor's Message," *Documents of the One Hundred and Second Legislature of the State of New Jersey* (Tom's River, N. J., 1878), p. 13.

121. *Minutes of the Board of Visitors of the Rutgers Scientific School*, June 14, 1878.

122. Ibid., June 10, 1879.

123. Weiss, *New Jersey State Board of Agriculture*, p. 23.

124. Ibid.

125. Woodward and Waller, *New Jersey's Experiment Station*, p. 34.

126. Ibid., p. 32.

127. Ibid., p. 34.

128. Ibid.

129. Connecticut established an agricultural experiment station by act of legislature in 1875 and North Carolina in 1877. A station in California using the funds of the State University was begun in 1875; in Massachusetts a station functioned from 1878 until 1880 at the Massachusetts Agricultural College and an unfunded station was in operation at Cornell University in New York State from 1879 until 1881.

NOTES FOR CHAPTER 10

1. True, *Experimentation and Research*, p. 82.

2. Albert S. Cook to G. H. C., March 30, 1880; True, *Experimentation and Research*, p. 84.

3. Trustees' minutes, October 27, 1885.

4. Ibid.

5. Ibid., March 9, 1886 and June 22, 1886.

6. *Report of the New Jersey State Agricultural Experiment Station for 1881*, p. 37f.

7. Woodward and Waller, *New Jersey's Experiment Station*, p. 152.

8. Ibid., pp. 154-155.

9. *Report of the Rutgers Scientific School for 1882*, p. 49.

10. True, *Agricultural Experimentation*, p. 150.

11. Ibid.

12. Woodward and Waller, *New Jersey's Experiment Station*, p. 349; "Report of the New Jersey Board of Agriculture for 1883-1884," Document #13, *Legislative Documents of New Jersey*, Vol. L, 1884, p. 18.

13. *Annual Report of the New Jersey State Agricultural Experiment Station for the Year 1880* (Trenton, N. J., 1880), p. 65. I am indebted to Dr. Edward Oleskie of the New Jersey Agricultural Experiment Station for the information on the taste of silage.

14. George H. Cook, *Bulletin 10*, New Jersey Agricultural Experiment Station, January 15, 1881; George H. Cook, *Bulletin 11*, New Jersey Agricultural Experiment Station, March 7, 1881; George H. Cook, *Bulletin 19*, New Jersey Agricultural Experiment Station, February 20, 1882.

15. *Report of the State Board of Agriculture*, April 18, 1883, p. 16.

16. *Report of the United States Commissioner of Agriculture for 1881-82*, p. 571.

17. Woodward and Waller, *New Jersey's Experiment Station*, p. 357.

18. *Minutes of the Board of Managers of the New Jersey Agricultural Experiment Station*, March 21, 1881.

19. *Report of the Agricultural Experiment Station for 1880*, p. 54ff.

20. Ibid., p. 55.

21. Ibid., p. 62.

22. Ibid., p. 149.

23. Cook, *Bulletin 10*.

24. *Report of the Agricultural Experiment Station for 1888*, pp. 114, 122-126.

25. Ibid., p. 119.

26. Woodward and Waller, *New Jersey's Experiment Station*, p. 136.

27. *Report of the Agricultural Experiment Station for 1886*, p. 29.

28. *Report of the Rutgers Scientific School for 1887*, pp. 169-171.

29. Woodward and Waller, *New Jersey's Experiment Station*, p. 133.

30. *Report of the Experiment Station for 1895*, p. 3 as noted in Woodward and Waller, p. 137.

31. Woodward and Waller, *New Jersey's Experiment Station*, p. 138.

32. Ibid., p. 45.

33. *Report of the Experiment Station for 1880*, p. 58, 65; *Report for 1881*, p. 60-68; *Report for 1882*, pp. 85-98; *Report for 1883*, pp. 16-17; *Report for 1885*, pp. 181-184.

34. H. C. Knoblauch et al., *State Agriculture Experiment Stations: A History of Research Policy and Procedure* (Washington, D. C., 1962), Misc. Pub. #904, U.S.D.A., p. 153.

35. True, *Experimentation and Research*, p. 142.

36. Edwin H. Bogardus to G. H. C., January 23, 1880.

37. George M. Rogers to G. H. C., February 5, 1880; J. G. Hitall to G. H. C., January 23, 1880.

38. Mary T. Cook to Elijah Thomas, March 9, 1883, Thomas papers.

39. Woodward and Waller, *New Jersey's Experiment Station*, p. 50.

40. Knoblauch, *Agriculture Experiment Stations*, p. 40.

41. *Proceedings of a Convention of Agriculturists Held by the Department of Agriculture, January 10-18, 1882* (Washington, D. C., 1882), p. 8.

42. Ibid., p. 9.

43. Ibid., p. 11.

44. Ibid.

45. Knoblauch, *Agriculture Experiment Stations*, p. 40.

46. Ibid., p. 41.

47. Ibid., p. 43.

48. True, *Experimentation and Research*, p. 123.

49. Knoblauch, *Agriculture Experiment Stations*, p. 47.

50. True, *Experimentation and Research*, p. 123.

51. Ibid., p. 124.

52. *Proceedings of a Convention of Delegates from Agricultural Colleges and Experiment Stations Held at the Department of Agriculture, July 8 and 9, 1885*, U.S.D.A., Misc. Special Report #9 (Washington, D. C., G.P.O., 1885), pp. 41-42.

53. Notes for an address before the Agricultural Committee in Washington, D. C., March 12, 1884, Cook papers.

54. Knoblauch, *Agriculture Experiment Stations*, p. 50.

55. Ibid., p. 52.

56. George Atherton to G. H. C., December 14, 1887.

57. Woodward and Waller, *New Jersey's Experiment Station*, p. 54.

58. *Report of the Agricultural Experiment Station for 1888*, p. 17.

59. Ibid., pp. 163-201, 202-212.

60. Ibid., p. 221; Woodward and Waller, *New Jersey's Experiment Station*, p. 156.

61. Knoblauch, *Agriculture Experiment Stations*, p. 55.

62. Circular letter from J. M. Gregory, Cook papers, 1871.

63. Knoblauch, *Agriculture Experiment Stations*, p. 58.

64. True, *Experimentation and Research*, p. 208.

65. John A. Myers to G. H. C., May 12, 1887.

66. John A. Myers to G. H. C., May 26, 1887; Knoblauch, *Agriculture Experiment Stations*, p. 64.

67. *Proceedings of the First Annual Convention of the Association of American Agricultural Colleges and Experiment Stations*, prepared from manuscript notes of the Secretary, C. E. Thorne (1941).

68. W. O. Atwater, S. W. Johnson and G. H. Cook, "Report of the Committee on Station Work," *Association of American Agricultural Colleges and Experiment Stations Convention*, held at the Department of Agriculture, Washington, D. C., October, 1887 (Washington: G.P.O., 1888).

69. Ibid., p. 27.

70. Ibid., p. 32.

71. Ibid., p. 3.

72. *Report of the State Geologist for 1884*, p. 12.

73. Ibid., p. 8.

74. Kemble Widmer, *Geology in New Jersey* (typescript, 1965), p. 17f.

75. W. P. Garrison to G. H. C., March 1882.

76. Henry F. Osborne to G. H. C., October 25, 1887.

77. T. C. Chamberlin to G. H. C., February 12, 1887.

78. James Geikie to G. H. C., July 9, 1883.

79. Charles Barrois to G. H. C., September 13, 1883.

80. Snyder, *Mapping of New Jersey*, p. 123.

81. C. C. Vermeule to G. H. C., June 17, 1888.

82. Frank L. Nason, "Geological Studies of the Archaean Rocks," *Annual Report of the State Geologist for 1889*, p. 12.

83. Ibid., p. 13.

84. Ibid., pp. 15, 16.

85. Woodward and Waller, *New Jersey's Experiment Station*, p. 79.

86. *Report of the State Geologist for 1888*, p. 5f.

87. Annual Report of the State Geologist for 1885, passim.

88. T. Sterry Hunt to G. H. C., May 6, 1883.

89. George H. Cook, "On the International Geological Congress, and Our Part In It As American Geologists," *Proceedings of the American Association for the Advancement of Science*, Vol. XXXVII (1888), p. 164.

90. Grove Karl Gilbert, "The Work of the International Congress of Geologists," *The American Journal of Arts and Science*, Vol. CXXXIV (1887), p. 446.

91. Ibid., p. 450.

92. Persifor Frazer, "A Short History of the Origin and Acts of the International Congress of Geologists, and of the American Committee Delegates to It," *The American Geologist*, Vol. I (1888), p. 100.

93. John C. Smock to G. H. C., April 1, 1887.

94. James Dwight Dana to G. H. C., December 12, 1887.

95. James Dwight Dana to G. H. C., December 12, 1887.

96. George H. Cook, "Report of the Sub Committee on the Mesozoic," *Fourth International Geological Congress*, London (1888), pp. A 161-165.

97. Persifor Frazer to G. H. C., April 21, 1887.

98. Ibid.

99. James Hall to G. H. C., October 14, 1887; Frazer, *Short History*, p. 98.

100. Frazer, *Short History*, p. 98.

101. Ibid.

102. Frazer to G. H. C., July 31, 1887; *American Journal of Arts and Science*, Vol. CXXXVI (1888), p. 470.

103. W. Boyd Dawkins to G. H. C., n.d., 1887.

104. Cook, Vice-Presidential Address. See footnote 89 above.

105. Ibid., p. 176.

106. Ibid., p. 177.

107. G. H. C. to J. P. Lesley, draft, 1887.

108. Trustees' minutes, June 19, 1888.

109. Merrill Gates to G. H. C., 1887.

110. Joseph Cannon Bailey, *Seaman A. Knapp: Schoolmaster of American Agriculture* (New York, 1945), p. 105.

111. Board of Visitors leaflet, 1887.
112. Paul Cook to G. H. C., March 3, 1888.
113. Merrill, *First Hundred Years*, p. 422.

Index